D0365270

HC
355
.M55
1991

Miller, Kenneth E.

Denmark, a troubled
welfare state.

$40.00

DATE			

DISCARD

BUSINESS/SCIENCE/TECHNOLOGY
DIVISION

© THE BAKER & TAYLOR CO.

DENMARK

DENMARK

A Troubled Welfare State

Kenneth E. Miller

Westview Press

BOULDER • SAN FRANCISCO • OXFORD

Westview Profiles/Nations of Contemporary Western Europe

Photo credits: Christiansborg Palace (copyright Lennard) and the countryside on Langeland (appears on cover; copyright the Danish Tourist Board), courtesy of the Danish Tourist Board. Photos of Queen Margrethe II, the political meeting, and senior citizens' housing (copyright Nordisk Pressefoto A/S), courtesy of Nordfoto.

All rights reserved. No part of this publication may be reproduced or transmitted in any form or by any means, electronic or mechanical, including photocopy, recording, or any information storage and retrieval system, without permission in writing from the publisher.

Copyright © 1991 by Westview Press, Inc.

Published in 1991 in the United States of America by Westview Press, Inc., 5500 Central Avenue, Boulder, Colorado 80301, and in the United Kingdom by Westview Press, 36 Lonsdale Road, Summertown, Oxford OX2 7EW

Library of Congress Cataloging-in-Publication Data
Miller, Kenneth E.
  Denmark : a troubled welfare state / Kenneth E. Miller.
    p. cm. — (Westview profiles/Nations of Contemporary
Western Europe)
  Includes bibliographical references and index.
  ISBN 0-8133-0834-8
  1. Denmark—Economic policy. 2. Denmark—Social policy.
3. Welfare state. I. Title. II. Series.
HC355.M55 1991
361.6′5′09489—dc20   90-20803
                                                              CIP

Printed and bound in the United States of America

The paper used in this publication meets the requirements
of the American National Standard for Permanence of Paper
for Printed Library Materials Z39.48-1984.

10   9   8   7   6   5   4   3   2   1

PST

$40.00

For Marilyn

Contents

Tables and Illustrations

Acknowledgments

I have had the opportunity to visit Denmark a number of times and to learn about the country through conversations and interviews with many people. I owe them all a debt of gratitude for their time, patience, and information. Especially helpful for this book have been Birte Weiss, M.F.; Viggo Fischer, M.F.; Poul Vorre of the Ministry of Social Affairs; Jens Chr. Pedersen of the Trade Union Federation; Annette Wegener and Jørgen Peter Skælm of the Ministry of Cultural Affairs; Helle Jacobsen and Vibeke Abel of the Equal Status Council; Marit Bakke, now of Norsk Rikskringkasting; and those in various government and nongovernment organizations who sent me reports and other publications about activities in their areas.

I am grateful to the Royal Danish Embassy Information Office in Washington, D.C., for its assistance in securing photographs for the book and to Bent Skou and Ellen Pittman of the embassy for their help in arranging my enjoyable stay at Nordisk Kollegium while I was conducting research in Copenhagen in the fall of 1988. Financial support from Rutgers for some of the research came from Dean Donald Stein of the Graduate School–Newark, Dean David Hosford of the Faculty of Arts and Sciences–Newark, and the President's Coordinating Council on International Programs. Grants in earlier years from the Rutgers Research Council also contributed to this work.

Some parts of the book are a family affair. My daughter, Susan, aided with information and suggestions on the Danish criminal justice system, and she supplied good Danish beer to celebrate the book's conclusion. My wife, Marilyn, acted not only as a friendly and encouraging critic and editor but also eased a hectic research schedule by conducting several interviews in Copenhagen. I am grateful to everyone for their assistance. The responsibility for any errors is mine, not theirs.

Kenneth E. Miller

1

Introduction

Denmark is a small country, and by no stretch of the imagination is it a major actor on the world stage. To many people, its mention brings thoughts of Hans Christian Andersen, the Little Mermaid, Danish pastry (a term not used in Denmark), or, perhaps, Isak Dinesen's Gothic tales or Victor Borge's monologues. More informed observers may think of the nation as one of the Scandinavian "social laboratories" where programs of the welfare state were pioneered.

It is certainly true that for many years Denmark has offered the world an outstanding example of political democracy and social progress. Its people have had a passion for liberty and social justice and have adopted the goal set forth by the nineteenth-century poet and theologian N.F.S. Grundtvig: a nation where "few have too much, and fewer have need." At the beginning of the twentieth century, Denmark was hardly considered one of the world's advanced states. Today, however, the freedom and openness of its society, its quest for equality, and its public policies are often admired.

But Denmark is no utopia, and in recent decades there have been political, economic, and international challenges to its governmental stability and social gains. By the 1970s, through measures adopted over an eighty-year span, Denmark had become an advanced welfare state, providing many services for its people along with a heavy tax burden to pay for those services. Then both economic and political adversity struck. The oil price increases by the Organization of Petroleum Exporting Countries (OPEC) and the consequent international recession hit Denmark hard, dependent as the country is on its export trade. Welfare costs that could be borne in a thriving economy became heavier with economic decline. Taxes and public spending were high; bureaucracy was growing; and critics of social, economic, and cultural policies became more vociferous. A revolt against taxes, bureaucrats, and the existing political party system came in the parliamentary election of 1973, when voters deserted their old allegiances and gave new political parties (notably

1

the Progress party of Mogens Glistrup) 25 percent of the seats in the Folketing, the Danish parliament.

Since 1973, governing Denmark has been extremely difficult. Instead of four or five parties in parliament, now there are often ten or eleven. No coalition has been able to put together a majority, and elections have been frequent. The minority cabinets in office since 1982 have usually been able to work out compromises on domestic legislation, but sustained action to meet Denmark's serious economic problems has been very difficult to achieve. Political decisions that used to be channeled through the "four old parties" and the traditional interest organizations (business, labor, and agriculture) are now affected by new political parties and grass-roots organizations (environmental, consumer, peace, feminist, and others). On international questions involving policies of the North Atlantic Treaty Organization (NATO), defense and disarmament, and some European Community issues, a parliamentary majority from the opposition parties often prevailed over the cabinet until 1988.

In its foreign relations Denmark has moved in the past century from neutrality to alliance and from economic independence to membership in the European Community. After its defeat by Prussia in 1864, the nation chose to be a peaceful neutral rather than to become involved in European politics. Although disputes over security arrangements continued, the basic policy became neutrality and disarmament. The country remained a bystander during World War I, but neutrality proved no safeguard against the threat of Nazi Germany. The Nazi invasion and occupation during World War II stimulated a change in outlook, and, after considerable debate, Denmark joined NATO in 1949. Much sentiment for pacifism and neutrality remained, however; although majority support for NATO membership has continued, Danish policies within the alliance have often seemed to other NATO states faint-hearted or inadequate. As left-wing political parties grew stronger in the 1970s and 1980s and as the dominant Social Democratic party, a NATO advocate, lost ground and modified its stand on some policies, Denmark's role in the alliance became a troubling issue.

To the disagreements on NATO has been added a deeper division: that over membership in the European Community (EC). Although the question was legally resolved in 1972 when a substantial majority of Danes voted in a national referendum to join the Community, a large segment of the population and a number of political parties continue to oppose membership. The initial controversy cut across party lines, divided the trade union movement, and left a residue of political bitterness and antagonism. Participation in the EC and the continuing arguments about it affect the party system, national economic and social policies, and the policy-making process. Legislation on agriculture, fisheries, conditions of trade, patents and copyrights, and so on, must be enacted in conformity with EC guidelines.

The Denmark of the 1990s is in many ways a sharp contrast to the Denmark of fifty years ago. Contrary to its twentieth-century beginnings as a neutral in world politics, detached politically (if not economically) from Europe and interested primarily in Nordic regional cooperation, the nation has become a member of NATO and of the European Community. From the model of a politically stable, advanced welfare state, with a broad consensus for social programs, the nation has become a fragmented and divided polity. These international and domestic changes have profoundly affected the level of agreement in society, brought controversial issues to the public agenda, and stimulated the formation of new political parties and new kinds of interest organizations and popular movements. Decision making is more complicated, and some outsiders have even said that Denmark has become ungovernable.

That judgment, however, is too extreme. Danish cabinets do not collapse like houses of cards. Controversies and divisions exist, but Denmark remains a vibrant democratic society with a rich cultural life. The welfare state endures, although there have been marginal changes and some reductions in government expenditures. Pioneering efforts have been undertaken in fields like consumer protection and the promotion of equal rights for women. New departures, such as economic democracy, are widely debated. Denmark remains a prime example of the "Scandinavian model," that mix of social welfare, economic planning, labor market and industrial relations policies, and political democracy that seeks to provide the good life in a modern industrial society.

The story of Denmark is, therefore, one of stability and change; of a welfare state in times of challenge and adversity; and of a small nation that, though buffeted by international political and economic storms, strives to maintain its own identity, autonomy, and domestic freedom.

2

The Nation and Its People

GEOGRAPHICAL FEATURES

The glaciers were the architects of the Danish landform. Their slow retreat (by about 10,000 B.C.) and the subsequent upheavals, submergences, and levelings of the earth shaped the contours of the landscape. The kingdom today consists of Denmark proper—an archipelago with the peninsula of Jutland (Jylland) and 406 islands, 90 of which are inhabited—plus the Faroe Islands in the North Atlantic, about 200 miles (320 kilometers) north of Scotland, and the huge island of Greenland. Jutland and its neighboring islands to the east comprise an area of some 16,600 square miles (43,000 square kilometers, which is slightly larger than Switzerland and about twice the area of Massachusetts), with Jutland itself providing nearly 70 percent of the land area.[1] The largest islands are Funen, or Fyn (1,152 square miles, or 2,984 square kilometers); Zealand, or Sjælland (2,709 square miles, or 7,015 square kilometers); and Lolland (480 square miles, or 1,234 square kilometers). Bornholm, in the Baltic some 90 miles (145 kilometers) to the east of Denmark and 22 miles (35 kilometers) off the south coast of Sweden, is considerably smaller (227 square miles, or 588 square kilometers). Excluding Greenland's nearly 840,000 square miles (2,175,590 square kilometers), Denmark is the smallest of the Northern countries.[2]

The nation's only land frontier, with the Federal Republic of Germany, is 42 miles (68 kilometers) long; but its total coastline amounts to more than 4,500 miles (7,240 kilometers), about one-sixth of the earth's circumference. No place in Denmark is more than 33 miles (53 kilometers) from the sea. Aside from Germany, Norway (125 miles, or 201 kilometers, away across the Skagerrak) and Sweden (12 miles, or 19 kilometers, away, over the Sound) are Denmark's closest neighbors.

The topography is characterized by glacial moraine deposits that form undulating plains and gently rolling hills. Essentially the surface is flat; the highest elevation—Yding Skovhøj in East Jutland—is only 568 feet (nearly 175 meters) above sea level. (There is a mountain, called

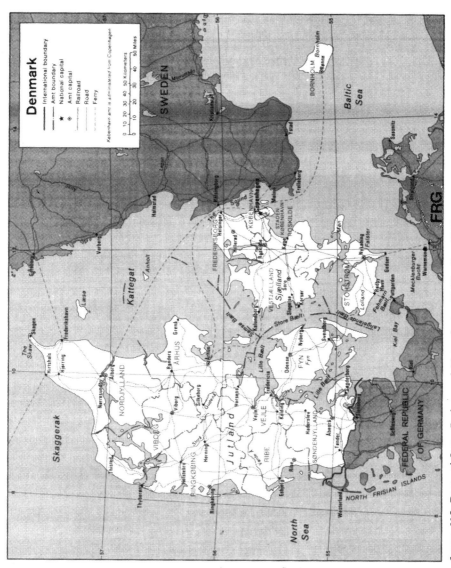

Source: U.S. Dept. of State, Background Notes Series, Publication 8298

Himmelbjerget, or Heaven's Mountain, all of 490 feet, or about 150 meters, high, near Silkeborg in Jutland's lake district.) The sea has always been a dominant influence in Danish life. From the North Sea to the west of Jutland, the Skagerrak divides Denmark from Norway; the Kattegat and the Sound (Øresund) separate Denmark and Sweden. The waters of the Great Belt (Storebælt) are between Zealand and Funen, and those of the Little Belt (Lillebælt), between Funen and Jutland. The country's insular nature has made maritime occupations like fishing and shipbuilding important since the days of the Vikings. Its location, at the intersection of the east-west sea routes connecting the Baltic and the North seas and the north-south land routes between Scandinavia and Germany, has made the nation the "crossroads of Europe" ever since the Bronze Age. Through this region have moved ideas, trade, and, occasionally, armies.

The surrounding waters temper the climate to Denmark's advantage. The Gulf Stream moderates the winters so that, though gray and misty, they are not as severe as in other countries of the same latitude, and the Baltic separates Denmark from the continental climate of Eastern Europe. Copenhagen, the warmest of the Northern capitals, had an average temperature of 49 degrees Fahrenheit (9.4 degrees Celsius) in 1988, with the coldest month, March, averaging about 36 degrees (2.1 degrees Celsius) and the warmest month, July, averaging about 64 degrees (17.8 degrees Celsius). Although the climate is not ideal for agriculture (the rainiest season is during the harvest months), the relatively mild winters allow farm animals to stay in pasture for much of the year, and the growing season is fairly long. Because of the small size of the country there are few regional differences, though the west tends to be wetter and the east colder in winter. It can rain any day of the year—and sometimes seems to.

Denmark's basically insular nature has made the building of bridges and the provision of ferries vitally important in linking the various parts of the country. Ferry service is provided across the Sound, the Great Belt, and the Kattegat. The Storstrøm Bridge, built in 1937 to connect the islands of Zealand and Falster, was for many years the longest bridge in Europe, measuring nearly 2 miles (3,211 meters). The Little Belt Bridge joined Funen and Jutland. In 1970 a suspension bridge was built near the Little Belt Bridge to help handle the increased traffic flow. A new bridge across the Great Belt between Zealand and Funen is scheduled for completion by 1996.

Sixty percent of Denmark's area is in arable lands and gardens, with forests accounting for only 11 percent of the territory. The farmland produces mainly fodder crops, although grain (primarily barley but also some wheat), sugar beets, and potatoes are also important. In 1988 there were some 84,000 agricultural holdings, a sharp drop from more than

184,000 in 1951. Moderate-size farms are still the rule, with one-third of them under 37 acres (15 hectares). Only about 3 percent of the farms are 250 acres (100 hectares) or larger.

It is indeed fortunate that the climate favors Danish agriculture, for raw materials needed for industry are almost entirely lacking. There are no metals, no coal, and no water power of any significance. Until the early 1980s Denmark was heavily dependent on imports of oil and other energy sources—in 1972 those imports accounted for 98 percent of all energy consumed, with oil alone accounting for more than 90 percent. The discovery and exploitation of oil and natural gas in the Danish sector of the North Sea, about 130 miles west of Jutland, has changed the energy picture considerably. Today domestic production covers 60 percent of total consumption of oil and natural gas, with 85 percent coverage expected in the near future.[3] Aside from oil and gas, about the only raw materials in good domestic supply are chalk, limestone, and clay. As a result, Denmark must import the essentials for its industry and rely on its skilled population to compensate for deficiencies in raw materials.

THE PEOPLE

Denmark is inhabited by a vigorous and energetic people. Though the population has never been large, it has contributed to the world many notable individuals in the arts and sciences. Among Danish writers, composers, artists, and philosophers have been Hans Christian Andersen, Søren Kierkegaard, Carl Nielsen, Isak Dinesen (Karen Blixen), Bertil Thorvaldsen, Ludvig Holberg, Martin Andersen Nexø, Johannes V. Jensen, and William Heinesen. Prominent scientists have included Tycho Brahe, Hans Christian Ørsted, August Krogh, Henrik Dam, and Niels Bohr. Worldwide audiences have enjoyed the comedy of Victor Borge and the dancing of Peter Martins.

At the end of 1989 the population of Denmark (excluding the Faroes and Greenland) was 5,135,409. Projections show a slow population growth into the twenty-first century and then a gradual decline to a number smaller than today's, with 4,760,000 as the estimated figure for the year 2025. The national birth rate declined in the 1930s, rose in the 1940s, then declined again and reached its lowest point in the 1980s. In 1988 it was 11.5 per thousand inhabitants, and the death rate was also 11.5. Life expectancy is now 71.8 years for men and 77.7 years for women. Within the population women outnumber men by about 74,000. Children below the age of fifteen make up nearly 18 percent of the present population, and people over the age of sixty-five constitute 15 percent of it (up from 7 percent in 1935).

More Danes got married in the 1980s, and more also entered into "paperless" marriages, or consensual unions: living together without having had a legal ceremony.[4] Weddings seem to be returning to favor, with an increase in the number each year since 1982. In addition, the number of those choosing church weddings, rather than civil ceremonies, has been growing. Along with changes in the marriage pattern has come an increase in the number of extramarital births, in 1988 amounting to 45 percent of all live births. The annual number of divorces has remained fairly stable in the 1980s but shows a twofold increase over the average in the 1960s. Abortions peaked numerically in 1980 and then began a gradual decline, with a rate of 4.1 per 1,000 inhabitants in 1987. (This was the same as the Swedish figure, a little higher than the Norwegian, and higher than those in Iceland and Finland.)[5] The suicide rate in Denmark is high, twice that in the United States, but for reasons that seem unconnected to the impact of the welfare state on the individual, which some critics see as the culprit.[6]

Denmark is the most densely populated of the Scandinavian countries, with 308 persons per square mile (119 per square kilometer). (Norway has 34 per square mile—13 per square kilometer—and Sweden, 49 per square mile—19 per square kilometer.) The people are not evenly distributed throughout the land; the density increases from west to east. There has been a growing migration from the farms to the cities and from the smaller islands to the larger ones. By the 1920s nearly half the Danes lived in cities, and by the 1980s this figure was more than 80 percent. Presently, fewer than 2 Danes out of 20 are engaged directly in agriculture, forestry, or fishing; 7 out of 20 work in manufacturing or commercial establishments; and 8 out of 20 are employed in the service sector. The number of women working outside the home has been rapidly increasing.

Around one-quarter of the total population live in the capital, Copenhagen, and its suburbs, which had 1,343,916 people in 1988. Only three other cities—Århus, Odense, and Ålborg—have more than 100,000 people. Despite the urban concentrations a great many Danes still live in small towns: Of some 1,400 local units with populations of more than 200, nearly 1,200 had fewer than 10,000 inhabitants. Copenhagen and the other larger cities have experienced a decline in population as the move from the central cities to the suburbs continues.

Among Danish cities Copenhagen predominates, and not just because of its size or its role as the national capital. True, it is the center of government and politics, with the Folketing (parliament) at Christiansborg, the royal palace of Amalienborg, the Supreme Court, and the administrative departments. But it is also the center of business and industry (being the home of about one-third of Danish industry), the

Countryside on Langeland. Along with mechanization and modern buildings, centuries-old farm traditions still thrive. Thatched and half-timbered farm buildings are in good repair. Many are admirably constructed and have been in family possession for generations. (Photo by Ole Akhøj)

leading port in Northern Europe, and a transportation crossroads with a major international airport at Kastrup. It is a center for culture and entertainment, too, with the Royal Theatre presentations of opera, ballet, and drama; the jazz clubs; and the world-famous Tivoli amusement park. Often called the "Paris of the North," Copenhagen has also been less flatteringly described as "a large head too big for a small body."

Other cities have their importance and attractions as well. Århus, second largest city and frequently referred to as Jutland's capital, has an important university. Ålborg, located within a sheltered fiord, is an industrial center, known, among other things, for its production of Ålborg Akvavit, a fiery liquor that is a national favorite. Odense, Hans Christian Andersen's birthplace, is the principal city of Funen and also a university center. Esbjerg, Denmark's "gateway to the west," has a deep-water harbor constructed in the 1870s and is a major fishing and general cargo port, with nearly half of the nation's food exports passing through it. A smaller town in Jutland, Billund, is famous with children throughout Europe for Legoland, a miniature world that includes castles, villages, ships and harbors, cathedrals, even Mount Rushmore and the New York City skyline, all constructed with the tiny Lego plastic building bricks.

Immigration and emigration have been fairly minimal in recent years. Both 1985 and 1986 saw sizable increases in the net migration figures, with surpluses of immigrants over emigrants of about 11,000 in 1986 and 6,600 in 1987 (but only 500 in 1988). In large part the increased immigration was from Asian countries and included Turks, Iranians, and Tamils from Sri Lanka, with many of the last two groups coming as political refugees. Asia (including the Middle East) provided nearly 30 percent of the immigrants in 1987. The other Nordic countries, the United States, and the United Kingdom accounted for nearly the same percentage.

Prior to 1986 the laws on political refugees were fairly liberal. As the numbers of those seeking asylum increased in the 1980s, public opinion polls indicated a growing concern both with the costs of caring for the refugees and with their assimilation into Danish society. In 1986 parliament revised the laws to make it more difficult for refugees to obtain asylum in Denmark. Nevertheless, it was estimated in mid-1988 that as many as 4,000 refugees might enter Denmark in that year, instead of the 1,500 anticipated. The right-wing Progress party has been outspoken in its belief that immigration must be sharply restricted, and the party's gains in the 1988 parliamentary election were attributable partly to that stand.

Despite this increased immigration the population is homogeneous. A German minority of some 30,000 lives just north of the border with Germany, in South Jutland, and there is a Danish minority on the other side of the border, in North Slesvig. Of the 1987 population, 98 percent had been born in Denmark, the Faroes, or Greenland. Though there have been numerous local dialects, which are mostly fading away, no language problem exists. Danish, Norwegian, and Swedish are such closely related tongues that the citizen of one country typically finds little linguistic difficulty when traveling or living in the others, though to the non-Scandinavian there seems a great deal of truth in the old saw that Danish is not a language but a disease of the throat. Most Danes seem to enjoy asking foreigners to say "rødgrød med fløde" or other tongue-twisters. In recent years a greater informality in language has developed. The familiar form of "you," du, has largely replaced the formal or polite form, de, in Danish discourse.

SOCIAL CONDITIONS

The returns from industry and agriculture have given Denmark one of the highest standards of living in the world. In per capita gross national product (GNP), Denmark stands high among Common Market members, its Scandinavian neighbors, and the United States: It ranked eighth in the world in 1980. Although there is some evidence of a limited trend toward greater equalization of incomes, differences remain. The richest 10 percent of the population received 25.5 percent of the national income in 1980 and the poorest 40 percent received 16.9 percent. Progressive taxation and welfare services provide some redistribution of income to the advantage of the poorer groups, but a differential remains between the incomes of men and women.[7] The great majority of Danes feel that there are class differences in Denmark, and they mention three or more specific classes, according to various sociological studies. In an extensive examination of prestige, class, and mobility, Professor Kaare Svalastoga of Copenhagen University concluded that Danish society could be divided into three main strata—upper, middle, and lower—each with three subdivisions (also upper, middle, and lower). The upper stratum included 0.3 percent of the population; the middle stratum, 40.4 percent; and the lower, 59 percent. Professor Svalastoga's survey, made some thirty years ago but still cited as a basic study, indicated that the Danes felt class divisions were revealed by differences in wealth, power, education, and prestige. He concluded tentatively that the most important single determinant of social status was level of education.[8]

Svalastoga commented that the use of occupational titles as symbols of status was "more, probably vastly more, frequent in Denmark than in [the United States, England, or Norway]. . . . a rather dominant attitude seems to be that a person's full name consists of title, first name, and last name."[9] Why this emphasis on titles? In part, they help with social identification, and they indicate a person's status in terms of position, education, or social origin. Also they serve a more prosaic identifying purpose. With numerous persons in Denmark having the same first and last names, occupation is an essential clue in trying to locate a particular individual. Danish telephone books include occupational titles and use the occupation, not the first name, as the second alphabetizing word. Even this may not be much help: In 1988 there were 287 closely printed columns of Hansens in the Copenhagen phone directory.

A recent study by the Social Research Institute divides the population into five social groups, based on the control the individual has over others' (and his/her own) work situations, as indicated by the number of people directed or supervised, and on the level of education required for jobs in each group. The first three groups—entrepreneurs, administrators, and professionals—constitute about 32 percent of the population; the lower two groups—small farmers and skilled and unskilled workers—

constitute about 68 percent. The study finds a strong relationship between parents' places in the social group structure and the places that their children later reach as adults.[10]

One cannot, by statistical measures, capture the spirit of a people or the ways in which they view themselves and their lives; generalizations, of course, are full of exceptions. The Danes have reason to be pleased with themselves and their accomplishments, but at times there is a certain smugness in their attitude, although that has been somewhat diminished by the economic buffetings of recent years. They are fond of material things and enjoy the comforts of life—the favorite Danish word seems to be *hyggelig*, meaning "cozy" or "comfortable." They think of themselves as an informal people, and they are more so than they used to be, though a U.S. visitor may still find an unfamiliar degree of formality.

The Danes pride themselves on their sense of humor and like to poke sly fun at what they consider the excessive stiffness and solemnity of their neighbors, the Swedes. A story has it that if two Norwegians, two Danes, and two Swedes were shipwrecked on a desert island, by the time rescuers arrived the Norwegians would be fighting, the Danes would have started a cooperative, and the Swedes would still be waiting to be introduced. Madeleine Gustafsson, a Swedish writer, makes a somewhat similar point. Imagine a parlor game, she suggests, in which one says quickly the first thing that a word brings to mind:

> "The Danes?"
> "Tenderness. Humor. Melancholy. The most civilized people among us."
> "The Finns?"
> "Warmth. A kind of—I don't know what to call it—lack of self-preservation instinct, directness."
> "The Norwegians?"
> "Youth. Everything that's part of it: vitality, the capacity for indignation and enthusiasm and—yes, the lack of perspective."
> "What about the Swedes?"
> "I don't know that one."
> "There, you see?"[11]

Proud of their freedom of expression the Danes often cultivate a critical and skeptical approach. As one anonymous Dane put it: "In Denmark, it's bad manners to talk about death. Otherwise, people talk about everything, but nobody listens, nobody pays any attention. This is thought to be liberal."[12] Irony and wit are used to pull down those who seem pretentious or behave ostentatiously. A contemporary Danish politician sums up: "The Dane is (relatively) tolerant. If I were to generalize, I would say the Dane is earthbound, balanced, self-ironic and considerably skeptical of ideologies and ideologues. . . . We are not melancholic, but it is difficult to incite Danes to a high degree of enthusiasm. They would rather hear a joke than rally round a speaker."[13]

THE FAROE ISLANDS

Located in the North Atlantic about 190 miles (about 300 kilometers) north of the Shetlands and northwest of Scotland, the Faroes are a group of islands of volcanic origin, with high cliffs, rock pinnacles, deep valleys, and narrow fiords. The distance by sea from Copenhagen is more than 900 miles (1,450 kilometers). Eighteen of some 30 islands are inhabited, with a total area in these 18 of 540 square miles (1,399 square kilometers). The population in 1987 was 46,700; the largest city, Thorshavn, had 14,300 people.

Although the Gulf Stream moderates the temperatures, the climate is unfriendly to agriculture. Winter storms are often fierce, and rainfall is heavy. Of some importance in the past (an old proverb says, "Sheep's wool is the gold of the Faroes"), sheep farming has been declining. The greatest proportion of meat, milk, poultry, and other foodstuffs has to be imported. Fisheries are the main source of income for the islands, and fish products make up more than 90 percent of their exports. When Denmark entered the European Community, the Faroes stayed out through their own choice because they feared that the EC's fisheries policy might be harmful to their local economy. They negotiated a trade agreement with the Community in 1974.

Vikings from Norway settled the Faroes in the ninth and tenth centuries, but after the separation of Norway and Denmark in 1814 the islands remained under Danish rule. The British occupied the Faroes during World War II. During the war years an independence movement developed, but a postwar plebiscite on separation from Denmark was inconclusive. Another solution, home rule, came into force in 1948. The Faroes have self-government within the Danish kingdom, with many local affairs directed by their own legislature, the Lagting (which dates back as far as A.D. 1000), and an executive responsible to that body. The Danish national government continues to be in charge of foreign policy, defense, the courts, and other common interests. Two representatives from the Faroes sit in the Danish parliament.

The language of the islands, Faroese, stems from Old Norse. Danish is a required language in school, and all adults speak Danish. There is a thriving cultural life, and the Faroese author William Heinesen has an international reputation.

GREENLAND

The largest but least densely populated part of the Danish realm is Greenland, the world's largest island. Its area of about 840,000 square miles (2,175,590 square kilometers) is 50 times that of Denmark proper. The distance from north to south is 1,660 miles (2,670 kilometers) and from east to west, 625 miles (about 1,050 kilometers). Most of the island is ice-covered (in some places the ice is more than 9,000 feet, or about 2,750 meters, thick); only about 15 percent is ice-free (the ice-free areas are about half the size of Texas). Most of Greenland is north of the Arctic circle, and the climate as a whole is arctic, with great variations in winter's length and temperatures between northern and southern Greenland and only slight variations in average summer temperatures. In 1988 the average temperature in Godthåb in the warmest month, August, was 44 degrees Fahrenheit (6.6 degrees Celsius) and in the coldest month, January, was 18 degrees (minus 8 degrees Celsius). The average temperature for the year was 30 degrees (minus 0.9 degrees Celsius), and Godthåb is in the warmest part of the island. No crops or trees grow, but many plants survive the chilling weather, and wildflowers bloom even in the north in the brief summertime. Much of the surrounding seas are ice-covered year-round; only the waters off the southwestern coast are normally ice-free all year.

The population is limited to the coastal areas and especially to a southwestern strip from Cape Farewell to Upernavik, which stretches a distance equal to that between Rome and Copenhagen. The population in 1988 was 54,100; a projection estimated that the total in the year 2005 will not be very different from this figure. Population density is less than 0.4 persons per square mile (0.1 per square kilometer).

Greenlanders live in 121 populated localities, a majority of which are sheep farming settlements of fewer than 100 inhabitants. Of 56 towns and villages, 40 had fewer than 500 people, and only 3 had more than 4,000. Godthåb (Nuuk in the Greenlandic language), the administrative center, is the biggest town, with 12,100 people.

The birth rate is almost double that in Denmark proper (most births—73.2 percent in 1986—are out of wedlock), and the abortion rate is much higher than Denmark's. Life expectancy figures are lower: 60.4 years for men and 66.3 years for women. Health conditions are improving, but alcoholism is a problem. About 9,000 of the inhabitants were born outside Greenland. Most Danes remain for only a few years, but new arrivals keep the Danish element at an almost stable 20 percent of the population.

In Greenlandic, Greenland is Kalaallet Nunaat, "the land of the Greenlanders." Related to the Eskimo languages of northern Canada,

Alaska, and eastern Siberia, Greenlandic is a polysynthetic language, that is, one in which words are formed by adding suffixes, so that a single word may express what requires several sentences in another language. Danish is spoken by a large part of the population and is a compulsory subject in the schools. Few Danes in Greenland learn Greenlandic, so the working language in business, teaching, and administration is often Danish. Greenland authorities have now designated Greenlandic as the principal language.

Fishing is the most important single industry in Greenland, with about one-fourth of the population dependent directly or indirectly on it for their livelihood. Mining is of modest proportions. The cryolite reserves have been exhausted, but there are deposits of iron ore (of low purity), low-grade coal, lead, zinc, chromium, molybdenum, scheelite, and uranium. Climatic conditions and transportation problems and the consequent cost of production raise difficulties for the exploitation of many of these resources. Oil exploration in southwest Greenland has been disappointing, but there are better possibilities on the continental shelf in the southeast and on land in east Greenland. Even if oil is found, production costs will be heavy. Seven hundred or eight hundred people are still active in sealing and other forms of hunting; some sheep are raised in south Greenland, albeit under difficult conditions; and handicraft production supplements the incomes of some people. In 1986 fishing, sealing, and agricultural products accounted for 82 percent of exports; lead, zinc, and chrome ore made up 14 percent.

Eskimos (the preferred word is Inuit, meaning "people") have lived in Greenland for more than 4,000 years. As hunters of seals, walruses, polar bears, reindeer, and whales, they crossed the ice from North America. The harsh northern conditions made survival difficult, and the population often nearly vanished completely. The ancestors of the present Inuit population probably arrived around A.D. 1000.

At about the same time the first European settlers came to Greenland. These were Norse who under the leadership of Erik the Red landed in southern Greenland in A.D. 982. The climate was considerably warmer than it is today, and by 1300 there was a population of 3,000 to 4,000. The settlers remained for about 500 years, and then the European population vanished for reasons that remain uncertain. Greenland came under Danish rule in the fourteenth century when the kingdoms of Norway and Denmark were united. Efforts at resettlement met with little success until 1721, when the Danish missionary Hans Egede arrived at Godthåb, converted many Inuit to the Lutheran faith, and set up trading posts.

Norway challenged Danish sovereignty over northwest Greenland in the 1920s, but in 1933 the International Court of Justice ruled in

Denmark's favor. During World War II U.S. troops occupied Greenland following an agreement between the United States and the Danish ambassador in Washington, D.C.—Denmark was then occupied by the Germans. U.S. air bases continue to exist at Thule and Søndre Strømfjord, and the United States operates various warning systems on the inland ice, all as a result of agreements with the Danish government.

Since the adoption of the new Danish constitution in 1953, Greenland has no longer been a colony but an integral part of the kingdom, with two representatives in the Danish parliament. By the early 1970s Greenland politicians were talking about home rule, and in 1975 a home rule commission made up of equal numbers of Danes and Greenlanders recommended autonomy. In a referendum in January 1979, with a turnout of 63 percent of the electorate, 12,754 Greenlanders (73 percent of those voting) voted for home rule, with 4,705 voting against.

The Home Rule Act became effective on May 1, 1979, and Greenland today is a self-governing part of the Danish kingdom. The Folketing delegated many of its powers over Greenlandic affairs to the island's legislature, but the Danish government retains responsibility for foreign policy, defense, and justice. The two governments exercise joint authority over Greenland's oil and mineral resources. Denmark continues to provide a large subsidy to the island in the form of a block grant.

Within Greenland, legislative power rests with the Landsting, a unicameral legislature of 27 members elected for four-year terms. Four parties compete for Landsting seats. Permanent residents who are eighteen years of age and older have the right to vote. The executive branch, the Landstyre, led by the "home government head," is chosen by and responsible to the Landsting. The High Court of Greenland and 18 circuit courts exercise judicial authority. With the consent of the minister for justice, decisions by the high court may be appealed to the Danish Supreme Court in Copenhagen.

In 1973 Greenland joined the European Community along with Denmark proper (but not the Faroes), even though 69 percent of Greenland's voters had rejected membership in the 1972 referendum. Many Greenlanders felt that EC membership would restrict the development of their economy and that they lacked the necessary power to get their interests and needs recognized within the Community. In a referendum in 1982, Greenlanders endorsed withdrawal from the EC by a narrow margin, and Greenland left the European Community in 1985, though an affiliation was retained: The EC promised to pay compensation over a five-year period for its members' continued access to fishing in Greenland waters, and Greenlanders won the right to sell fish in EC countries without tariff barriers.

3

History

The first scanty traces of human habitation in what is now Denmark appear about 100,000 years ago. More substantial evidence of human life appeared during the Old Stone Age (around 10,000 B.C.), after the last retreat of the glacial ice, when wandering hunters followed the ever-northward course of reindeer migration. By the early Stone Ages there were many small inland settlements of people engaged in hunting and fishing.

In the New Stone Age (about 2500 B.C.) came a revolutionary change: the introduction of agriculture, perhaps as the consequence of a wave of immigration from the south. Oxen, sheep, goats, and pigs were domesticated. Flint-working reached a high peak of excellence and artistry, and flint axes, knives, and other products, as well as Danish amber, were exported to the Mediterranean countries. Immigrant craftsmen brought to Denmark the skills of working with bronze. Shipbuilding progressed from simple canoes to seagoing craft requiring twenty to thirty oarsmen, making possible trade with Baltic areas. Danes began to learn from southern peoples the techniques of making iron from the "bog ore" found in the marshes. Farmers cut or burned off forests and turned to grain crops like wheat and barley. Trading connections with other parts of Europe were periodically interrupted but always restored, and Denmark proved able to withstand the pressures of itinerant peoples from the south.

The Viking era, lasting to about A.D. 1050, was a period of Scandinavian expansion. For the Danes, dislocations in trade with the south, caused in part by transfer of the capital of the Roman Empire to Constantinople, forced them to turn more attention to the east-west trade routes through the Baltic, and Denmark became increasingly a maritime nation. Around A.D. 500–600, a major wave of attacks and invasions began. Danish Vikings conquered the Frisian coast and by about A.D. 800 had embarked on their major campaigns against England.

In 886 the king of Wessex had to give up his lands north of a line from London to Chester, and thousands of Danes settled permanently in that territory in an independent Viking kingdom, the "Danelaw." The raids and the inflow of Danish peasants were not checked until the reign of Alfred the Great (871–901), who regained the Danelaw but permitted its inhabitants to keep their Danish laws and customs. The last great attacks on England came during the reign of Sweyn Forkbeard (ca. 985–1014). After a series of battles Sweyn conquered all the English provinces and forced London to surrender, whereupon the English king fled to France. Upon Sweyn's death the English monarch returned, but in 1015 Sweyn's son Knud (or Canute) won control of the entire country. Canute was crowned king of England; shortly thereafter he became king of Denmark upon the death of his brother and soon added southern Norway to his domain. His empire fell to pieces after the demise of his second son, Hardeknud (or Hardicanute), in 1042, and England was lost to the Danes.

An earlier monarch, King Harald Bluetooth (ca. 935–985), aware of the danger of attacks from the south, had succeeded in consolidating the several Danish kingdoms into one domain under his rule. In Jelling, a small town in Jutland, may be seen today two runic stones, one set up by Harald and one by his father, Gorm. Harald's stone, dating from about A.D. 960, has this finely carved inscription: "Harald, the king, ordered this memorial made for his father Gorm and his mother Thyra, the Harald who won all of Denmark, and also Norway, and [made] the Danes Christian." Harald was the first Danish king to become Christian, in an act of political realism rather than piety, and Christianity may be regarded as a major import of the Viking age. The Church did not become firmly established till the reign of Sweyn Estridson (1047–1074); as a result, Christianity and paganism coexisted for a considerable period.

THE MONARCH AND THE NOBILITY

The Church and the king were both forces for national unity. The institution of the monarchy spans Danish history from the beginnings of written records to the present, but a king in early times was not always a man of great power. *Primus inter pares*, he was elected by the *tings*, or popular assemblies, mainly for purposes of leadership in war. One of the early kings, Gorm the Old (who died in A.D. 950) is considered the ancestor of all subsequent Danish monarchs. By Viking times the property-owning farmers were the core of the society, and it was they who gathered in the village *tings* to choose leaders and to administer justice. Excluded from any influence were free men without property, women, and serfs.

Throughout the eleventh and twelfth centuries and despite a bloody and unstable period from 1131 to 1157 when there were many contenders for the throne, the kings continued to grow in power as the needs for executive action increased. Gradually the kings began to gain a share with the national assemblies, or *landstings*, in the rudimentary legislative field as well. By the end of the reign of Valdemar II, the Victorious (1202–1241), written laws had been promulgated for Denmark's three lands. The relations of the king and the groups who dominated the *landstings* were clearly changing, and gradually the *landstings'* role in electing the king became a mere formality.

The traditional origin of the Danish flag goes back to the reign of Valdemar II. Legend has it that the first flag, the Dannebrog, dropped from heaven as Valdemar the Victorious battled in Estonia in 1219 and turned defeat into victory. (The actual date of the flag, with its white cross on a red field, is some eighty years later; nevertheless, it is the oldest European national banner still in use.) The country's coat of arms—a yellow field with three blue lions and nine small red hearts—dates from about 1190.

The developing class of nobles gained a victory in 1282 when they forced King Erik Klipping to sign the Great Charter (Håndfæstning). By the provisions of this charter, often considered Denmark's first consti-tution, the king recognized important restrictions on his power, agreeing to an annual "parlamentum" or *hof* and accepting limitations on his judicial powers. New kings made similar agreements at the beginning of their reigns, and so Denmark had a series of "constitutions" of this type until the establishment of royal absolutism in 1660. The charters assured the nobles a stronger and often decisive voice in government and made them a counterbalance to the monarch.

By the end of the fourteenth century the Danehof, the annual assembly provided for in the Charter of 1282, had lost out to a small inner circle of nobles and clergy, the Rigsråd. This council, together with the king, exercised more and more legislative and judicial authority and over the course of time acquired the real power to select a new monarch upon the death of the old one. The national government rested upon the cooperation of king and council, an arrangement that from reign to reign reflected a shifting balance of power: At one time the king was the stronger party, at another, it was the council.

Tests of strength for the Danish state came throughout the twelfth and thirteenth centuries, in struggles against the princes and towns of northern Germany and in civil wars at home. After periods in which national independence and unity seemed almost hopelessly lost, a strong ruler, Valdemar Atterdag, succeeded by about 1370 in reuniting and consolidating the kingdom and in restoring to Denmark the Scanian provinces in Sweden. After his death his daughter Margrethe ruled Denmark on behalf of her younger son. Married to the king of Norway, she gained control there upon her husband's death in 1380. When her son died, the Danish and Norwegian nobles recognized Margrethe as their ruler, and after her army defeated the Swedes, she assumed power in Sweden as well. She arranged for the permanence of the three-nation union by providing a successor, Erik, her sister's grandson. A convention at Kalmar proclaimed him king of the three countries in 1397. The union of Kalmar lasted, with intervals, until 1523, when Sweden finally succeeded in effecting a permanent separation; the union of Denmark and Norway endured until 1814. With Danish rule over Norway also had come sovereignty over the Shetland, Orkney, and Faroe islands; Iceland; and Greenland.

The changes occurring in Denmark were not solely political. The towns were beginning to draw laborers from the countryside, and many peasants, during times of civil war and other disturbances, voluntarily gave up their lands and accepted tenancy from owners of larger estates in exchange for protection. In the course of their struggles with the king, the nobles had won privileges of exemption from taxation that were extended to their tenants, and so there was an additional incentive for freeholders to accept tenancy. The sixteenth century was one of economic progress in Denmark; a large number of the manor houses that still dot the countryside date from this period. But it was a time of progress and prosperity for the large landowners, not the small ones. It has been estimated that between 1250 and 1400 the proportion of the population made up of independent farmers decreased from 50 percent to 15 percent.

Market towns began to replace peasant villages as trading centers and in time acquired monopoly privileges over trade. As a result, peasants were forced to bring their products to these market centers. In Zealand the town of Copenhagen (founded in 1167 by Bishop Absalon) had developed as a maritime center with an export trade in salted herring. Hoping for support from the Church, Queen Margrethe gave the town to the bishop of Roskilde, but her successor, Erik VII, reacquired it and made its castle his residence, so that Copenhagen became the national capital in about 1417.

The Church in Denmark in the late Middle Ages seemed as concerned with material goods as with spiritual ones. King Christian II (1513–1523) had begun reforms in church administration even before Luther's protests were heard in Germany. A young Danish student and former monk, Hans Tavsen, returned home from Wittenberg and began preaching Lutheran doctrines in the towns, and others soon followed his example. King Frederik I (1523–1533) extended his protection to Tavsen and granted the reformer permission to continue preaching despite the protests of the Church.

The controversy over the Reformation was in Denmark a mild one, though religious matters were partly involved in a civil war over the succession to the throne after Frederik's death. The winner in this bloody "Count's War" was Frederik's son, a Lutheran. As Christian III, he called together in Copenhagen in 1536 a national assembly, the Rigsdag, whose 1,200 members, drawn from the nobles, the burghers, and the peasants, voted to abolish the old Church organization and to eliminate the political and religious powers of the Catholic clergy. The king forced bishops from office, confiscated Church property, and took steps to organize the new Lutheran Church as a state church with the monarch at its head.

Christian III's grandson, Christian IV (who reigned from 1588 to 1648), is perhaps the best known of Danish kings, recalled whenever Danes sing the national anthem, "King Christian Stood by Lofty Mast." A master builder, he created new towns and fortified old ones, reconstructed the old castle of Frederiksborg and built the new Rosenborg Palace, and developed a new commercial harbor and a naval base in Copenhagen while expanding the city's area to twice its former size.

> He personally checked timber measurements when ships were under construction, personally bought up the stone and timber required for his castles, personally completed both rough sketches and finished architectural drawings, personally tested the mortar used at building sites and criticized it, conducted negotiations with foreign ambassadors, wrote and spoke several languages, loved good music and was the founder of a distinguished era in Danish organ-building.[1]

Christian IV's handiwork can still be seen in Copenhagen today in the Stock Exchange, a residence for university students (Regensen), the Round Tower, Rosenborg Palace, and housing built originally for workers in the royal shipyard (Nyboder).

In foreign affairs the long series of wars between Denmark and Sweden continued, with dominance in Scandinavia as the prize. In the long run Denmark was at a disadvantage in the contests with its rival: Internal differences between king and nobles, failure to reorganize and modernize sufficiently the political and military structure, class dissensions, the lessened value of Danish agricultural products as an element of national power—all these were factors in the decline of Danish leadership. A decisive defeat came in the Thirty Years' War (1618–1648), and after a further and even more serious defeat in the Danish-Swedish War (1657–1660), the nation had to yield. By the peace settlement

Denmark gave up her rich Scanian provinces to Sweden and recognized the Sound as the boundary between the two countries.

ROYAL ABSOLUTISM

The Swedish wars left Denmark prostrate, exhausted, and impoverished. Reform and reorganization were imperative. The kings had increasingly felt themselves fettered by their council, the Rigsråd, and the nobility, and the low status to which Denmark had sunk offered an opportunity to strike off the bonds, especially because the nobles had by no means distinguished themselves in the wars.

In 1660 Frederik III summoned a Rigsdag, composed of members of the nobility and representatives of the burghers and the clergy. (The peasants, who constituted 80 percent or more of the population, were neither invited nor represented.) When the nobility proved hesitant to vote for new taxes, the other estates, with the king's encouragement, decided to move against them. Supported by the army, the representatives of the towns and the Church offered to the king and his heirs the establishment of a hereditary monarchy, to be ruled "as should seem best to his majesty for the general good." The nobles, made hostages when the king closed the city gates, were forced to yield, and the monarch no longer had to agree before taking office to a charter with restrictions on his power.

The constitutional document, the Royal Law, or Kongeloven, issued by Frederik in 1665, was an unequivocal statement of absolutism. The king possessed all power as head of both state and church. He was above the laws of man, with only God as his judge; he was limited only by the obligation to defend the Augsburg Confession.

Of course, the king could not in practice exercise all power by himself, and a consequence of the absolute monarchy was the development of a centralized bureaucracy. In the course of time some of the civil servants were granted titles, and a new aristocracy developed, tied to the monarch and with no roots in the old system. As the civil servants' role became more and more important, rule by bureaucracy rather than absolute monarchy was perhaps a more accurate description of Denmark's system of government.

Among the major groups that comprised the Danish population, the nobility, with its infusion of new blood and because many of its members possessed large estates, continued to be important. The bourgeoisie as a group were also thriving and gaining in political and economic importance with the expansion of mercantile capitalism. They educated their sons, who often found positions in the Church and the administration; they invested in land as well as in manufacturing and commerce; they gained social approval; and some were granted titles and peerages.

For the peasants, tenancy remained the rule. Even after the abolition of serfdom in 1702 they were tied to the soil through a militia system that forced them to live in the same area or on the same estate as long as they were eligible for service. Toward the end of the eighteenth century, however, agricultural reforms began to be initiated from above by members of the nobility. By the close of the century all forms of compulsory labor had been abolished, and the peasant gained protection against expulsion from his farm as well as the rights to move and to live where he chose.

In economic policy the Danish state had adopted mercantilism. But the first Danish edition of *The Wealth of Nations* appeared in 1779, and soon the revolutionary principles of laissez-faire had become a part of the conventional wisdom. The government abolished or restricted monopolies and in 1797 enacted the most liberal tariff arrangements in Europe. Mercantilism had encouraged continuation of craftsmen's guilds in the towns, but the reaction against the old economic theory led to actions against these monopolies, although the guild system was not finally ended until 1862. Other reforms included abolition of the slave trade (1792), full civil rights for the Jews (1814), and compulsory education for children between the ages of seven and fourteen (1814).

In the midst of the period of reform came a further disastrous involvement in international affairs. Efforts to keep Denmark neutral in the wars that accompanied and followed the American and French revolutions ultimately failed, as circumstances led to an alliance with France. When the Danes sought to evade an ultimatum from Britain in 1807, a British squadron bombarded Copenhagen, occupied the harbor, and seized the Danish fleet. From then on, Denmark stood with Napoleon until forced to surrender in 1814. By the Treaty of Kiel, Norway was lost to Sweden, which had joined the victorious coalition before the war's end. Denmark managed to retain Greenland, Iceland, and the Faroe Islands.

THE STRUGGLE FOR CONSTITUTIONAL REFORM

After the defeat in the Napoleonic wars and the loss of Norway, the Danes might have been expected to avoid foreign entanglements and to center their interests and activities within their own boundaries. Any desire to devote full attention to domestic problems had to be left unfulfilled, however, because of growing troubles in the south with the duchies of Slesvig and Holstein. The relationship between Denmark and the two territories was a complicated one—Lord Palmerston is supposed to have remarked that only three persons really understood the Slesvig-Holstein question: one was dead, one was in an asylum, and the third, he himself, had forgotten it. Slesvig belonged to the Danish Crown as a personal possession of the king, but Holstein was part of the Holy Roman Empire and the king ruled there as an imperial duke. Danish influence predominated in northern Slesvig, but the Germans were strong in the south, and Holstein was overwhelmingly German in composition and sympathies.

The question of the duchies was made even more complicated by involvement of their status in the struggle for a democratic constitution in Denmark. Earlier reforms had helped bring into existence a large group of independent farmers. Hard-headed, realistic, and practical in their political attitudes, they began to find that some of their interests and goals coincided with those of the bourgeoisie. The farmers embraced the idea of the folk high school, first proposed by N.F.S. Grundtvig in the 1830s, as a means of improving their lot, and the national movement in Slesvig seized upon it as a way to carry on the cultural struggle against the Germans. The first such school opened at Rødding in 1844. There was also a religious revival in the countryside, which expressed itself partly in opposition to the established Church. This revival also had social and political significance, as it increased contacts among the farmers in different localities. Urban liberals identified themselves with the attempt to promote the Danish language and culture in Slesvig and associated the demand for a new constitution with settlement of the Slesvig problem.

The problems of Slesvig-Holstein and constitutional reform, intertwined because any basic constitutional change would also affect relationships between the Danish state and the duchies, can only be touched upon here. Under pressure from students, merchants, and farmers, Christian VIII (1839–1848) directed one of his ministers to prepare a constitution. That task was not completed by the king's death on January 20, 1848, but the new king, Frederik VII, informed the liberals that henceforth he would rule as a constitutional monarch, with his ministers responsible for government policies.

Prussia then backed a revolt by Holstein separatists, but the Danes were able to hold their own in the First Slesvig War, which ended in 1850 without change in the status of the duchies. During the war a national assembly drafted a constitution, which the king approved on June 5, 1849. The "June Constitution" (Junigrundloven) recognized a division of powers, with the legislative power vested in the king and the Rigsdag; the executive, in the king; and the judicial, in the courts of law. Notable was the provision that the king's signature was valid only if countersigned by one or more ministers. The exact relationship between the king and his ministers remained to be worked out in practice, and Danish politics in the rest of the century was to center on this question.

The Rigsdag was to have two chambers, the Folketing and the Landsting, equal in power but not identical in composition. The right to vote belonged to all "independent" males over the age of thirty; this meant about 15 percent of the population. Members of the Folketing were chosen in direct elections for three-year terms; they had to be at least twenty-five years old. Landsting members were elected indirectly for terms of eight years, with half the body renewable every four years; they had to be at least forty years of age and have an income, or pay taxes, of a certain amount. Among other provisions the constitution guaranteed the rights and liberties of the individual and promised judicial reform.

When the Danes acted in 1863 to incorporate Slesvig into the kingdom, Prussia and Austria joined forces and decisively defeated the Danish troops. By the Treaty of Vienna in 1864, Denmark had to yield Slesvig, including the Danish-speaking parts, to Prussia and Holstein to Austria (Prussia soon acquired it).

CONTINUING POLITICAL PROBLEMS, 1864–1939

Defeat had showed Denmark to be no match for its southern neighbor, and policies had to be adjusted accordingly. With no allies to count on, the country would have to play the role of a small power, accept neutrality, and avoid offending Germany. To many it appeared that any attempt at defense was futile, and there was a growing sentiment for disarmament and pacifism.

Conservative forces took advantage of the shock of national defeat to revise the constitution in their favor in July 1866. The rest of the century was marked by political conflict, often bitter, between the forces of conservatism and reform. First among the latter stood the independent farmers, politically organized as the Venstre, or Liberal, party.[2] By the 1870s the industrial revolution had come to Denmark and with it an urban working class, a trade union movement, and a socialist political party. The first Social Democrats appeared in the Folketing in 1884, and in the quest for reform this new group soon joined with the Liberals. In addition to the Social Democrats, support for democratic reforms came from representatives of tenants and other small farmers and from some of the urban intellectuals.

From 1872 on, the reform groups had a majority in the Folketing, though the conservatives controlled the Landsting. The crux of the constitutional and political dispute was the Liberal and Social Democratic demand for acceptance of the basic principle of parliamentary government, the selection of the king's ministers from the party with a majority in the lower house. The conservatives, organized as the Højre (or Right) party, maintained that the king could choose his ministers freely, without reference to party strengths in the Rigsdag or to election results. The king agreed with the conservatives and drew his ministers from the majority in the Landsting.

With a stalemate between the two houses, government could only be carried on by resort to a constitutional provision enabling the king to issue temporary or "provisional" laws without the Rigsdag's approval. In the long run this was an impossible situation, and finally, when the elections of 1901 virtually eliminated the Right from the Folketing, the king had to yield and appoint the first Liberal cabinet. With this "change of system" (systemskifte) a major goal for which the opposition groups had been fighting was attained, and henceforth the principle of cabinet responsibility to the majority in the Folketing was established.

In 1915 a new constitution did away with the special privileged requirements for voting or serving in the Landsting: It abolished both property qualifications for membership and the exceptional treatment given to the wealthier voters. All citizens of thirty-five or over, including women and servants, acquired the right to vote for the electors who chose the Landsting, and the king's power to appoint some members was ended, though the Landsting itself was to choose one-fourth of its members. The term of office was set at eight years. For the Folketing, universal suffrage also applied, with a reduction of the voting age to twenty-five. For both houses proportional representation replaced the earlier system of plurality elections in single-member districts. World War I delayed the implementation of the new constitution, and not until 1918 were the first elections held under it.

Constitutional reform and the competition among the Danish political parties were closely intertwined. On the Left the Social Democrats had continued to grow in strength, and in 1913 for the first time they passed the Liberals in popular votes. The Liberals were no longer a party of the Left but a party moving to the Center and Right. Between the Social Democrats and the Liberals a new party had emerged, the Radicals (Det Radikale Venstre), which had split off from the Liberals in 1905. Backed by smallholders and some urban intellectuals and professional people, the Radicals allied themselves with the Social Democrats, and the Radical minority cabinets of 1909–1910 and 1913–1920 received the support of the socialists. To the political Right of the Liberals the old conservative party underwent a change of name and program and emerged in 1915 as the Conservative Peoples party (Det Konservative Folkeparti). Increasingly party rivalry involved competition between two sets of alliances: Social Democrat–Radical vs. Liberal-Conservative.

World War I brought pressure upon Denmark from both belligerent sides. The nation was in a vulnerable geographic and economic position, and its survival seemed to require neutrality. The country suffered as a result of heavy shipping losses, economic dislocations, inflation, and speculation. In 1916 a plebiscite upheld the government's decision to sell the Danish West Indies (now the Virgin Islands) to the United States. In 1918 Iceland's independence was acknowledged, but with the king of Denmark remaining king of Iceland as well. The principal territorial change came at the end of the war when, after a plebiscite that showed a 75 percent pro-Danish majority, North Slesvig was reunited with Denmark.

Domestically the immediate postwar years were times of economic unrest and political crisis. After resolution of a cabinet crisis in 1920 Liberal and Social Democratic minority cabinets alternated in power until 1929, when the Social Democrats and the Radicals united to form a coalition government headed by the Social Democratic leader, Thorvald Stauning. This coalition, with a majority behind it in the Folketing, was to endure until 1940. The Landsting remained a more conservative body, however, and the Social Democratic–Radical combination lacked a majority there until 1936. Although several new parties made their appearances after World War I—both the Communist party and the Justice party were founded in 1919—politics continued to center on the competition of the "four old parties" and on the cooperation of Social Democrats and Radicals against Liberals and Conservatives.

After the 1929 election the Social Democrats and Radicals agreed upon a common legislative program, and the groundwork was laid for fruitful cooperation on social and economic reform. With the onset of the world economic crisis of the 1930s, the krone had to be devalued, the purchase and sale of foreign currency had to be controlled by the state, and the government increasingly intervened in economic life and sought to stimulate domestic industry and employment. An attempt to revise the constitution failed in 1938, when voting in a national referendum produced an overwhelming majority for the change but not the 45 percent of all eligible voters required by the amending process.

DENMARK DURING WORLD WAR II

The struggle over constitutional reform had been overshadowed by the menacing international situation. With the remilitarization of Germany and its increasingly aggressive stance, there was once again a strong and potentially hostile neighbor to the south. Popular feelings were anti-Nazi, but the government had to be cautious, especially since there seemed no likelihood of external aid against Germany if trouble should develop.

Neutrality appeared the only reasonable policy. The government sought to maintain normal relations with Germany, even though this meant persuading Danish newspapers to soften their attacks on the Nazi regime. A Nazi movement among the German minority in South Jutland had become increasingly active. Its numbers were not great, but its ties with the German Nazis, its demands for the incorporation of South Jutland into the Third Reich, the actions of its uniformed militants, and the dominant position it gradually obtained within the German population of the border areas made it a troublesome element and a persistent nuisance.

On September 1, 1939, Germany attacked Poland. Denmark proclaimed its neutrality and took what steps it could to ensure its defenses. No one really believed that, if a test of arms should come, the nation would be able to hold off an invading army. The declaration of neutrality offered no protection when the Nazis decided the occupation of Denmark was essential for their war effort. On April 8 there were reports of German troop movements on the Jutland border; on the 9th, those troops entered Denmark, while German warships and transports appeared in Danish harbors and German planes flew overhead. A few shots were exchanged, but the Danish government quickly concluded that there was no alternative but to yield to a German ultimatum. Before Germany could take any action against Denmark's outlying territories, Henrik Kauffmann, the Danish ambassador in Washington, placed Greenland under U.S. protection, and the British occupied the Faroe Islands and Iceland.[3]

The Nazis, intent on making Denmark a "model protectorate," allowed the governmental institutions and the political parties to carry on. King Christian X, a man in his seventies, continued his morning horseback rides through the streets of Copenhagen without attendants or escort and became the symbol of the Danish national spirit, as well as of the attempt to keep the situation as normal and stable as possible. To Danish political leaders it seemed better to make necessary but limited concessions to the occupiers than to risk a complete takeover of authority by the Germans. Only after the tide of the war began to turn, and as Nazi demands became increasingly severe and extreme, did resistance become well organized and significant.

Political interference by the occupying authorities began almost immediately, however, despite the pledges and assurances. After the invasion of the Soviet Union in June 1941, the Germans demanded the arrest of the leading Danish Communists, and the government felt compelled to comply. In August the Rigsdag passed a statute outlawing the Communist party and providing a basis for detention of the arrested Communists. This was unconstitutional, but it was considered necessary to placate the Germans, who also insisted on Danish adherence to the Anti-Comintern Pact. The cabinet succeeded in limiting Denmark's obligation under the pact to its own territory and in avoiding any commitment to other political duties or to participation in the war. Danes were allowed to volunteer for military service with the Germans on the Russian front. In 1942 the Germans insisted on changes in the Danish cabinet and on the imposition of Erik Scavenius as prime minister.

An election for the Folketing was constitutionally required in 1943, and the Germans allowed the vote, probably believing that the results could be interpreted as popular support for the Scavenius government and its policy of conciliation with Germany. So March of 1943 provided the strange spectacle of the democratic process at work in a Nazi-occupied land. All political parties participated save the outlawed Communists. The democratic parties called for a heavy vote to show Danish support for democracy and national independence, and the elections became a patriotic demonstration. Nearly 90 percent of the electorate cast their ballots, and almost 95 percent of those voting supported the principal democratic parties—Social Democratic, Radical, Liberal, Conservative, and Justice. The Danish Nazi party, despite, or perhaps because of, the favor of the occupying power, received only about 2.7 percent of the total.

Almost from the beginnings of the occupation some Danes had disapproved of the government's policy of accommodation toward Germany, and small groups, acting without coordination, engaged in acts of sabotage and in the circulation of anti-German propaganda and illegal newspapers. As the resistance movement developed, its organization improved, and British planes supplied it with arms and equipment by parachute drops. Danes in London formed the Danish Council in September 1940 to direct the actions of their countrymen who had escaped the Nazi yoke. A significant part of the Danish merchant marine had avoided German seizure and served the Allies well during the rest of the war. Some 150 ships with their Danish crews were in the Battle of the Atlantic.

Within Denmark opposition to the Nazi occupiers intensified. Strikes hampered production in factories serving the Germans; especially significant were those in the fall of 1943, including a six-day work stoppage in Odense. In response the Germans demanded the imposition of martial law and the surrender of all accused saboteurs to them for trial. When the government and the Rigsdag refused, the Nazis began to use harsher methods. They brought in more troops, and they turned loose on the

Danish population bands of armed ruffians. On August 28, 1943, Werner Best, the Nazi representative in Denmark, issued a list of repressive demands. Backed by all the democratic parties the cabinet flatly rejected the ultimatum, and the German military commander declared martial law. The Gestapo rounded up numerous leading citizens, and German forces moved against military units and overcame spirited but futile resistance. The Danish Navy scuttled itself, and only a few ships fell into German hands.

For the Nazis, Best insisted that a new and more subservient government be formed. Again the Danes refused, and the king indicated that he could appoint no ministry without parliamentary approval. Administrators remained at their posts, however, so that essential services could be carried out. The Germans imposed more stringent control over the economy to make sure it served their war needs, and they instituted increasingly repressive measures against those suspected of sabotage, espionage, or resistance in any form.

The Nazis also decided that the time had come to dispose of the 8,000 Danish Jews, apparently on orders from Hitler himself. Seizure of the Jews was set for October 1, 1943, but by that time most of them had been warned and already had gone into hiding, aided by all segments of the Danish population. Individual acts of heroism were numerous. In Hannah Arendt's words:

> The story of the Danish Jews is sui generis, and the behavior of the Danish people and their government was unique among all the countries of Europe. . . . One is tempted to recommend the story as required reading in political science for all students who wish to learn something about the enormous power potential inherent in non-violent action and in resistance to an opponent possessing vastly superior means of violence.[4]

Of the Jewish population, both citizen and refugee, about half were smuggled to Sweden during October, nearly half remained safely in Denmark throughout the rest of the war, and only about 500 were taken by the Germans.

The four largest underground groups combined in September 1943 to form the Freedom Council, which from then on directed and coordinated the resistance movement. Increased sabotage brought brutal counter-sabotage from the Germans, including murders, such as the killing of the respected clergyman, poet, and dramatist Kai Munk, and the destruction of property, such as the near-devastation of the famous Tivoli in Copenhagen. The German authorities ordered a curfew in Copenhagen in June 1944. In protest, workers began leaving their jobs early, saying that they had to go home to tend their gardens during the daylight hours. When news came of the execution of eight saboteurs, a spontaneous general strike developed in the capital. Workers left their factories, the populace ignored the curfew and began to erect barricades in the streets, and shots were exchanged. The Germans cut off gas, water, and electricity to the city and moved in more soldiers, but the beleaguered citizens refused to yield. The Freedom Council set a number of conditions for a cessation of the strike: abolition of the curfew, restoration of normal public services, and no reprisals. As the strike began to spread to other cities, the Germans gave in and agreed to the council's conditions.

The authorities in Berlin blamed their representatives in Denmark, Best and General Hermann von Hanneken, for failure to control the situation, and the Gestapo took over, with more raids, shootings, attacks, arrests, and deportations the result. Meanwhile the resistance movement improved its organization and increased its activities. Especially important was the very successful sabotage and disruption of rail traffic through Jutland, important because of its delaying effect on the movement of German troops from Norway to other fronts. The Freedom Council became a kind of "illegal" government that exercised general direction of anti-German activities, maintained contact with the Allied forces, issued instructions to the population that were generally followed, and kept in touch with the leaders of the Danish political parties. In Sweden Danish refugees were organized and trained as military units, with the covert assistance of the Swedish government.

Cooperation between the Freedom Council and the political party leadership proved difficult at times. Both groups realized, however, that cooperation was essential for the unity of the nation, and a working relationship gradually developed. As the tides of war turned, the question of Denmark's postwar government came to the fore, and in the spring of 1945 representatives of the Freedom Council and the parties agreed on a coalition regime with ministers drawn from the Social Democratic, Conservative, Liberal, and Radical parties and from the resistance movement.

On May 4, 1945, London radio announced that German forces in Denmark, Holland, and North Germany had surrendered to Field Marshall Bernard Montgomery. There was jubilation in Denmark, and spontaneously people put lighted candles on their window sills. Unfortunately the Germans on the island of Bornholm in the Baltic refused to surrender until they were severely bombed by Soviet planes. Soviet soldiers then occupied the island and remained for nearly a year.

POSTWAR PROBLEMS

The king immediately called upon Vilhelm Buhl, a Social Democrat, to head a cabinet based on the formula agreed upon by the parties and the Freedom Council. The new government had to face immediately a number of complex and difficult problems. Upon the German surrender people accused as Nazi collaborators or traitors to Denmark were arrested, and arrangements had to be made for their speedy trial and for punishment of the guilty. The anti-Communist laws were almost immediately repealed by the Rigsdag, and the Anti-Comintern Pact was declared invalid. A law passed on May 16, 1945, gave the Communist party three seats in the Folketing, the same number it had won in the 1939 election.

The end of the war brought the question of Denmark's southern boundary and the status of South Slesvig into Danish politics once more. The people there had voted in 1920 to stay with Germany, although the region had a substantial Danish minority. A considerable body of opinion in the Liberal and Conservative parties favored incorporation of the territory, but Social Democrats and Radicals argued that the sentiment for union in South Slesvig might not prove lasting once the ravages of war had been forgotten and that Denmark should avoid territorial changes that could lead to future unrest. All parties desired to promote "Danish-mindedness" among the minority south of the border, and as a result the government provided aid to schools and cultural activities there. The issue of annexation gradually faded away. In South Slesvig the sentiment for union with Denmark diminished, and at the same time the German minority in Denmark, some of whom had collaborated with the German occupation forces, was restored to its place in the Danish community.

Politically, socialist and nonsocialist governments alternated in the early postwar years, with no cabinet having any continuing majority support in the Folketing. Following the election of May 1957 the old coalition of Social Democrats and Radicals reappeared, but this time with a surprising third partner, the Justice or "single tax" party. For the first time since the 1930s (discounting the abnormal World War II period), a cabinet had a majority behind it in the Folketing. The coalition lost seats in the 1960 election, however, and its successor, a Social Democratic–Radical cabinet, kept a majority only by the appointment of a nonparty Folketing member from Greenland as minister for that territory. After the 1964 election the Social Democrats formed a minority ministry that continued after the election of November 1966. No striking changes in domestic policy occurred during any of these governments. Economic controls had to remain during the immediate postwar period, but after Marshall Plan aid began arriving in the summer of 1948, restrictions could be removed, and real economic recovery and expansion could begin.

Denmark quickly joined the United Nations (U.N.), and postwar foreign policy was at first based on hopes for the attainment of security through the international organization. Gradually it became apparent to many Danes that the U.N. could not serve this purpose. At the same time it appeared that neither the old policy of neutrality nor isolation were possible or desirable. After the failure of negotiations for a Scandinavian alliance, Denmark and Norway joined the North Atlantic Treaty Organization (NATO), but Sweden remained free of alliances.

As the movement for European economic integration developed, the importance of exports to both Britain and West Germany placed Denmark in a difficult position. The nation remained outside the European Economic Community (EEC) but became a member of the European Free Trade Association along with the other Scandinavian states. The government continued to seek good trade relations with the "Six" (the members of the EEC), however, and hoped to bring the two international groupings together.

The end of the war brought a renewed effort at constitutional revision, a task that was to take more than seven years. After a number of compromises the major parties agreed on a new basic law, with revisions including the introduction of unicameralism, provisions for use of the referendum, and the establishment of an ombudsman. The voters endorsed the document on May 28, 1953, and on June 5, the traditional "Constitution Day," King Frederik IX signed the new constitution.[5]

TIMES OF CHANGE: POLITICAL, SOCIAL, AND INTERNATIONAL

The 1950s and 1960s were a period of economic growth that brought the "affluent society" to Denmark. Although heavy industry lost ground in the economy, relatively speaking, light industry for the production of consumer goods—furniture, home furnishings, radios, TV sets, and plastic wares—flourished. The number and proportion of white-collar workers and employees in the service trades increased, as did the number of public employees as educational, cultural, and social institutions and general administration expanded. With rising incomes Danes began to enjoy the benefits of a consumer society. For many families this meant the first car, a TV, better housing, and more leisure time for holiday trips and enough money to afford them. People became accustomed to a steady rise in the standard of living.

Times were also changing politically. In November 1958, after several years of infighting, the Communist party expelled Aksel Larsen, who had been its leader for twenty-six years. Larsen moved quickly to organize a new party, the Socialist Peoples party (SF), and in the November 1960 election the voters gave SF 6 percent of the votes and 11 members in the new Folketing. The Social Democrats now faced a threat on the Left from a more radical socialist party. After rejecting SF overtures for cooperation, the Social Democrats found themselves forced into exactly that when the 1966 election produced a parliamentary majority for the two parties. A Social Democratic minority cabinet remained in office, but the informal alliance among the socialists impelled the nonsocialist parties to closer cooperation, and after the 1968 election a Liberal-Conservative-Radical majority coalition took power. This was the first time the Radicals and Conservatives had sat in the same cabinet except for the grand coalitions of the two World Wars.

The youth rebellion that had rocked France and other countries struck Denmark toward the end of the 1960s. Demonstrations against nuclear weapons and against U.S. policies in Vietnam had become rather common, but by 1968 these were joined by wider anti-authority outbursts from a younger generation that repudiated what it deemed the materialistic self-satisfaction of its elders. The rebels included a considerable variety of groups and viewpoints, and their challenges were not manifested only by differences in clothing and hairstyle. University students demanded a share in running their institutions and brought pressure on the authorities through sit-ins and building occupations, to the delight of the media. Government concessions on university governance seemed to satisfy most of the student demands, although more radical young people demanded an alternative society. The most concrete manifestation of these more extreme demands was the takeover of some unused military barracks in Copenhagen and the establishment there of the "free city of Christiania," hailed by some as an important social experiment and condemned by others as a haven for hippies and drugs. Christiania's continued existence remains a controversial issue in Danish politics.

Much more important as a political issue was the question of Denmark's membership in the Common Market. The Conservative and Liberal parties strongly favored entry, the Communist and Socialist Peoples parties strongly opposed it, and the Radical and Social Democratic parties were officially in favor but there were divisions in their ranks. Under these circumstances, turning the issue over to the people for a decision made sense, and in 1972, after a vigorous campaign and with a record turnout of the electorate, nearly two-thirds of those voting endorsed entry. Disagreements over Denmark's international role as a member of the European Community and of NATO continued to mark Danish politics in the years after the referendum.

Meanwhile the society's good times were threatened by growing economic and political difficulties. The world prices of raw materials were rising sharply, and export earnings failed to overcome the deficit in the balance of trade. Denmark had to resort to heavy foreign borrowing to meet the gap. Wages were going up, but so were prices and taxes, and inflation was becoming a serious problem.

Politically, new fissions appeared in the party system. By the time of the 1973 election four new parties were on the scene. A small Left Socialist party had split off from the Socialist Peoples party in 1968, and a Christian Peoples party, founded in 1970, expressed the dissatisfaction of some of the population with liberalization of the laws on abortion, pornography, and sex education. Much more of a threat to the established party system was the Progress (Fremskridt) party of a flamboyant and wealthy tax lawyer, Mogens Glistrup. His dramatic expressions of opposition to taxes and bureaucracy attracted a great deal of attention. He called for abolition of income taxes and a burning of tax records, for as few and as simple laws as possible, for restrictions on the bureaucracy (fire half the civil servants, he advised), and for reductions and eliminations of government programs. Glistrup suggested that the ministry of defense should be replaced by a recorded announcement that said "We surrender" in Russian. The four old parties were not just old, he declared—they were senile. By the spring of 1973 public opinion polls showed support for Glistrup's new party as high as 20 percent of the voters.

The fourth new party grew out of discord among Social Democrats and the secession from the party by Erhard Jakobsen, a right-wing socialist. On November 7, 1973, Jakobsen announced formation of a Center Democratic party, with a program of substantial tax reductions and protection of home owners. When Jakobsen's absence from a key vote produced a tie in the Folketing, the prime minister, Anker Jørgensen, immediately called a new election for December 4.

That election—the "political earthquake" of 1973—shook the "old parties" to their foundations. All the established parties lost very heavily in votes and seats—the Social Democrats, for example, though remaining the largest party in the Folketing, received only one-quarter of the votes, their lowest percentage since before World War I. Glistrup's Progressives won 16 percent of the votes and Jakobsen's Center Democrats, 8 percent, nearly one-fourth of the votes thus going to two brand new parties in their first tries for office. The Christian Peoples party entered the Folketing for the first time, and the Communist and Justice parties returned after a thirteen-year absence. Only the Left Socialists failed to pass the 2 percent threshold of the electoral law.

The explanation of the massive shifts of voters in 1973 must be multifaceted. Many voters seemed fed up with the bickerings, maneuvers, and compromises of the old parties. Judging from the success of the antitax and anti-spending parties, high taxes and rising inflation were certainly on the minds of the voters. The new parties, as well as the older ones that had been unrepresented in the Folketing for some time, could disclaim responsibility, blame those parties that had had parliamentary representation, and, in some cases, offer easy solutions to the problems. Public opinion polls had indicated a growing alienation from the politicians. Party membership and party identification had been declining over the previous decade so that traditional party ties were weakened. And Glistrup and Jakobsen showed themselves adept at using the media both to promote themselves and as a substitute for the party organizations they had yet to develop.

The Danish political landscape has been quite different since the 1973 cataclysm. With sometimes as many as eleven parties represented in parliament, with even the largest party having less than 40 percent of the seats and frequently only one-third of them, and with sharp policy and/or ideological differences dividing many of the parties, finding political combinations that can put together a Folketing majority has generally been an arduous enterprise. All cabinets since 1973 have been minority ministries, dependent for their tenure on the often shaky and short-term support of other parliamentary parties. Compromises have been numerous and essential but often short-lived. Parliamentary elections have been frequent—there were eight between 1973 and 1988, or, on average, one about every twenty-two months—but their results have produced no solid majority administrations.

All of these cabinets had to operate against a backdrop of serious economic difficulties: slow or stagnant economic growth, high unemployment (especially among young people), inflation, severe balance of payments deficits, and a large and growing foreign debt. By the early 1980s some of these economic conditions had improved, and the Schlüter government—a "four-leaf clover" coalition of the Conservative, Liberal, Center Democratic, and Christian Peoples parties—was quite happy to take credit for the gains, even though international factors, including the fall in both oil prices and interest rates, were certainly contributory.

In defense and foreign policy issues the "four-leaf clover" parties frequently found themselves outvoted by opposition parties in the Folketing. As neither the cabinet nor the Social Democrats wanted to consider these parliamentary setbacks as votes of no-confidence that would precipitate an election, the coalition remained in office, whatever the embarrassments and the effects of the defeats upon its authority.

In 1986, when the Folketing rejected the Luxembourg Agreement on European Community reforms, the government went over the heads of parliament to the people and secured a popular endorsement of the agreement in a referendum. In April 1988, the Schlüter cabinet suffered its twenty-third defeat on a national security issue, this time involving Denmark and NATO, and the prime minister again went to the voters, calling a new parliamentary election. The outcome was, as usual, confusing, but after three weeks of negotiations Schlüter was able to form a coalition of Conservatives, Liberals, and Radicals. Like its post-1973 predecessors, however, the new cabinet lacked a Folketing majority and depended for its life on support from either the Social Democrats or the Progressives. A parliamentary election in December 1990 brought substantial gains for the Social Democrats. A Schlüter minority government, backed only by the Conservatives and Liberals, continued in office. The Radicals left the coalition to resume their independent position as a Center party in Danish politics.

4

Government

THE CONSTITUTION

The present Danish constitution, which went into effect in 1953, has a number of provisions not contained in previous basic laws, including unicameralism, the referendum on legislative enactments, and the establishment of an ombudsman. For the first time the principle of parliamentarism appears explicitly: "The King shall not be answerable for his actions. . . . The Ministers shall be responsible for the conduct of the government. . . . A Minister shall not remain in office after the Folketing has passed a vote of no confidence in him. Where the Folketing passes a vote of no confidence in the Prime Minister, he shall ask for the dismissal of the Ministry unless writs are to be issued for a general election."[1]

The procedure for constitutional amendment remains complicated, though it is slightly easier than before. The Folketing must pass an amendment twice, with an election intervening between the actions. The proposal then goes to the voters, and it is adopted if a majority of those voting on the amendment favor it and if this majority includes at least 40 percent of the eligible voters (45 percent was required in the previous constitution).

The 1953 constitution and the Succession to the Throne Act, recognizing male precedence in the succession, now allow females to inherit the throne if there is no male heir. Women's groups had long argued for such a change, maintaining that full equality between the sexes would not be achieved without it. Interest in this modification of the succession law was enhanced by the fact that the reigning monarch, Frederik IX, had three daughters but no son. King Frederik died in 1972 and was succeeded by his eldest daughter, Margrethe II.

THE MONARCHY

The constitution gives the king significant legislative and executive powers but provides that he exercise them through his ministers.[2] All government bills must be discussed in a Council of State (Rigsråd) made up of the king and his ministers, and after passage by the Folketing the monarch must give his assent to bills before they go into effect. He has formal responsibility for the realm in international affairs, and he has the prerogative of granting amnesty. In all these actions, however, he is a limited constitutional monarch whose acts require not only his own signature but also those of one or more ministers, and it is the minister who is held responsible. The constitution says nothing about one of the king's most important roles, that of national symbol. The monarchy is deeply rooted in Danish life and history and, now above political battles, is a source of stability and confidence for the nation.

The king must be a member of the Evangelical Lutheran Church. The throne may be lost by a king's leaving the established Church, by his failure to make the required declaration of support for the constitution, by abdication, or by marriage without the Folketing's consent. If there is no successor, then the Folketing must elect a new king and determine the future order of succession.

Lord David Cecil wrote that the Danes, Norwegians, and Swedes "do not like the idea that the royal family is something apart, leading an existence of courtly formality and stately splendor. . . . The kings and queens of these countries perform their public functions with traditional state and dignity; but when these are over, they return to a home life which differs in no essentials from that of their subjects."[3] According to stories, Frederik IX occasionally startled people by answering his own telephone or by calling up journalists who wanted to interview him. He was an accomplished musician who frequently conducted the Royal Danish and State Radio orchestras.

Queen Margrethe II is the first woman on the Danish throne since her namesake, Margrethe I (1353–1412), ruled over Denmark, Sweden, and Norway. Educated in political science, law, and archeology at Copenhagen University, Cambridge, Århus University, the Sorbonne, and the London School of Economics, she also studied *cordon bleu* cooking. She is a person of broad interests that include archeology, theology, and literature. A creative artist and illustrator, she has contributed drawings for J.R.R. Tolkien's *Lord of the Rings* and for various Danish works, such as one of the oldest heroic poems, *Bjarkemål*. One year she created the Christmas seals used by Danes along with the postage stamps on their holiday mail, and in 1985 she designed the stamps that commemorated the fortieth anniversary of Denmark's liberation from the German occupation.

The queen meets weekly with the prime minister and the foreign minister, and these meetings are not mere courtesy visits but opportunities for real discussion. Through her annual New Year's address on television

Queen Margrethe II
(Photo by Poul Ainow)

and radio she speaks to the Danish people on broad matters of public concern but not in any partisan political sense. She and her consort frequently undertake state visits abroad, and, together or singly, they often journey to the other parts of the Danish realm, Greenland and the Faroes.

In 1967 Queen Margrethe married Count Henri de Laborde de Monpesat, a French diplomat, who assumed the title of Prince Henrik. The prince shares his wife's literary and artistic interests, and he is an accomplished pianist. Together the royal couple translated into Danish Simone de Beauvoir's *Tous Les Hommes Sont Mortels*. A consort must be prepared for a life that is overshadowed by the monarch, and Prince Henrik has apparently adjusted well to this, as well as to the changes in language, religion, and tradition that his marriage imposed. He once compared the skills of a prince consort to those of a tightrope walker:

If he is too restrained, people wonder whether he is of any use; but if he seeks the limelight, they think he has a swelled head. The couple has two children: the heir to the throne, Crown Prince Frederik, born in 1968, and Prince Joachim, born in 1969. (Since 1513 every king has been named either Frederik or Christian.)

It has frequently been said that if Denmark were to become a republic—a contingency on which one would not want to wager a great deal of money—Margrethe would be elected its first president. Public opinion polls often have found her to be the most popular Dane. But, it must be emphasized, her role is a nonpolitical one, despite the language of laws and constitution.[4]

THE FOLKETING

The 1953 constitution replaced the bicameral Rigsdag that had existed since 1849 with a one-house legislature, the Folketing. Legislation has set the parliamentary membership at the constitutional maximum of 179, of whom 2 are from Greenland and 2 are from the Faroes. Any person qualified to vote in Folketing elections is eligible for election as a member of the Folketing (abbreviated M.F.). The term of office is four years, unless the legislature is dissolved before the expiration of that period, as nearly always happens. A government whose term is drawing to an end may use its discretion to set the election date at a time favorable to its fortunes.

The Folketing sits in the palace of Christiansborg. Places in its meeting hall are arranged in a semicircle, with seats and desks for ministers on the extreme left of the Speaker's desk and with those for members arranged by party groups running the rest of the way around the chamber to the Speaker's extreme right. Its regular session begins each year at noon on the first Tuesday in October, except for a newly elected Folketing, which assembles on the twelfth weekday after the election unless convened earlier by the king. At its first meeting the prime minister reports on the state of the nation and a general debate follows. Sessions are organized on the basis of the "Folketing year," which runs from the first Tuesday in October to the same date in the following year. The Folketing tries to finish its labors by Constitution Day, June 5, but many committees must continue to work, and sometimes there is a special session of the entire body in the summer or early fall.

At their first meeting in each Folketing year the members elect a Speaker (*formand*, which means simply "chairman"), four vice-speakers, and six secretaries. The Speaker and vice-speakers constitute the Folketing's presidium, a group that has some importance on procedural matters. The Speaker has usually come from the largest party and since

Christiansborg Palace and a part of Højbro Plads. The statue on Højbro Plads depicts Bishop Absalon, the founder of Copenhagen, who erected the first castle on this site. The present palace contains the royal reception rooms, the premises of the Folketing (the Danish parliament), and the Supreme Court. (Photo by Lennard)

1924 has most often been a Social Democrat, although the last two have been Conservatives. Although the Speaker is reelected annually, the tradition (occasionally broken) is one of continuity until the incumbent decides to resign or retire. (Women are equally eligible for the post, but no woman has yet been elected; therefore, the following language uses *he* when referring to the Speaker—and also when referring to members of the Folketing—rather than *he or she*.)

The Speaker is an important figure in the legislative process. As presiding officer of the Folketing he sees that the rules are respected and order is maintained. He recognizes members but allows party spokesmen and initiators of proposals to speak before others. He may call to order a member who has spoken past the time allocated to him or one who uses disorderly language. The Speaker interprets the rules and can only be overruled by election of a new Speaker. He determines the time and the agenda of meetings, consulting with the party leaders but having the power of final decision and usually giving precedence to government measures. He retains his own voting right in the chamber and may participate in the debates, turning over the chair to one of the vice-speakers. On two occasions in recent years the Speaker has been designated the royal investigator (*kongelig undersøger*) to lead the search for a coalition government.

Meetings of the Folketing are public, except on rare occasions when the body votes to have a closed session. Members usually speak from a rostrum to the left of the Speaker's desk, though since 1982 they have been able to speak from their places in the chamber. The rules set strict limits on the amount of time a member may talk on various types of questions before the house. The Speaker sees that these time limits are enforced, using a bell rather than a gavel.

A pamphlet published by the Folketing's presidium notes that the parliament is not a very lively assembly. Speeches tend to be dry and unemotional, and no one bangs on his desk.

> The reasons for the absence of manifestations of temperament are a native tradition that is bound up with popular dislike of exaggeration, together with the simple fact that expressions of approval and disapproval are regarded, according to the Standing Orders, as contrary to good order. This does not mean that a debate cannot be tough and ruthless. Even the most cutting remark can be soft-tongued.[5]

Visitors to the Folketing may be disappointed to find the chamber nearly empty, with few members seeming to be engrossed in the legislative business. Indeed, someone once said that if a person wanted to keep a piece of news secret, he should announce it from the rostrum of the

Folketing because then nobody would hear it. Members not present on the floor are likely to be in party or committee meetings, talking with constituents or delegations from outside groups, or working in their offices. They will be on hand for major debates and certainly for votes.

THE LEGISLATIVE PROCESS

The initiative in lawmaking rests with the cabinet, although every M.F. has the constitutional right to introduce a bill. The number of government bills (those sponsored and introduced by a minister and backed by the cabinet) greatly surpasses the number of private bills (those introduced by an individual or a group of members without government sponsorship). The legislative workload has been increasing: in 1954–1955 the Folketing dealt with 148 bills and passed 103 of them. Thirty years later the comparable figures were 237 and 154.[6]

Government measures may originate with a ministry's civil servants, who are aware of problems of coverage and interpretation in existing laws; with a special commission appointed to study problems in a specific policy area; or with the political party or parties included in the government. Regardless of origin, the measure must secure the endorsement of the cabinet before being submitted to the Folketing.

Opposition to the government's proposals is ordinarily expressed through amendments to them, rather than by the introduction of competing bills. Or an opposition party or parties may seek passage of a resolution (folketingsbeslutning) calling on the government to introduce a bill of a certain kind or to appoint a commission to study or investigate a particular legislative problem. The number of such resolutions has greatly increased in recent years.

Virtually all bills are introduced in written form rather than orally. A minister ordinarily introduces a government bill by sending a copy, along with a summary and a discussion of its principal points, to the Folketing's Speaker. Shortly thereafter, printed copies of the bill and the minister's statement are available to members (the Folketing has its own printing plant in the Christiansborg basements). No obligatory deadline exists for the introduction of bills except that set by the constitution for the annual Finance Act.

The constitution requires three readings of a bill before final passage. At First Reading there is a debate on the measure's general principles, with no amendments permitted. In this as in subsequent stages, debate is led by the official spokesmen (ordførere) for each party group and by the minister who has introduced the bill. If it is approved on First Reading, the bill goes to one of the twenty-two regular standing committees for detailed consideration. These include committees on finance, defense, social welfare, education, energy, and so on. Each committee has seventeen members chosen by proportional representation. A party with only a few Folketing members may have no one on a committee unless a larger party is willing to relinquish a seat. Committee chairs are mostly shared among the bigger parties, with the nongovernment parties receiving some of the posts.

The constitution provides specifically for a special Foreign Affairs Committee, which the government must consult before making any important decision in foreign policy. This is separate from the standing Committee on Foreign Relations. Covering another aspect of international affairs is the standing Committee on Market Relations, which exercises supervision over Denmark's relations with the European Community. A committee, meeting in private, considers a bill in detail, paragraph by paragraph. It may seek additional information and explanations from the ministry, and it may invite the minister to attend the meeting to discuss various points. Reports indicate that ministers are often given a rough time, especially by opposition party members. The committee may receive written statements, and even delegations, from organizations wishing to express their views on the measure. It may make amendments, though usually the ones approved by the committee majority are acceptable to, or have even been prepared by, the ministry. Members keep in close touch with their respective party groups throughout the deliberations. Both members and outsiders believe that closed committee meetings enable the M.F.s to work informally and objectively and to reach acceptable compromises that might be impossible in the glare of publicity. The committee publishes no record of its work but makes a written report to the Folketing with its recommendations on the bill, and perhaps with minority proposals as well.

Debate on the Second Reading is a detailed consideration of the bill, and this is the decisive stage for most proposals. The Folketing votes on any amendments offered and then decides whether the bill is to go to Third Reading. At that stage amendments are again in order. After these have been voted on, the measure is once more debated as a whole, and the Folketing decides on final passage. On important measures where there is considerable disagreement among the parties, Third Reading may be a crucial stage, but in many cases it is a pure formality, with little or no debate occurring before approval. A bill is lost if not finally passed before the end of the Folketing year.

Voting in the Folketing is now done electronically. Each member's desk has a voting machine with three buttons, enabling a vote of yes, no, or an abstention. On most bills, votes follow party lines rather strictly; it is rare for a member to vote against the position taken by her or his party group. Many votes are unanimous or nearly so. For example, in the 1984–1985 Folketing, 37 of 140 government bills received a unanimous vote. The proportion of unanimous votes has decreased as more parties have had Folketing representation in the years since the 1973 election. A bill becomes law after receiving the royal assent. The minister who has been in charge of the measure reports in writing on it to the king; the king signs, and the minister countersigns.

THE FOLKETING AND THE PUBLIC PURSE

According to the constitution, the Folketing must receive the Finance Bill no later than four months before the beginning of the fiscal year (which runs from January 1 to December 31). The bill contains a detailed account of the state's anticipated income and expenditures for the fiscal year. Prepared in the finance ministry, it is guided by the finance minister through the Folketing. It is considered by the Finance Committee, one of the strongest and hardest-working legislative units, once called by its secretary "a little Folketing" because of its workload. If the budget is not approved by January 1, the Folketing must adopt a provisional appropriations act.

The principal parties in the Folketing have usually gone along on the final budget vote, though sometimes abstaining rather than casting an affirmative ballot. On occasion particular items of income or expenditure may stir up controversy, and once in a while opposition parties have combined to vote the budget down and force a new parliamentary election.

Unforeseen spending needs may arise during the fiscal year, and, following a practice dating back to the 1849 constitution, the Finance Committee can approve government requests for funds to cover unexpected items. Of course, this gives the committee a considerable amount of power, especially if a minority cabinet is in office. At the end of the fiscal year the Folketing must adopt a supplementary appropriations act to include all these allocations.

THE REFERENDUM

Because there is no longer a second legislative chamber, other safeguards have been designed to prevent hasty action, give an opportunity for second thoughts, or allow the people to overrule their legislators. The constitution provides in Section 42 that one-third of the members can request a referendum on a bill passed by the Folketing. Rejection of a bill by the people requires a majority vote against it, and this negative majority must include at least 30 percent of the eligible voters. If this is not the case or if a majority endorses the bill, it is submitted to the king for approval like any other measure. A number of bills, including finance and tax measures, are not subject to referendum.

The only use of this type of referendum since the new constitution's adoption came in 1963 when the two chief opposition parties, the Liberals and the Conservatives, challenged four laws dealing with land use in Denmark. The voters turned down all four proposals. Thus, through the referendum procedure, a government with a majority in the Folketing may find some of its legislation turned down by the voters. If this happens, the cabinet does not have to resign, even though it has suffered a major political defeat. A referendum has no direct effect on the life of the government, although it certainly may increase the ministry's political difficulties.

Section 29 of the constitution requires a referendum on any law changing the voting age, and the Danes have voted four times on this, finally lowering the age to eighteen in 1978. The Folketing may also adopt a special law providing for a referendum on an issue not covered by any of the constitutional provisions or as a means of determining public opinion before parliamentary or government action is taken. For example, the nation's decisions to join the European Community and to accept the "EC package" were made through referendums in 1972 and 1986.[7]

THE FOLKETING AND THE CABINET

Many of the actions of the cabinet can be taken only with the legislature's consent or cooperation. The government must present its program at the Folketing's first meeting; it must prepare and defend its budget and see that it is enacted; it must answer to the Folketing in frequent debates; it must consult with the Foreign Affairs Committee and the Market Relations Committee on important matters of external relations; and it must open the public accounting records to Folketing-appointed auditors.

The Folketing may use a variety of methods to influence or control the government. To secure information in order to judge the executive's policies, an M.F. may submit a question (*spørgsmål*) in writing to a minister, requesting either a written or an oral reply. A regular period is set aside each week for brief oral answers—there is no debate and no vote. If the M.F. has requested a written reply, both question and answer are printed in the Folketing's journal. The number of questions has been increasing rapidly—in the 1953–1954 session there were 60; in 1968–1969, 308; in 1984–1985, 1,750. With the rise in the total number of questions and the consequent problem of time, the proportion of written questions is growing; 1,613 of the 1,750 were written in 1984–1985. Question time serves as a quest for information; it is not a means to bring down a government nor to seek the redress of individual grievances.

If the M.F. finds the answer unsatisfactory and wishes to pursue the matter further, he or she may decide to follow with an interpellation (*forespørgsel*). Or the leaders of a party group or groups may resort to the interpellation to bring about a debate on an issue or a general policy or perhaps to challenge the government. Often the discussion is not pressed to a vote. When a debate is held, time is allotted to the questioner (or, if a number of members have submitted the question, to their spokesman), the minister, the spokesmen for the other parties, and individual members. The rules are strict on the amount of time each one may speak except for the minister, who is not limited.

The interpellation differs from the ordinary question in that there is a debate, possibly ending in a vote; it brings up "a rather heavy political artillery" and is used infrequently.[8] Though the aim of some interpellations is to bring the downfall of a ministry or at least to put it under heavy pressure, others may serve simply as the basis for general debate on a matter of public importance, without the questioners intending any challenge to the government's existence. A party or parties desiring a vote at the end of the debate can have it only by moving its own resolution concerning the Folketing's agenda (*dagsorden*—the resolution is a "motivated order of the day," or *motiveret dagsorden*); similar motions may be made after a debate on a minister's report on matters within his jurisdiction or after a debate on a bill. There may be so many proposals and counterproposals that it is difficult to tell which express confidence and which, no-confidence; both the formulation of such resolutions and the interpretations of their nuances are parliamentary arts. The number of interpellations also has grown in the 1970s and 1980s—they averaged about six a year from 1953 to 1973 but about twenty-five a year from 1973 to 1985. A direct motion of lack of confidence may also be used. In October 1947, for example, Prime Minister Knud Kristensen was defeated on a confidence motion over his South Slesvig policy, and the ensuing election brought the replacement of his Liberal government by a Social Democratic one.

THE OMBUDSMAN

An institution new to Denmark under the 1953 constitution is the Folketing's *ombudsmand*, seen by the constitution framers as a means of supplementing traditional checks on abuses of power by government agencies. The Folketing established the position in 1954 and the first Danish ombudsman, Stephan Hurwitz, a professor of criminal law at Copenhagen University, began his duties in 1955.

The Folketing wanted the new office to serve two main purposes. First, it would act on behalf of the legislature to strengthen the traditional controls over the administration, which were deemed inadequate because of the growing power and increasing complexity of the administrative branch. Second, the ombudsman would protect the citizen by serving as a kind of court of appeals, to which individuals with complaints against administrative agencies might apply for a redress of grievances. In the words of one M.F., the ombudsman should be "the protector of the man in the street against injustices, against arbitrariness, and against the abuse of power" by the executive.[9] In actual practice, this function of the ombudsman has occupied most of his time and that of his small staff, and the first objective—controlling the powers delegated by the Folketing—has been of lesser importance.

The ombudsman, who under the statutes must have a law degree, is chosen by the Folketing after each general election and is responsible to it. If at any time he loses the confidence of the Folketing, he may be dismissed and a new ombudsman chosen. Although responsible to the Folketing, he is also guaranteed an independent status. The Folketing cannot interfere in his day-to-day operations, order him to take up a particular case, or tell him what his decision shall be. The legislative control, aside from the power of appointment and dismissal, resides in the ability to establish the general regulations under which the ombudsman operates. In setting these rules, the Folketing has not sought to undermine his independence.

The ombudsman's authority extends over the regular civil and military services of the state (except for the courts and the parliament itself) and over a great deal of local administration. He may investigate problems either on his own initiative or as a result of a citizen's complaint. Most investigations stem from the latter source. Access to the ombudsman is simple, easy, and cost-free—the rules say that a complaint must be in writing, but if the complainant has difficulty with this, the ombudsman's staff will help. The only limitations are that the case must first have gone through the regular avenues of administrative appeal and that the complaint is not anonymous.

During 1988 the ombudsman received 1,875 cases or complaints. Many were not pursued, either because they fell outside the ombudsman's jurisdiction or because a preliminary scrutiny showed no cause for investigation. In the course of the year, work was completed on 913 cases, including some carried over from previous years. The ombudsman found cause for criticism of administrators in 130 cases and made other types of representations or recommendations in 40 more.[10]

What can the ombudsman do about a problem? He lacks the power to change administrative decisions, to award damages, or to punish civil servants. He can order the appropriate authority to begin criminal proceedings if these are warranted, or he may direct an agency to start disciplinary action against a civil servant, but such actions are unlikely to be used. Instead, the ombudsman has relied on a third alternative—publicity—and this has worked very well. Under the law, he may "state his view of the case," and in doing so, he not only communicates with the parties to the case but also informs the Folketing, the agencies concerned, and, through the press, the public at large. He will also include the case in his annual report, which receives a great deal of attention from the legislature, the government, the press, and the public. A Folketing committee regularly scrutinizes the report.

There seems to be agreement in Denmark that the institution of the ombudsman has been effective. No serious faults have been revealed in Danish public administration, but the existence of an officer who can effectively and impartially investigate complaints seems to have a salutary effect upon administrative officials and a reassuring influence on the citizenry.[11]

THE PARTIES IN THE FOLKETING

"The Danish Folketing is no longer *the* legislative assembly, as the constitution's fathers and their later revisers imagined, but only a puppet-show, which plays to the gallery, press, television, and people, kicking about on threads that are pulled by the party headquarters." So wrote an Independent party member of the Folketing in 1961.[12] It is certainly true that party organization is very important in the Folketing and that the party groups have a great deal to do with its operations and decisions. It is equally true that members rarely take a stand contrary to their group.

Each political party represented in the Folketing has its own parliamentary organization that annually elects a chair and a steering committee. The group normally meets each day the Folketing is in session, usually in the hour prior to the general meeting. Its chair plays a key role in the discussions and compromises that are so essential in the Danish parliamentary system. He or she meets often with the prime minister and the other group chairs, reports back to the party group, and frequently returns with its sentiments to subsequent meetings until general agreement can be reached. The chair and others from the Folketing group are represented in the congresses and conferences of the extra-parliamentary party organization and in the top party committees.

The party group chooses its spokespersons for the various debates in the Folketing and fills its share of committee posts. In discussions behind closed doors it decides on its position on the bills and other matters before the Folketing, considers the desirability and possibility of compromises with other parties, tries to reconcile divergent views within the group, and determines the tactics to be used in the Folketing. During the committee stage of the bill the group may hold frequent discussions as its committee members report on proposed amendments and the views of the other parties.

Once the group has reached a decision by majority vote after a free discussion, those in the minority are expected normally to accept the outcome and vote with the group. A member who feels unable to do so is expected to notify the group before abstaining or voting against its position. Abstention is more likely than a vote against one's party; and it seems that an occasional exercise of such an independent spirit will not jeopardize chances for renomination by the party for the next election. For a persistent dissenter, the situation might be different, but by the very nature of Danish politics, such an individual is not very likely to be in the Folketing. A person would seldom join or remain in a party unless in basic agreement with its program and principles, and a person with a reputation as a frequent dissenter or troublemaker is unlikely to be nominated as a Folketing candidate. Any picture of M.F.s dragooned into voting the party line by the threats of party bureaucrats is highly inaccurate.

There is in the Folketing no real equivalent to Her Majesty's Loyal Opposition in the British House of Commons. There is no "shadow cabinet" and no Leader of the Opposition. The procedure of parliamentary spokesmen focuses attention on the leaders of each of the parties in the general political debates, rather than on a dialogue between prime minister and opposition leader. As Professor Poul Meyer has suggested, it is often very difficult to decide just which *are* the opposition parties in the Folketing, as parties change sides from time to time in the course of decision making.

It cannot be assumed that, in Denmark, "the role of the opposition is to oppose." Parliamentary compromise is essential and, aside from considerations of the national interest, a party that acquires a reputation as inflexible and uncompromising may suffer at the polls. The role given to compromise and conciliation, rather than frequent overt confrontation, becomes even more important when the government lacks a Folketing majority and has to try to create one from issue to issue.

FORMING A GOVERNMENT

The constitution states that the monarch appoints and dismisses his ministers, but it also makes those ministers responsible to the Folketing. This means that the king must appoint a government that a majority of the Folketing will either accept or tolerate. If an existing coalition regime with a majority keeps or increases its following in the Folketing, the king's task is easy. But generally the problem of government formation is involved and complicated, and the more parties there are in the Folketing, the greater the number of possible combinations that might provide a Folketing majority.

The outgoing prime minister advises the king to meet with the leaders of the various parliamentary parties, and, consulting with each set of leaders separately, the monarch receives their advice on the appointment of a royal investigator. The royal investigator, usually the leader of one of the parties but on two recent occasions the Speaker of the Folketing, then begins discussions with the parties in a search for a new government. These talks, and the negotiations between parties to which they may lead, are often lengthy and complicated. Sometimes the royal investigator must report failure, and the king must again call in the party leaders for advice. If several parties that together have a Folketing majority can agree to form a cabinet, then the issue is decided and the king will appoint the leader they agree upon as prime minister.

If no majority coalition can be found, then the king has the task of appointing a prime minister to head a minority government. No firm rules exist to guide the monarch in this difficult situation. The party with the largest number of members in the Folketing may insist that it has a right to office; the party that has gained the most seats in the election may feel that it has the right to constitute the government; or several parties that together fall short of a majority may still feel that they will be able to govern. In any case, both the king and the party leaders will have to make sure that the Folketing will not meet a minority ministry with an immediate vote of no-confidence. In this complicated situation the king will be guided by the advice of the party leaders and remains subject to the ultimate check of the Folketing's possible rejection of his choice. Always the aim will be to keep the monarch's role nonpartisan and nonpolitical.

Sometimes the process of government formation may take two to three weeks; on other occasions a few days suffice. Other problems arise when a government meets defeat in the Folketing. A prime minister then has two choices: he may resign, whereupon the consultations concerning a new government will begin, or he may ask the king to dissolve the Folketing and call new elections. It is well established that the king will not make a personal decision regarding dissolution that conflicts with the wish of the prime minister. In other words, the king will not deny such a request. The defeated ministry continues in office until the new one is named, but only as a caretaker.

Mastery of the art of compromise is a prerequisite for Danish political leaders. The art is essential in both typical forms of Danish ministries, the minority government (the most frequent form) and the majority coalition government. In these two general types of governments (which have had many variations), there are differences as to where the necessary compromises take place. A minority cabinet must seek the support or at least the forbearance of enough of the other parties so that its measures may be enacted; sometimes it may have a tacit agreement on aid from one or more "supporting" parties outside the government. This means frequent negotiations between the cabinet's leaders and the leaders of some or all of the other parties, negotiations in which the cabinet must at times be willing to yield. The constitution does not require a ministry to resign if one of its bills is defeated, but no cabinet can endure a long series of legislative discomfitures. The government's life depends in part on its ability to maneuver, to concede where concession is required, to keep within the lines set by its "supporting" party or parties when they exist, to change allies when necessary, and yet to retain its own identity and promote the interests of its supporters.

Of course, even a minority government is not totally disarmed and at the mercy of the other parties. It has the power to dissolve the Folketing and call new elections, and it may itself be able to choose the most opportune time to do so. Also, some of the opposition parties may dislike each other more than they dislike the cabinet and may not find it easy to combine against the ministry. They may not all find it desirable at the same time to vote against a government or to precipitate a new election.

For a coalition government with a parliamentary majority, compromises must take place in the first instance among the governing parties. Not only must there be accord upon policies but also upon the posts that each party is to have and the individuals who are to fill them. The smaller parties in the coalition typically will have several more ministers than their numbers in the Folketing would seem to justify. After negotiations among the leaders have settled the number of posts for each of the government parties, each party then decides which of its members should serve, and further negotiations match the individuals and the ministries. The prime minister will accept the names suggested by the parties unless they include persons with whom he cannot work, and he may be able to insist on the inclusion of a particular individual.

If the coalition has a Folketing majority behind it, compromise with the opposition parties is not as essential as for a minority government. Yet it will often be to the advantage of the ministry to get as broad a measure of agreement as possible, especially on controversial or painful proposals, so that the blame may be shared as widely as possible, or on defense or foreign policy measures for which it is desirable that the major parties speak with one voice. The government must also keep in mind the possible negative reaction from the voters if it appears to push its program through without due regard to the rights of the opposition parties or to pay no heed to their suggestions and alternatives.

THE PRIME MINISTER AND THE CABINET

Besides considerations of party representation, coalition leaders must also take into account in cabinet making a number of other factors, including the abilities required in specific departments and the needs of the parties in the Folketing. Ministers cannot participate in the general legislative work, and some talented members are required as party spokespersons and committee members. Both the claims of experienced politicians and the desirability of training and experience for younger members must be considered. Ministers must meet few formal requirements, however. It is customary for the justice minister to have had a legal education, for the minister of agriculture to have had some connection with farming, and for the minister of ecclesiastical affairs to be a member of the Evangelical Lutheran Church. Sometimes several departments are combined under one minister, and occasionally there is a minister without portfolio, that is, without specific departmental responsibilities. Nearly all ministers are members of the Folketing.

The prime minister is, of course, the dominant figure in the ministry, with responsibility for taking the lead in presenting its legislative program. To allow him to concentrate on his role as political leader and coordinator, many functions previously assigned to the prime minister's department (*statsministeriet*) have been transferred to other ministries in recent years—only matters pertaining to the Faroes, Greenland, and official relations with the press remain. He has the assistance of a capable secretariat, through which he keeps in touch with the important ministries and committees.

The cabinet—made up of twenty-one members in 1990—meets for several hours each Tuesday morning to discuss important matters facing the government. The meeting can also be used to work out any conflicts arising between ministries. Every government bill goes to the cabinet for approval before submission to the Folketing. After discussion the prime minister sums up and states the consensus that has been reached. Legally speaking, government decisions are made by the king in the State Council (the monarch plus the cabinet). The council meets on Wednesdays for about half an hour several times a month. Its deliberations are a pure formality, although the queen may ask a few questions. Anker Jørgensen, a Social Democratic prime minister, once said that he liked the State Council—it was about the only time he could be sure of getting a half hour's rest. The prime minister meets with the queen following the council sessions and on the Wednesday mornings when no council is held, and the two discuss whatever topics they wish.

Each minister is politically responsible to the Folketing for what occurs within his or her jurisdiction. The constitution guarantees the minister's access to the legislative sittings and a right to participate in the debates even if he or she is not a member of the Folketing (voting, however, is allowed only for members).

The minister is the administrative head of the department, and the number of independent decisions that must be made in that capacity increase year by year. Another ministerial task is to coordinate the many separate activities within the department. Many responsibilities must be delegated to the higher civil servants. After recent moves toward decentralization, a minister has tended to have fewer strictly administrative tasks and more time for overall planning and policy.

Besides the prime minister's department, ministries in 1990 included foreign affairs, finance, interior, defense, ecclesiastical affairs, public works, social welfare, industry, Nordic affairs, labor, housing, justice, agriculture, education and research, cultural affairs, fisheries, economics, health, taxation, energy, communications, and environment. The interior minister also held the Nordic affairs portfolio, and the church minister was also minister for communications.

A ministry usually has one or more departments within it, and there may be several directorates as well. Departments are divided into offices and lesser units staffed by civil servants. Most of the administrative work of the central government is carried on through the ministries, some of which employ fairly large numbers of people. A few agencies are more or less independent of direct ministerial control and supervision, though a minister may have power to appoint some members of such an agency's governing board or may serve on it him or herself.

The constitution requires that civil servants be Danish citizens; it orders those appointed by the king to make a solemn declaration of adherence to the constitution; and it provides that a civil servant may be transferred without his or her consent only if there is no loss of income in the transfer and if he or she has been given a choice of transfer or retirement on pension. Civil servants may belong to political parties and may be elected to the Folketing.

Those in the higher ranks of the civil service are normally expected to have a university education or its equivalent; degrees in law and economics tend to predominate. There is no civil service commission and no system of general open entrance examinations. The major administrative units take care of their own merit appointments, usually on the basis of the candidate's qualifications and references; no spoils system exists. The principle of seniority is important in promotions but is not usually applied to the highest administrative posts. Laws provide detailed regulations on rights, salaries, pensions, classification of positions, and so on, and they protect civil servants against arbitrary dismissal or transfer. Public employees have the right to organize and to bargain collectively on salaries and working conditions, but civil servants have no right to strike.

COURTS AND JUDGES

The history of Danish law has been one of great stability and continuity. Written law goes back at least to A.D. 1200, when three codes—the Jutland, the Zealand, and the Scanian—were in use in different parts of the country. Gradually the Jutland version superseded the other two and became used throughout the realm. A comprehensive code of laws, known as the Danish Law of Christian V, marked no break with the past but built upon the Jutland code and other enactments. Supplemented by other legislation, Christian V's code of 1683 remained largely in force until the twentieth century, and parts of it are valid today.

Throughout the seventeenth and eighteenth centuries the authors of Danish legal textbooks had a significant influence on the development of the law. Christian V's code was inadequate, incomplete, and often inconsistent in many of its provisions, and in their efforts to clarify and systematize, text writers, partly influenced by Roman law, sometimes introduced legal principles previously unknown in Denmark but that became accepted as supplements to the code.

Legal change since 1683 has come through the adoption of separate statutes, rather than by amendments to a code. Some of these statutes are very comprehensive and entailed a long period of study and consideration before final enactment. Thus, efforts at a general reform of the administration of justice began around the middle of the nineteenth century and culminated in 1916 with the passage of the Administration of Justice Act (*retsplejeloven*), which went into force in 1919. This lengthy and often amended statute, with more than a thousand sections, covers basic points in civil law, as well as procedure in both civil and criminal cases. The Criminal Statute (*straffelov*) likewise was developed by a series of commissions and was finally enacted in 1930.

Detailed statutory provisions are supplemented by detailed administrative regulations. The courts are careful about proclaiming general rules in their decisions, preferring to approach cases as concrete problems for which settlement requires consideration of all the particular points that have been raised. Precedent plays a lesser role in Danish courts than in English and U.S. ones. Judges will heed existing practice, and they will study earlier rulings that have been brought up in the hearing of a case, but they do not consider that prior rulings are necessarily binding.[13]

The constitution leaves the organization and structure of the courts in the hands of the legislature, and the Act of 1916, with later amendments, provides the basis for the present judicial system. Within the regular judicial structure are three kinds of courts: the lower courts (*underretter*), the high courts (*landsretter*), and the Supreme Court (*højesteret*).

In each of the 84 legal districts the lower courts hear the great majority of cases; their jurisdiction covers civil and criminal cases of lesser importance as well as marriage and paternity cases. Usually each district has one judge, but the larger districts may have several (the Copenhagen city court has some thirty judges)—however, only one judge sits in each case. In districts with more than one judge, the workload is usually divided on the basis of subject matter, perhaps with one judge hearing civil cases and another hearing criminal cases. A lower court judge may also have a number of other duties as notary, bailiff, estate administrator, or custodian of various records.

The Western High Court, sitting in Viborg, has jurisdiction in Jutland; the Eastern High Court in Copenhagen hears cases from the rest of Denmark. In jury cases the two courts hold trials in other cities in their districts so as to allow a fair selection of jurors and to permit more convenient attendance by witnesses and the parties to a case. In 1983 the Eastern High Court had fifty-six judges, the Western High Court, twenty-nine. At least three judges sit in every high court case. They hear civil cases involving larger amounts of money than those in the lower courts and all criminal cases involving trial by jury. They also have appellate jurisdiction over civil and criminal cases heard in the lower courts.

Denmark's highest court, the Supreme Court, has fifteen judges, five of whom must sit in any case. The court works in two divisions of at least five judges each, though important cases will be heard by more than five judges and extremely important cases, by all fifteen. The Supreme Court has only appellate jurisdiction. Appeals come from the high courts and from some special tribunals. A case that has begun in a lower court and then has been appealed to a high court can be heard on appeal by the Supreme Court only with permission from the minister of justice, for cases he considers of major significance.

Danish jurists seem agreed that the Supreme Court has the power of judicial review over statutes—that is, if a law is deemed in conflict with the constitution, the court can declare the statute void. The constitution makes no explicit statement of this power, however, and there has yet been no example of its use. The Supreme Court and other courts do review administrative actions that have been challenged as contrary to the constitution or to statute. Judicial scrutiny in these cases may operate under various limitations: The statutes may forbid review of some kinds of administrative actions, and the court is restricted to the legality of the decision and not to considerations of its adequacy or soundness. The courts follow their usual procedures in such cases, so judicial review of administrative actions may be slow and expensive.

Judges express their decisions in writing but traditionally in a brief and often somewhat vague form. Supreme Court opinions have become more complete since 1937, however, when for the first time dissents were indicated and a rule was enforced that the opinions of the several judges be cited in the decision. Since 1958 the names of the individual judges have had to be stated in connection with the opinions; before then, both majority and minority opinions were anonymous.

The constitution guarantees the independence of the judiciary. In the performance of their duties, judges are to be directed solely by the law. They can be dismissed from office only by a trial and judgment and cannot be transferred against their will except as the result of court reorganization. A judge may be retired after the age of sixty-five but without loss of the income he or she would have received up to the time of statutory retirement, which occurs at the end of the month in which a judge reaches the age of seventy. Judges are independent of the executive and outside the supervision of the ministry of justice; the judiciary is responsible for its own discipline.

Judges are appointed by the king, which means the government, acting on the recommendation of the minister of justice. In practice, when a judicial vacancy occurs, qualified persons may apply for appointment. The presiding judge of the high court in the district where the vacancy exists or, if the applicant is from outside that district, the presiding judge of the high court in the district in which the applicant resides comments in writing on the application, as does the president of the Supreme Court. An application for a position on the Supreme Court goes directly from the court's president to the minister of justice. In either situation the minister has, in effect, the final decision and is not bound by the judges' recommendations. Laws set certain qualifications of prior judicial, legal, or administrative service for judges in the various courts, and since 1919 most Supreme Court judges have had previous service on a high court.

The constitution requires that judicial proceedings be "public and oral to the widest possible extent." A closed trial is a rarity, except in some marriage and paternity cases or in cases of sexual crimes. In all cases evidence must be directly presented to the trial court. This includes the examination of the witnesses and the parties to the case, except in the Supreme Court, where written evidence provides the basis for decisions, although the proceedings are oral. The law makes available a mediation procedure before a regular trial in a civil case, so that unnecessary actions may be avoided.

There are no juvenile courts in Denmark. A child under the age of fifteen who commits a criminal act may be placed under the care of a voluntary child welfare association, which may either assist the parents or, in a difficult situation, place the child in a foster home or children's institution. It is rare that anyone under the age of eighteen is prosecuted; it is much more likely that the case will be taken care of by a child welfare association. The case of a person between the ages of eighteen and twenty-one may be handled by one of the associations, or the offender may be sent to a youth home for rehabilitation.

Under the constitution an individual who is taken into custody must be brought before a judge within twenty-four hours. If the person cannot be released immediately, the judge must decide within three days whether the individual should be held in prison or released on bail. The judge determines the amount and nature of the bail, which is not granted for serious offenses. During the period of detention the suspect may, subject to supervision, use the telephone and receive those visitors he or she needs to see to run a business or to manage private affairs. If the judge orders the individual held, he or she may appeal to the high court. The accused person may not be remanded for an offense that can involve only a fine or mitigated imprisonment (*hæfte*) as punishment. If charges are brought, the defendant may anticipate a speedy trial.

Juries are not used in civil cases, but any criminal case with a penalty of at least eight years' imprisonment must have a jury trial in a high court. Twelve jurors and three judges take part in the trial. Only the jury may give a verdict of guilty, by a vote of at least eight of the twelve jurors. If the jury finds the accused person not guilty, its verdict is final. The jury may ask the presiding judge for advice, but it alone decides. The judges may set aside a verdict of guilty, however, if they feel it was reached on insufficient evidence. The accused may then be given a new trial (before different judges and jury), although in such a situation the public prosecutor will frequently drop the case. The jury and judges together determine the sentence to be imposed after a guilty verdict, with the votes of the three judges having the same weight as the twelve votes of the jurors. In the event of a tie vote between judges and jury, the court imposes the lighter of the two proposed sentences.

Even more extensively used than juries, which are reserved for serious criminal cases, are the lay judges, or assessors (*domsmænd*).

Assessors do not sit in any jury trial or in minor criminal cases for which the penalty is a fine, such as traffic offenses, nor do they sit in criminal cases in which the accused has made a confession that the judge considers supported by the evidence. In the trial of other criminal cases two assessors sit with a judge in the lower courts, and three assessors sit with three judges in high court appeals. They need no specialized training, and their powers in the trial are generally the same as those of the regular judges. The Supreme Court does not use lay assessors, but it cannot, on grounds of a different interpretation of the evidence, reverse a high court decision in which assessors have taken part. The system of lay participation in the administration of justice has sometimes come under fire, but it seems generally to work well.

Penalties under the criminal law are either fines or imprisonment. The court may impose fines without any legally prescribed maximum unless the law definitely fixes one. It may use the so-called day-fine system, under which the fine is a multiple (from 1 to 60) of the average daily pay of the offender, though this is imposed in only a small proportion of cases. The criminal code sets a wide range of penalties for particular offenses, and in sentencing the court will consider such things as extenuating circumstances and the age of the offender.

Prosecution of cases is under the supervision of the ministry of justice. General responsibility rests with a public prosecutor (*rigsadvo-katen*), who is aided by a number of assistant prosecutors. The public prosecutor presents the state's case before the Supreme Court; supervises all the other prosecuting authorities; and decides on instituting proceedings, subject to the rare intervention of the minister of justice. In practice, the local public prosecutors (*statsadvokater*) make the decision to prosecute. They also represent the state in the trials, especially before the high courts, or designate other lawyers to do so.

Unlike the procedure in some other European countries, the courts have no role in the preliminary inquiries that may lead to the decision to prosecute. In a few instances the injured party may begin proceedings and in some, such as libel, must do so. In minor criminal cases the chief of police may initiate or withdraw proceedings, and the case often may be settled without trial upon the payment of a fine prescribed by law. In lower court trials, police authorities often perform the function of prosecutor.

The accused person has a right to counsel or may serve as his own lawyer. If he declares that he cannot pay for an attorney, the state will provide him with one, to be selected by the defendant himself from a panel drawn up by the ministry of justice. The list often includes some of the most experienced criminal lawyers in Denmark. No financial means test is applied to the defendant, and the attorney who is appointed for the defense is paid from public funds administered by the justice ministry. The prosecution supplies the defense attorney with the complete government file against his client, and he may use government laboratories and consult with necessary experts at public expense. If the accused person is acquitted, no attempt is made to assess the costs of his defense against him. If he is convicted, an investigation of his financial resources will be made, and if he is found able to afford it, he will be charged for the cost of the legal services provided to him.

The practice of law requires a letter of appointment from the ministry of justice, which is granted to law graduates from Danish universities who have had three years of practical training under the supervision of another lawyer. University study for a law degree usually requires six to six and a half years. Since 1958, all lawyers have had the common title of advocate (*advokat*), but it is still not possible for every attorney to appear before all courts unless he has met certain requirements. To appear before a high court, an attorney must have passed a special examination, and to appear before the Supreme Court, he must have been a lawyer for at least five years and be certified by a high court as experienced in pleading before it.

All of the some 2,300 attorneys in Denmark are members of the Society of Counsels, whose Board of Counsels watches over the standards of the legal profession and may reprimand or fine an attorney or, as a last resort, suspend his right to practice. The board arbitrates disputes on fees between lawyers and clients. A court may suspend or cancel any attorney's right to practice if he has committed a punishable offense that makes him unworthy of the bar.

Besides the regular judicial hierarchy, a number of special courts exist. The High Court of the Realm (Rigsretten), provided for in the constitution for the trial of impeachments, has fallen into disuse. Certain maritime and commercial cases arising in Copenhagen fall under the jurisdiction of the Maritime and Commercial Court (Sø- og Handelsret). Cases that require a specialized knowledge in those fields are heard by a tribunal constituted in each instance of a regular judge, who presides, and usually two nonjudicial experts in the case's subject matter. Similar cases arising in the provinces may be tried by the Copenhagen court with the consent of both parties, although occasionally they are heard in the high or lower courts, which add the necessary experts for the trial. Appeals from the Maritime and Commercial Court go directly to the Supreme Court.

A special Court of Appeals (Den særlige Klageret), established in 1939 outside the regular court system, hears cases involving charges against a judge and those dealing with criminal cases that cannot be opened for reconsideration through the ordinary channels of appeal. An

Industrial Court (Arbejdsretten) handles alleged violations of contracts and agreements in the labor market. Prior to 1919 there was a separate system of military courts, but since then military cases have fallen within the jurisdiction of the regular courts. Certain matters involving the clergy and other officials of the established Church may be heard by ecclesiastical courts.

Denmark has no separate hierarchy of administrative courts, such as exists in France. Administrative decisions may be appealed to higher levels within the agency and ultimately to the minister, and in recent years some more or less independent administrative appeal boards have been created. Some administrative decisions may be reviewed in the regular courts, and, of course, the ombudsman also stands guard against abuses. The ombudsman's authority does not extend over the courts and their personnel, however.

THE RIGHTS OF THE INDIVIDUAL

Part VIII of the constitution provides extensive coverage of the rights of the individual; most of these rights have remained basically unchanged through all the constitutional revisions from 1849 to 1953, though several new guarantees have been added during the twentieth century. One of the new provisions, resulting from Danish experience with Nazi policies and concentration camps, declares that no citizen may be deprived of liberty because of political or religious convictions or descent. The constitution explicitly protects expression by speech, writing, or in print against censorship, but an individual may have to answer in court for misuses of these rights, such as libel or slander. The constitution does not forbid censorship of other forms of expression. There is a rating system for movies, and censorship of theatrical performances ended only in 1953.

Citizens have the right to form associations for any lawful purposes, with no prior approval from the government. However, associations using or threatening violence may be dissolved through court action. Those who take part in a rebellion or who otherwise act in an unconstitutional way to change the basic law may, upon conviction, be imprisoned for up to eight years. Citizens may assemble, unarmed, without prior permission, but the police are entitled to be present at public meetings, and open-air gatherings may be banned if it is feared that such assemblies may present a danger to the public peace. Reasonable restrictions may be imposed—for example, the police may require at least a day's notice of meetings and processions on the public streets.

Although a national church exists, citizens have the right to form other congregations for the worship of God, and they cannot be required to contribute to a denomination to which they do not belong. Freedom of religion does not allow the citizen to avoid compliance with "any common civic duties." Nor does the right to form a religious congregation permit the teaching or practice of actions "at variance with good morals or public order"—a church could not teach that God approved theft or incest or murder, but it would be the practical societal consequences of such teachings that would lead to their condemnation, not the religion per se.

Under the constitution's sections 71 and 72, the search of a house; the seizure and examination of letters and other papers; and a breach of the secrecy of postal, telegraph, and telephone communications can only take place as the result of a court order or through certain specific statutory exceptions.

The right of property is declared "inviolable," and a person can be required to yield property only when the "public weal" requires it and only under legal procedures that provide full compensation. The courts determine questions of the legality of expropriation and the amount of compensation. Any restriction on "free and equal access to trade which is not based on the public weal" is to be abolished, according to the constitution. This does not prohibit requirement of a license, a certain educational achievement, an appropriate apprenticeship, passing of an examination, or other evidence to show that one is qualified for a particular profession or occupation.

New in the 1953 constitution is the statement that "in order to advance the public weal efforts should be made to afford work to every able-bodied citizen on terms that will secure his existence." Resulting from the experience of the Great Depression, this provision does not guarantee work but rather emphasizes the government's responsibility to follow policies that maintain employment opportunities. The basic law guarantees public assistance to individuals who cannot support themselves or their dependents, provided that statutory obligations are complied with. School-age children are entitled to a free public elementary education, and their parents are obligated to see that they receive it, either in the public schools or in other schools with equivalent standards. Under Section 81 of the constitution all male citizens who are able to bear arms are liable to military service. Section 83 abolishes all privileges attached by law to nobility, title, and rank: It does not prohibit titles or ranks but denies them any legally established special status.

The rights of the individual are well protected in Denmark. They are clearly defined in law and practice going back well before the constitutions of the twentieth century, and they are safeguarded by the courts, the ombudsman and other governmental institutions, and especially by a public opinion that is alert to private and public acts that may infringe upon individual freedoms.

LOCAL GOVERNMENTS

Because Denmark is not a federation, the national government determines the organization, powers, and responsibilities of local governments. The basic law covering local units is the Local Government Reform Act of 1970, which consolidated 1,300 local authorities into 275.[14] With that consolidation have come major efforts at decentralization by transferring some functions from the central government to local and county authorities and by allocating most new public functions to those units.

The local government structure comprises 14 counties (*amter*) and 275 local authorities, or municipalities (*kommuner*). Every municipality belongs to a county except for the two ancient cities of Copenhagen and Frederiksberg, each of which has the functions both of a county and a municipality. With 620,000 people Copenhagen is the largest county; Bornholm is the smallest, with 48,000. The smallest local authority, Læso, has a population of 2,600; the largest, excluding Copenhagen, is Århus, with 258,000.

Both county and local authorities are governed by councils, elected at each level for four-year terms by all Danish citizens over the age of eighteen, aliens over eighteen who have lived in Denmark for at least three years, and resident citizens of the other Nordic countries. Local councils have at least five but no more than twenty-five members, and county councils (and the local councils of Odense, Ålborg, and Århus) may have from thirteen to thirty-one members. The Copenhagen City Council must have fifty-five members.

Each council elects a chairman—in the municipalities, the town mayor (*borgmesteren*); in the counties, the county mayor (*amtsborgmesteren*)—to preside over its meetings and to take general responsibility for the administration of the local government. The councils operate through a system of standing committees, of which the finance committee is the most active and important. The governments of the largest cities (Copenhagen, Odense, Ålborg, Århus) are somewhat different, with plural executives of mayor and aldermen. A regional body, the Greater Copenhagen Council, has 37 members chosen from the local and county councils of the metropolitan area. The council has coordinating functions over such things as environmental planning, mass transit, and water supply.

The largest single function of the county authorities is the operation of hospitals. In addition, they administer and pay the public health insurance and provide institutions for child and youth welfare and for the handicapped. They are generally responsible for the education and training of young people between the ages of sixteen and nineteen. Other functions include construction and maintenance of major roads; regional planning; and participation in the management of regional museums, orchestras, and theaters. County boards of appeal handle complaints against the decisions of local authorities in social welfare matters. These services are financed mainly by county income and land taxes (47.5 percent of revenues in 1984) and by grants from the central government (28.9 percent). County governments (excluding Copenhagen/Frederiksberg) employed 115,300 people in 1984, with 71,100 working in hospitals.

Local authorities provide a wide range of services. Practically all social security benefits pass through their treasury departments, and their social welfare committees oversee medical care in the schools, dental services for children, home nursing, children's day care centers, and institutions and homes for the elderly. The local units are responsible for general primary education; public libraries; sports fields and sports centers; the local road system; gas, electricity, and water supply; sewage treatment and disposal; firefighting; and local planning. They cooperate with the counties in employment programs and in traffic management. They provide the tax assessment that is used by both the central government and the counties in levying direct taxes. These services are financed by local income and land taxes, charges and fees, and equalization and block grants from the national government. Local governments had 288,700 employees in 1984. Together, local and county authorities are the largest employer in Denmark.

Central government–local government relations are a network of both cooperation and supervision. Areas of cooperation are often developed and altered through negotiations between the national government and organizations representing the local governments: the Association of County Councils (Amtsrådsforeningen) and the National Association of Local Authorities (Kommunernes Landsforening). Central government supervision comes in each county from a nationally appointed county prefect (*amtmand*), assisted in the oversight of local authorities by a five-member Supervisory Committee elected by the county council. The prefect reports to the minister of the interior, who can set general rules concerning the ways in which the powers of the committees can be exercised. National supervision is intended to ensure that local authorities act in accordance with the law. A Supervisory Committee can annul local government decisions that are inconsistent with the statutes and has the power to check the financial activities of the local authorities.[15]

5

Politics and Elections

Throughout the twentieth century Danish politics has been multiparty politics. Since 1909 no party has been able by itself to win a
parliamentary majority. An electoral system based on a complicated form
of proportional representation helps keep many small parties in existence.
Of necessity, politics is also coalition politics as parties seek to find
allies with sufficient strength to enable them to hold office or to influence
the policies of those in power.

THE ELECTORAL SYSTEM

The constitution, in Section 31, calls for an electoral system that
secures "equal representation of the various opinions of the Electorate"
and then leaves it to parliament to work out the details. The result, set
forth in the Electoral Law of 1953 and its subsequent amendments, is
an extremely complicated form of proportional representation. Its goal
is to provide a fair distribution of legislative seats—for example, a party
that receives 10 percent of the votes should receive 10 percent (or close
to it) of the seats. Of the Folketing's 175 members chosen from Denmark
proper, 135 are elected from constituencies and 40 are supplementary
members to ensure proportionality.[1]

The electoral law divides Denmark proper into three election areas
(Copenhagen, the islands, and Jutland), each of which is divided into
principal districts: 3 in Greater Copenhagen and 14 following county
lines. The 175 seats are divided among the three areas, with 135 of
them allocated to the 17 districts as constituency seats. Each party
normally presents one candidate in each of the nomination districts (103
in all) into which each county is divided.

Nominations rest in the hands of the parties and primarily with
the local party organizations. Few independent candidates run, and none
are elected. The ballot contains the names of all the candidates in a
district, grouped according to party. A party may choose one of several

ways in which to list its candidates, and its choice will have an effect on which individuals are elected.

The election law states that all parties represented in the Folketing may participate in the election. A party without Folketing members must secure the signatures of voters amounting to $\frac{1}{175}$th of the total votes cast in the last parliamentary election, a figure that is now around 20,000 signatures. Parties that have reached the ballot in this way are entitled to the same public funding and access to radio and television as the established parties.

In general, all Danish citizens who reside permanently in the kingdom and have reached the age of eighteen have the right to vote. Elections are held every four years or earlier if the Folketing has been dissolved. Voting at four-year intervals has been a rarity: From 1973 to 1990 there were nine Folketing elections. Voting turnout has ranged from 74.9 percent in July 1920 to 89.5 percent in 1943, when during the German occupation the election took the form of a demonstration of national patriotism. Turnout in the 1990 voting was 82.8 percent of those eligible.

The parties' campaigns are concentrated in the two or three weeks just before election day. The traditional campaign meeting at which speakers for all parties discuss, argue, and exchange opinions has increasingly given way to newer techniques: advertising, posters, leaflets, informal gatherings, and radio and television programs. The state radio and television facilities allocate small amounts of time by agreement with the parties, and no additional time may be purchased. Television has played an increasing role in election campaigns, with programs that feature debates among party leaders drawing the greatest attention.

On election day the citizen casts a vote either for a party or for a particular candidate. The vote for a candidate may be either for the person nominated in the voter's district or for any candidate in the larger constituency. Under the supervision of the interior ministry, a complicated procedure determines the number of constituency mandates won by each party, the division of supplementary mandates among the parties, and the individual candidates who have been elected. For a party to share in the supplementary mandates, it has to qualify under one of three provisions of the electoral law, the most important and relevant being that it has secured at least 2 percent of the valid votes cast in the entire country. This requirement is usually referred to as the threshold rule.

The interior ministry also prepares a list of substitute members from those candidates who fail to win election to the Folketing. That non-elected candidate in a district who came closest to winning a seat becomes the first substitute for his/her party there and will enter the

TABLE 5.1   Folketing Elections, 1988 and 1990

| | 1988 | | | 1990 | | |
Party	Percent of Popular Vote	Seats	Percent of Seats	Percent of Popular Vote	Seats	Percent of Seats
Conservative	19.3	35	20.0	16.0	30	17.1
Liberal	11.8	22	12.6	15.8	29	16.6
Social Democrat	29.8	55	31.4	37.4	69	39.4
Radical	5.6	10	5.7	3.5	7	4.0
Socialist Peoples	13.0	24	13.7	8.3	15	8.6
Center Democrat	4.7	9	5.1	5.1	9	5.1
Christian Peoples	2.0	4	2.3	2.3	4	2.3
Progress	9.0	16	9.1	6.4	12	6.9
Other	4.8	0	0	5.2	0	0

Folketing as a replacement for an elected member of the party from that district should a vacancy occur.

The end result of this rather involved electoral system is a distribution of seats in the Folketing that is almost exactly proportional to the share of the popular votes received by the parties. The last two general elections show this clearly (see Table 5.1). The slight overrepresentation for parties in the Folketing is accounted for by the votes "wasted" for parties that did not meet the minimum requirements for representation set forth in the electoral law.

THE POLITICAL PARTIES

By 1905 the main constituents of the twentieth-century Danish party system—the "four old parties," as they are usually called—had all appeared on the political scene. Although faced with new competitors from time to time and experiencing some adversity after the "political earthquake" of 1973, they have continued as the central elements in Danish politics. A pattern of competition between two blocs, the Social Democratic–Radical and the Liberal-Conservative, prevailed (with occasional temporary divergencies among allies) until the rise of the Socialist Peoples party in the 1960s.[2]

The Social Democrats

The Social Democratic party has been the largest Danish party since 1924, when it formed its first government under Thorvald Stauning. Nineteen of twenty-eight cabinets since 1924 have been led by Social Democrats. When not in office, it has been the principal opposition party.

The language of the party's first program—the "Gimle" program of 1876—was Marxist, but it emphasized that efforts would proceed "by all legal means" and went on to list immediate reforms that the socialists desired. Though the Marxist phrases persisted for a number of years, the emphasis from the beginning fell on changes that would benefit the working class in existing society. The party was clearly reformist, not revolutionary; its eyes were fixed on immediate political and economic problems.

As the party grew in strength, its representatives shared in government on both local and national levels, where their attention had to focus on practical problems of legislation and administration. The party membership and its voters seemed to have little interest in socialist ideology and long-term goals, but much concern with immediate social improvements. It was not until 1945 that there again appeared to be a swing to the Left, with a new program emphasizing the inequalities of capitalism, the need for economic planning, and the desirability of some public ownership. Rather than strengthening the position of the Social Democrats, the program created difficulties for continued cooperation with the Radicals and gave the Liberals and Conservatives a handy target at which to shoot. Subsequent statements of party principles and policies have been more moderate in language and recommendations than that of 1945.

The working program for 1988–1992 promises that the Social Democrats will defend and improve the welfare state; fight unemployment; work for better housing; give high priority to environmental protection; and expand political, social, and economic democracy. The party rejects the idea that economic development can be left to the play of market forces and calls for an incomes policy that is fair to all groups in society and for modernization of the Danish economy. There is no list of industries to be nationalized. The foreign policy section of the working program emphasizes the goals of a nuclear-weapons-free Denmark and Northern Europe, an open and cooperating Europe, and general nuclear disarmament.

The highest party authority is the party congress, which meets at least every four years. It adopts party programs, elects the party chair and other officers, and considers organizational problems. The present party leader, Svend Auken, was elected in 1987. An annual conference (*årsmøde* or *landsmøde*) discusses reports on party activities and finances. The national executive (*hovedbestyrelse*) handles party affairs between sessions of the congress or conference, while a smaller executive or steering committee (*forretningsudvalg*) provides leadership on pressing matters that arise between the meetings of the national executive. The

Danish Federation of Trade Unions (LO) is well represented in all these bodies.

All of the organizational structure is governed by the party's own rules, rather than by national statute, and this is true for the other Danish parties as well. Most of the other parties have structures similar to the Social Democrats' but less complicated, with a national conference as the highest authority, an executive committee, and sometimes additional councils or committees.

The Social Democratic party received its largest share of the popular vote, 46.1 percent, in the parliamentary election of 1935. It has been Denmark's largest party in both votes and seats since 1924 but has never attained a majority. Its vote was around the 40 percent line in elections in the post–World War II period until the disaster that struck all the established parties in 1973. Its support dropped to one-quarter of the electorate, then rose back to the 37 to 38 percent mark by the late 1970s, only to begin another decline in 1981. The decline was arrested when the Social Democrats polled 37.4 percent of the votes and captured fourteen new seats in the election of December 1990.

The Liberals

The Liberal party (or Venstre) lost its historical position as the leading Danish political party in 1924, when in that year's general election it fell into second place, where it remained until the 1960s. Since 1966, its share of the votes has generally been below 20 percent, dropping down to 10.5 percent in 1987 and 11.8 percent in 1988, which put the party in fourth place behind the Social Democratic, Conservative, and Socialist Peoples parties. It moved back into third place, and nearly into second, with 15.8 percent of the votes in 1990.

In recent years the Liberal party has sought to emphasize that it is no longer the farmers' party of its origin and heyday but a centrist party with a program appealing to all classes and interests—that it is Denmark's liberal party rather than Denmark's *agrarian* party. But Liberals have hastened to add that by "liberal," they do not mean nineteenth-century laissez-faire or rugged individualism. Their programs and policy statements emphasize both the importance of individual freedom and the values of fellowship and joint responsibility in the family, in the workplace, and in society. A free society, the party maintains, demands equality before the law, access to education, social welfare, and decentralization. It has been strongly in favor of Danish membership in NATO and the European Community.

Although overshadowed in recent years by their frequent ally, the Conservative party, the Liberals remain a principal element for any

A political meeting of the Conservative party, 1984. The speaker is Poul Schlüter, the party leader and prime minister.

nonsocialist coalition. Their one attempt at coalition with their Social Democratic rivals, in 1978–1979, lasted little more than a year. Their leader in 1991 was Uffe Ellemann-Jensen.

The Conservatives

The chief competitor for the Social Democrats in recent years has been the Conservative party (Det konservative Folkeparti). Throughout most of the twentieth century the party had to be content to accept third place, behind the Social Democrats and the Liberals. Since 1975, when its share of the popular vote reached a twentieth-century low of 5.5 percent, it has made a surprising comeback, reaching a twentieth-century high of 23.4 percent in 1984. Its vote share diminished slightly in the elections of 1987, 1988, and 1990. It was the largest non-socialist party throughout the 1980s and into the 1990s and the leading party in the non-socialist coalitions that have been in office since 1982. The Conservative leader, Poul Schlüter, has been the prime minister in all those governments.

Today the party stresses its belief in freedom and democracy, within a context of responsibility, and it points to the need for a reasonable balance between individual and society and between public and private.

Danish conservatism considers itself a centrist party that rejects both reaction and laissez-faire, as well as all kinds of socialism. It opposes Social Democratic and trade union plans for economic democracy because it believes this would give the unions too much power and the individual too few rights of ownership. It recognizes that the state has a role to play in economic life, and it approves the welfare state as long as social programs do not undermine individual liberty and opportunity. The party supports a strong national defense based on NATO. It was very much in favor of Danish entry into the European Community.

The Radicals

The fourth of the "old parties" is the Radical party (Det radikale Venstre). Always a small party, it has exceeded 10 percent of the popular vote in only three of twenty elections since World War II. In the elections in the 1980s it averaged 5.6 percent of the vote and dropped to 3.5 percent in 1990. Yet the Radical party has occupied a key position in Danish political life. Its strength has often been sufficient to determine which parties might take office, either alone or perhaps in coalition with the Radicals. Today it is still ardently courted by other parties desiring to form a cabinet. The Radicals consider themselves a "social liberal" party and, like so many of their competitors, see themselves near the Center of the political spectrum, a little to the Left of other nonsocialist parties. In 1968, after the Social Democrats had begun to cooperate with the Socialist Peoples party, the Radicals turned from their erstwhile ally and joined a coalition government with the Liberals and the Conservatives. This represented a new pattern of cooperation in Danish politics, one not to be repeated until 1988 when the three parties again took office together.

Because of its central and often decisive position, the party claims that both in and out of power it has been able to promote a socially conscious, democratic policy of reform. It has stressed the need for cooperation among the major economic decision makers in society—public and private—to promote stability. The Radicals' background in foreign policy and national defense has been one of neutrality and pacifism. Until the mid-1950s the party opposed Danish membership in NATO, and even today many Radicals are lukewarm supporters of NATO at best. Many also opposed Danish entry into the European Community. The party would like Denmark to keep military expenditures down, to work for international disarmament, and to continue aiding third world countries. The top position in the party is not the national chair but the chair of the Folketing group; in 1991 this post was held by Niels Helveg Petersen.

The Socialist Peoples Party

The Socialist Peoples party (Socialistisk Folkeparti, or SF) came into being in 1958 after the expulsion by the Communist party of its longtime leader, Aksel Larsen. A few weeks after his ouster Larsen joined with other former Communists to found a new and independent left-wing socialist party that accepted Marxism as its ideological base but held that socialism had to be related to Danish experience and suited to Danish conditions.

The 1960 election brought SF into the Folketing, but it was shunned by the Social Democrats until the 1966 election produced a "workers' majority" for the two parties and informal cooperation between them.[3] That majority was lost in 1968 when the secession of 6 SF members of parliament (who formed a new party, the Left Socialists) precipitated a new election. SF voting strength declined in the 1970s but increased substantially in the 1980s, and the party passed the Liberals in the voting in 1987 (14.6 percent) and 1988 (13.0 percent), to become the third largest party. It fell behind the Liberals in 1990 (8.3 percent). Its relations with the Social Democrats have been generally good, although there have been major differences on some international and defense policies; but none of the other parties have found SF acceptable as a coalition partner, and it has yet to serve in its first cabinet. Gert Petersen became the party chair in 1976.

The Socialist Peoples party considers itself a democratic socialist party of the working class, open to all who want to abolish human exploitation. It will seek to make Denmark disarmed and alliance-free; it wants to keep the nation independent of international capitalism; and it opposes Danish membership in both NATO and the European Community.

The Christian Peoples Party

During its tenure of office from 1968 to 1971, the Liberal-Conservative-Radical coalition secured the passage of legislation that liberalized access to abortion and eased restrictions on pornography. One consequence was the formation of a new political party, the Christian Peoples party (Kristeligt Folkeparti), which came into existence officially on April 13, 1970. It got on the ballot for the 1971 Folketing election and received 57,000 votes but fell 606 short of the minimum required for representation.

Entering the Folketing in the next election, in 1973, with 4 percent of the votes, it has retained a small representation (usually no more than 4 or 5 members) and a share of the popular vote barely above the 2 percent threshold in the five elections in the 1980s and 1990.

Despite its small size it was a member of the "four-leaf clover" coalition in office from 1982 to 1988.

In its statements and programs the party emphasizes that its policies rest upon the Christian view of life, charity, and stewardship. It urges expansion of democracy through decentralization of political decisions; calls for economic and social policies that eschew special interests and benefit all in society, with particular attention to the weak, the sick, and those in need; and advocates strong action to protect the environment and the quality of life.

The Center Democrats

The Center Democrats suddenly appeared on the political scene in 1973 with the defection of a leading right-wing Social Democrat and a successful effort to collect enough signatures to get his new party on the ballot in time for the parliamentary election. Erhard Jakobsen had been a Social Democratic member of the Folketing for twenty years and mayor of the Copenhagen suburb of Gladsaxe for most of the same period. Increasingly unhappy—and often vocally so—with what he perceived as the growing radicalism of the Social Democratic party (especially its cooperation with SF), he broke with the socialists on the immediate issue of increased taxes on home owners. As its name implied, his Center Democratic party would be middle-of-the-road, not Left of Center. Jakobsen was a well-known political figure and a colorful television speaker and political campaigner. Three weeks after its formation, his new party gained 7.8 percent of the votes and 14 seats in the Folketing (only 2 seats fewer than the Conservatives). In the recent elections the party seemed to have stabilized at around 5 percent of the voters.

Given the fragmentation of the Folketing, the party's strength was sufficient to enable it to be part of the Conservative-led "four-leaf clover" coalition from 1982 to 1988. Erhard Jakobsen held a cabinet post, as did his daughter, Mimi, who succeeded him as party leader in 1990. Both Jakobsens were quite bitter when the Center Democrats were left out of the Conservative-Liberal-Radical coalition after the 1988 election.

The party has maintained its position in the Center, cooperating from time to time with Social Democratic governments as well as with the nonsocialists. It prides itself on its nonideological and pragmatic character. (Erhard Jakobsen has been quoted as saying, "Our party promises the electorate nothing but, as distinct from our opponents, we keep our word to the letter.") It accepts a capitalist economy but wants to maintain a strong safety net of social welfare measures. It is a stalwart supporter of NATO and the European Community.

The Progress Party

Like the Center Democrats, the Progress party emerged on the Danish political horizon in the election of 1973—indeed, it was the principal victor in that election. Its founder, Mogens Glistrup, had caught the public eye in January 1971, when in a television interview he explained how companies he formed avoided taxes and went on to compare tax dodgers to the Resistance's railroad saboteurs during the Nazi occupation.[4]

In August 1972 Glistrup formed the Progress party. In its first try for office it sent 28 members to the Folketing, second only to the Social Democratic representation. Its right-wing stance and sometimes unruly behavior has caused it to be shunned by all the other parties, so it has had no opportunity to enter a governing coalition. Its electoral strength has gone up and down, remaining above 11 percent of the voters in three subsequent elections in the 1970s, then dropping and reaching a low of 3.6 percent in 1984. Though frequently troubled by internal disputes and occasional secessions, the party began to revive in the mid-1980s and polled 9 percent of the votes in 1988 but fell to 6.4 percent in 1990. Mogens Glistrup was convicted of tax fraud in 1983, disbarred, and sentenced to three years in prison. Released in March 1985 after serving eighteen months, he returned to politics as an active and often outspoken campaigner and was reelected to the Folketing.

Glistrup found himself increasingly out of step with his party and its parliamentary leader, Pia Kjærsgaard. The Progressives expelled him from membership in November 1990. He immediately formed the Prosperity party (Trivselspartiet) and joined in an electoral alliance with the left-wing Common Course party in the hopes of gaining Folketing representation. In the December 1990 election the alliance failed to win any parliamentary seats.

The Progress party maintains its antitax, anti-spending, antigovernment position. It stresses defense of individual freedom against an overpowering state, socialism, and the tyranny of the "paper-shufflers" of bureaucracy. It calls for preservation of the Danish way of life against foreign influences and demands tighter restrictions on immigration. (During the 1988 election campaign, Glistrup was quoted as saying, "So long as there are high taxes and Muslims, we've got something to fight for.")[5] Observers agree that the Progress party is not neofascist, but it is certainly far to the Right on the Danish political spectrum.

The Communists

Throughout the 1920s and 1930s the Danish Communists closely followed the Moscow line. They had no great success at the polls, though economic depression and unemployment helped them to elect their first 2 members of the Folketing in 1932. During the Nazi occupation, Communists played a notable part in the Resistance movement after Hitler's invasion of the Soviet Union, and their standing was high at the end of the war. Two Communists, including the party leader, Aksel Larsen, served in the first postwar coalition government, and in the Folketing election of 1945, the party reached its zenith in Danish politics: 12.5 percent of the votes and eighteen Folketing members, seven more than the Radicals.

But in the next election two years later, the party lost half its seats and nearly half its 1945 voters, as the Communist coup in Czechoslovakia, the Berlin blockade, the general Soviet position in the postwar world, and the close identity of Danish Communist views with the Soviet line had their effect on the electorate. By 1960, as a result of internal crisis, the party's expulsion of Aksel Larsen, and the competition of the Socialist Peoples party, its share of the votes was only 1.1 percent and its representatives had disappeared from the national legislature. In the years of political and economic crisis of the 1970s, the Communist party again sent a few members to the Folketing, but since the election of 1979 it has had no Folketing representation.

The Justice Party

The Justice party (Retsforbundet) bases its program on the single tax philosophy of Henry George, as well as on the ideas of such Danes as Severin Christensen, Axel Dam, and Christian Lambek. Organized in 1919, the party had representation in the Folketing from 1926 to 1960, with its greatest strength in the period between 1947 and 1960. Its best election was 1950, when it received 8.2 percent of the votes and elected 12 Folketing members. Political analysts attributed the party's progress in the 1940s and 1950s to its appeal to voters disenchanted with the major parties and to the oratorical abilities of one of its leaders, Viggo Starcke, rather than to any groundswell of conversions to Georgism.

Despite its generally individualistic philosophy, the Justice party joined in a coalition government with the Social Democrats and Radicals in 1957. The 1960 election eliminated it completely from the Folketing, and by 1966 it was receiving less than 1 percent of the popular votes. Its fortunes improved slightly in the 1970s and for a time it again had parliamentary representation, but by 1981 it was once more out of the legislature. In the 1987 election it polled only 0.5 percent of the votes; it put up no candidates in 1988. On the ballot again in 1990, it failed to win enough votes for parliamentary representation.

The Left Socialists

Formed by radical seceders from the Socialist Peoples party in 1968, the Left Socialists (Venstresocialisterne) have been in and out of the Folketing since that year. The party often has been troubled by party schisms, and its few M.F.s (never more than 4) have had no influence on the Folketing's activities. The Left Socialist share of the vote fell to 1.4 percent in the 1987 election and to 0.6 percent in 1988, so it won no seats in either election. In the 1990 election the party joined with the Communist and the Socialist Workers parties in an alliance that gained no Folketing seats.

Other Parties

In a way the Left Socialists' replacement in the Folketing was a new left-wing socialist party, Common Course (Arbejderpartiet Fælles Kurs), founded in April 1987. It is strongly opposed to NATO and hostile to the European Community, and it urges the total disarmament of Denmark. It polled 2.2 percent of the votes in 1987 and elected 4 M.F.s, but in 1988 its vote fell below the threshold (it received 1.9 percent), so it lost its representation.

From time to time other parties—such as the Danish Union (Dansk Samling), the Independent party (De uafhængige), and the Liberal Center party—have appeared, elected a few Folketing members, and then faded away. Before World War II and from 1953 to 1960, the Slesvig party represented the German minority in South Jutland with 1 M.F. Other minor parties—the Marxist-Leninist party, the Greens, the Humanist party, the Communist Workers party, the Socialist Workers party—have put up candidates in some recent elections but thus far with no success.

VOTING BEHAVIOR

A few generalizations used to explain, in an oversimplified way, much of the electoral support that each of the "four old parties" received. The Social Democrats were the party of the working class; the Radicals were the party of the small farmers and some urban intellectuals; the Liberals were the party of the larger farmers; and the Conservatives were the party of the urban middle classes. Social Democrats and Conservatives competed for the allegiance of the increasing number of white-collar employees.

Voting behavior in the 1970s and 1980s departed greatly from this traditional pattern. In the 1950s, four out of every five blue-collar workers voted Social Democratic; but by the election of 1971 it was three out of five, and by 1988, two out of five. Although the Social Democratic party and the trade unions have been closely linked, more than half of the trade unionist voters cast their ballots for a party other than the Social Democrats in 1984. A survey of voters in the 1987 Folketing election indicated that the Social Democrats retained the largest share of the working class vote (38 percent) but had fallen behind the Socialist Peoples party in the votes of public employees (the white-collar salariat) by 24 percent to 34 percent. The Social Democrats captured only 17 percent of the private salariat and 7 percent of the self-employed. In contrast, the government parties (Conservative, Liberal, Center Democrat, and Christian Peoples) and the Radicals had 79 percent of the self-employed vote, 61 percent of the private salariat's ballots, and about one-third of the public salariat and the workers. The votes for the Progressives were fairly evenly distributed among the various classes or occupational groups. Ole Borre, a Danish political scientist, suggests that a new type of class conflict may have emerged, "namely a conflict between the respective personnel of the private and the public sector, to compete with the older conflict between manual and non-manual occupations."[6]

Changes can also be seen in the behavior of young voters. Over the past several decades about one-third of each new cohort of voters has voted for a party to the Left of the Social Democrats, i.e., for the Communist, Left Socialist, Common Course, or Socialist Peoples parties. In the 1987 parliamentary election, 35 percent of voters between the ages of eighteen and twenty-seven voted for the left-wing parties, as against 18 percent for the Social Democrats (who in 1971 had received support from 45 percent of young voters).[7] The Social Democrats are an aging party that appears to have lost much of its appeal to the younger generation. Forty percent of young voters supported one of the four government parties or the Radicals in 1987. A 1989 study found that women voters, especially the generation that has become politicized in the past twenty years, were more radical than the males.[8]

Volatility—the fluctuation in voting results from election to election—is high. Party membership has shrunk, party identification has diminished, and voters seem much readier to move from one party to another. One study concluded that in the 1981 election one-fourth of the voters supported parties other than those they had voted for in 1979. Another study found that in 1988, some 600,000 voters (about 15 percent of the participating electorate) changed parties from their 1987 preferences.[9] Much of the voter movement seems to be within the same bloc or family of parties, however—that is, a defecting Social Democratic voter is much more likely to vote for another socialist party than for a nonsocialist one, and a dissident Liberal will go to a nonsocialist party instead of one in the socialist bloc.

POLITICAL COMBINATIONS AND TRENDS

Since 1909 Danish politics has been coalition politics. No party on its own has had a parliamentary majority, and governments have had to be either formal coalitions (majority or minority) or single-party minority cabinets. In both cases the governing party or parties needs allies. For formal coalitions this means partners who will agree on a common program and a sharing of cabinet posts. In minority coalitions or single-party minority governments, it means aid for the cabinet from what the Danes call "support parties," parties that will vote more or less regularly with the government but without sharing in cabinet posts or endorsing a common program. Sometimes the support is steady and long-term; often it is issue-to-issue, uncertain, and temporary.

World War II and its immediate aftermath temporarily disrupted old patterns of cooperation, and the prewar Social Democratic–Radical alliance could not be immediately revived. There was a period of alternating minority governments (Social Democratic, Liberal, and a Liberal-Conservative minority coalition). No majority coalition could again be created until 1957, and then it could only come about by adding an unexpected ally, the Justice party, to the old Social Democratic–Radical combination.

In the 1960s, Social Democratic tactical and policy changes to take into account the existence and strength of the Socialist Peoples party produced a new alliance and a new majority government of Radicals, Liberals, and Conservatives in 1968. This was the first coalition of those three parties in Danish political history—the Radicals had seen the Conservatives as their historic enemy and had been accustomed to the Social Democrats as friend and ally. This 1968–1971 coalition was also the last majority government that Denmark has had.

The two alliances—Social Democrats–SF and Liberal-Radical-Conservative—dominated the political scene from 1966 to 1973, though plagued by voting shifts, party splits, and frequent difficulties in establishing governments that could last for more than a few years. The "political earthquake" of 1973 created a new party system, with at least eight and sometimes as many as eleven parties represented in the Folketing. Securing a majority coalition has been an impossible task, and all governments since 1973 have been minority regimes.

All sorts of combinations have been tried: minority Social Democratic governments, supported by Radicals, Christian Peoples, Center Democrats; a minority Liberal–Social Democratic coalition; minority Conservative–Liberal–Center Democrat–Christian Peoples coalitions, supported by the Radicals; a minority Social Democratic government, backed tenuously by SF and the Radicals; a minority Conservative-

Liberal-Radical coalition; and a minority Conservative-Liberal coalition. Except for one of the "four-leaf clover" governments, none has lasted very long. Lacking a majority, each cabinet has had to seek compromises with a number of parties, and those compromises generally tend to be short-term, leaving difficulties temporarily alleviated but unresolved. Elections have not solved problems because they have produced no feasible majority combinations. The immediate task, after any election, is not so much to find a government that has a Folketing majority supporting it as to find one that will not have a majority at once against it.

What the future holds is a highly speculative question. The Social Democratic party has new young leadership and made sizable gains in the 1990 election. After major advances in the early 1980s the Conservative party has lost ground in recent elections. The Liberals are making some progress, but the Radicals, though continuing to occupy a key political position, do well to hold on to the small share of the votes that they have. The Progressives represent an extreme in the system and have generally been shunned as a coalition partner by the other parties. Electoral alignments are weakening, and an increasingly issue-oriented electorate finds no difficulty in shifting allegiances from one party to another.

Over the years Denmark has maintained its political stability despite the multiparty system and the inability of any party to attain a majority among the voters or in parliament. The fragmentation of the parties and the electorate since 1973 have called that stability into question. Few expect it to disappear, but certainly the changes in the party system in the past several decades have not made the task of governing Denmark an easy one.

6

Interest Groups and Public Policy

Denmark is a land of organizations. A survey in 1980 found 1,990 voluntary associations operating on a national basis, and to that total must be added their branches, as well as all sorts of more local, independent organizations.[1] Ninety percent of the population belong to at least one organization (the comparable figure for the United States is 62 percent), and 75 percent are members of more than one. Nearly every interest in society—from hobby to foreign language study to religion—has its own association. The constitution explicitly recognizes the right of citizens "to form associations for any lawful purpose." When that purpose includes efforts to influence public policy, the organizations become interest groups. The great development of group power and influence began with the appearance of the major economic organizations in the last years of the nineteenth century and the early years of the twentieth. Even before World War II those associations seemed so important and influential that they were often called the "third house" of parliament.

THE MAJOR ECONOMIC ORGANIZATIONS

Labor

The first trade unions appeared in Denmark in 1871. As part of the socialist movement they almost immediately came into conflict with the authorities and found their growth hampered both by government repression and by conditions of depression and unemployment in the late 1870s. As the economy improved, unions increased in number, and in 1898 they came together to form the Cooperating Trade Union Federation (De Samvirkende Fagforbund) with some 70,000 members. In 1899 the Danish Employers Association imposed a lock-out that

81

affected more than half the organized workers. This "Hunger Strike," which attracted international attention and brought humanitarian aid to Denmark from all over Europe, was settled by conciliation in September 1899. The unions considered this a great victory that won recognition of the rights to organize and to strike and established the framework for future labor market negotiations. The next decades saw additional gains for the workers: the eight-hour day and the forty-eight-hour week in 1920; cultural and educational activities through labor clubs, choral societies, and the Workers Educational Association (Arbejdernes Oplysningsforbund, or AOF); the forty-five-hour work week in 1959; four-week holidays in 1972 and five weeks in 1979; and in 1987, the thirty-seven-hour work week, to be put fully into effect by 1990.

Under a new name, the Danish Federation of Trade Unions (Landsorganisationen i Danmark, or LO) now includes thirty unions with 1,413,000 members (about 48 percent are women). Mainly craft unions, they range in size from the 1,878 members of the National Union of Photographers to the 317,000 members of the Union of Commercial and Clerical Employees. Other large organizations are the Union of General Workers (Specialarbejderforbundet), with 306,000 members, and the Union of Metalworkers, with 143,000. About one-third of the union membership are public sector employees, including the National Union of Enlisted Military Personnel in the Army; one-third work for companies affiliated with the employers' organization, the Danish Employers Confederation (Dansk Arbejdsgiverforening, or DA); and one-third are employed in private sector companies outside DA. The rate of unionization is very high, about 82 percent.[2]

LO's sovereign body is its congress (1,363 delegates in 1987), which convenes every four years to choose the president (in 1991, Finn Thorgrimson), other officers, and the executive committee and to adopt the organization's program. A general council, made up of the executive committee and representatives from the unions based on their membership, is the decision-making unit between congresses. Day-to-day activities are in the hands of the executive committee. In 1989 a special congress voted to create a new structure, to be based on five "cartels" of unions in related fields and set up during a five-year trial period.

LO is critical of the economic policies of the Conservative-led cabinets since 1982 and urges the establishment of a government that will follow Social Democratic policies. Although there are occasional differences of opinion, LO and the Social Democratic party consider themselves and the cooperatives as elements in the same labor movement.

Outside LO are two other labor organizations, the Joint Council of Salaried Employees and Civil Servants (Fællesrådet for Tjenestemænd og Funktionærer, or FTF) and the Central Organization of Danish

Professional Workers (Akademikernes Centralorganisation, or AC). Today FTF comprises ninety organizations, essentially white-collar and civil service groups, with 335,000 members. About one-fourth work in the private sector, and the rest are employed by the national and local governments and by public utilities like the telephone company. The largest constituent organizations are the Danish Teachers Union (65,000 members), the Danish Nurses Union (40,000), and the National Union of Danish Bank Employees (31,000).

Politically independent, FTF has worked closely with LO since 1973 when the two organizations reached an agreement to avoid jurisdictional disputes. FTF and LO cooperate on collective bargaining policy, but each FTF union negotiates individually with employers, with assistance and advice from FTF. FTF represents its members on matters of common concern, such as taxes, education, working conditions, and social policy.

Like FTF, the Central Organization of Danish Professional Workers (AC) is an umbrella association. It now has some 122,000 members in twenty different unions. Members are mainly salaried employees in both the public and the private sectors; they include lawyers, economists, engineers, dentists, architects, pastors, doctors, veterinarians, surveyors, and holders of advanced degrees. The organizations bargain separately with their employers, and the national association speaks for them on general issues of pay, employment, training, and education. AC is nonpolitical but cooperates on some practical matters (safety in the workplace, for example) with LO and FTF.[3]

Employers, Industry, and Business

On the employers' side the most powerful and influential organization is the Danish Employers Confederation (DA). At about the same time that labor unions appeared in Denmark, employers began to form associations, less for collective bargaining or antiunion activity than for promotion of their commercial interests. By 1895, however, with the increase in unionism and strikes, the belief grew among employers that an association for mutual assistance was desirable. The Danish Employers Confederation was formed in 1896, and the Association of Manufacturers in the Copenhagen Metal Trades and the Joint Council for Danish Industries and Handicrafts soon joined.

DA today is the central organization of employers' associations in industry, construction, transportation, crafts, and trade and commerce. It represents the common interests of its members in labor matters and in relations with government, determines general policy for the wage negotiations with LO, and engages in many public relations activities on behalf of employers. Its membership in 1983 comprised 22,177 enterprises, employing 460,000 people, and included 155 member associations. DA's policy-making authority rests with a 600-member general assembly, which elects a general council of 54 members and an executive committee of 9, including the chairman.

The Federation of Danish Industries (Industrirådet) represents about 2,300 industrial firms. It speaks for its members to government and has representatives on many boards and commissions concerned with economic matters; it leaves collective bargaining and labor agreements to DA. The Danish Federation of Crafts and Smaller Industries (Handværksrådet) has 44 member organizations that included 70,000 small and medium-sized enterprises with 430,000 employees in 1983. Many of its members also belong directly or indirectly to DA. It provides advice and assistance to its affiliates and is concerned with taxes, prices and costs, environmental and energy legislation, technology and research, and education. Businesspeople are also organized in the Danish Chamber of Commerce (Det Danske Handelskammer).

Agriculture

Danish farmers were at the forefront of the nineteenth-century struggle for democracy and parliamentarism, and in the twentieth century their organizations have been directly involved in making agricultural policy. Although today farmers are only a small part of the population, they continue to have an important role in the Danish economy, and their organizations have considerable economic power. Their principal representative is the Agricultural Council (Landbrugsrådet). It is a federation of associations that together cover almost all agricultural activity: the larger farmers, in the Federation of Danish Agricultural Societies; the small farmers, in the Federation of Danish Smallholders' Societies; the Federation of Danish Cooperative Societies; the exporters of bacon, butter, and cheese; the Poultry Council; the Fur Producers Association; and so on. It purports to speak for most of Danish agriculture and so has an important influence, especially on export questions. Representing the largest landowners, the Federation of Large-Scale Farmers' Societies does not belong to the Agricultural Council; but most of its members are also members of local branches of the Federation of Danish Agricultural Societies.

A founder-member of the Agricultural Council is the Federation of Danish Cooperative Societies, an umbrella association of 32 cooperative societies and organizations in grain, machinery purchasing and farm supplies, processing, sales and services, banking and insurance, and fishermen's and market gardeners' cooperatives. As the main organization in the cooperative movement, the federation represents a very significant part of the farming industry: In 1985, cooperative enterprises accounted for 91 percent of milk production, 93 percent of butter production, 96 percent of pig production, 79 percent of cheese production, 65 percent of egg sales, 98 percent of fur sales, and so on. It does not include consumers' cooperatives or workers' cooperatives, which have their own national associations.[4]

LOCAL GOVERNMENT AND OTHER INTEREST ORGANIZATIONS

All these major organizations in agriculture, business, and labor might be called "establishment" groups, because for many years they have been accepted and integrated into public policy making and administration. To them should be added another set of associations, those representing local government authorities. As a result of local government reform, attempts to decentralize public functions, and growing numbers of employees at local and county levels, these associations have been important parts of the interest group system since the 1970s. The National Association of Local Authorities represents all local governments except Copenhagen and Frederiksberg (which have county as well as municipal status). According to the National Association's constitution, its tasks are to look after the common interests of Danish local authorities, to promote cooperation among them, and to aid them in their activities.

The association's governing body is an annual delegate meeting that elects an eleven-member board of directors. Seats on the board are allotted to the political parties by a method of proportional representation that uses as its basis the total number of votes obtained in the county council elections. A similar organization exists for the counties: the Danish County Council Association.

The major economic interest groups and the local government associations fall into the category that Jacob A. Buksti and Lars Nørby Johansen have called "pure insiders": those deeply involved in the political and administrative process.[5] They all have interests in a wide range of governmental activities, as well as fairly easy access to the policy makers. Other interest groups exist—indeed, the group system has broadened considerably in the past three decades—and some have won "insider" status in their particular areas of concern. Still other organizations remain outside or on the periphery of the consultative or corporate process in which the "insiders" are involved. Government agencies may not recognize them as entitled to share in that process because of their newness, their limited membership, their tactics, or their policies. Some groups may eschew the formal consultative procedures for fear of co-option by the state. In a number of areas of concern, an established organization with "insider" status may have been challenged or supplemented in recent years by new and sometimes more radical groups.

The Nature Conservation Association of Denmark (Danmarks Naturfredningsforening) clearly is an "insider." Its activities date back to 1911 when a conservation association was established for Zealand and the southern Danish islands. When its activities became nationwide, it adopted the present name in 1925. The organization was instrumental in securing passage of Denmark's first conservation laws in 1917 and 1937, and its influence has been felt in revisions of those laws and the adoption of substantial new legislation in the 1970s.

The Nature Conservation Association works for the preservation of areas that have great value for the public because of their natural beauty, location, or distinctive character or that have scientific importance because of their flora, fauna, or geological structures. It fights against pollution of the air, land, and water, and it seeks to guide land planning so as to protect the natural environment. The association has a special legal right to challenge government decisions that may cause excessive damage to nature and to force an appeals board to re-examine such decisions. It keeps a wary eye on politicians, believing that their "fair words" often end up more in "unfulfilled declarations of good intentions than in proposals for concrete action."[6]

Today the association boasts that it has more members than all the Danish political parties combined. The total in September 1988 was estimated at 280,000 in 200 local societies, with 700 new members joining each week. Independent of parties and economic interests, the association depends for its financing solely on member contributions.

In recent years several new organizations have joined the battle for the environment. Greenpeace, an affiliate of the international movement, focuses its attention on air and ocean pollution, the need to halt the exhaustion of natural resources, and the imperative of an end to nuclear testing and the arms race. Not averse to direct action, it has a membership of about 52,000. Another environmental group, NOAH, began in Copenhagen in 1969 and has about fifty local units throughout Denmark. It has put particular stress on campaigns against specific evils: "Blue Mondays" to focus public attention on additives in foods and a "Car-Free Day" to create public debate on air pollution and transportation policy.

Denmark has no nuclear power plants (though many Danes worry about the ones in nearby Sweden), but the 1970s oil crisis brought a proposal to build a plant in the Jutland-Funen area. This set off a national debate, one concomitant of which was the formation in January 1974 of Energy Movement OOA.[7] The organization set as its goals a critical evaluation of information about all problems connected with the use of nuclear energy and the dissemination of this information; increased research on other forms of energy; and formation of a long-range energy policy that would take social and ecological needs into account. OOA considered that it had won a great victory when the Folketing decided in March 1985 that the nation's energy policy would exclude nuclear power. It has seventy-five local branches and about 7,000 regular contributors to its finances. A similar emphasis on an environment-protective energy policy and on provision of information about renewable energy sources (sun, wind, waterpower, etc.) comes from the Organization for Lasting Energy, formed in 1975.

The principal consumers' organization, the Consumer Council (Forbrugerrådet), differs from other Danish interest groups in that it is largely financed by the public treasury. In effect, the government pays the council to act as an independent, nonparty representative of consumers. The council began in 1947 when a number of organizations—all the national women's groups, as well as the Workers Educational Association, or AOF—formed the Danish Housewives' Consumer Council in protest against the unfair impact of rationing and import restrictions: "The goods one could get were poor and expensive; and since the government gave permission for the import of roller-skates and orange marmalade at a time when it was impossible to get ordinary children's clothing, not to mention shoes, this was the straw that broke the camel's back."[8] The new organization managed to survive on a financial shoestring until the government, starting with the 1963/64 budget, began to provide an annual subsidy. The additional income enabled the launching in 1964 of a magazine, *Tænk* (*Think*), a journal much like *Consumer Reports* in the United States.

In the mid-1960s the council reorganized, dropped "Housewives" from its name, and became simply the Consumer Council. The name change reflected the national debate on equality between the sexes and was intended to emphasize that the council's work concerned all consumers. Its bylaws stress its independence from both public authorities and trade and industry. There is no government representation in any part of its organizational structure, although a subsidy from the national treasury covers more than 80 percent of its expenditures. In 1984 the council's membership was twenty-two national organizations—including AC, FTF,. LO, AOF, the National Council of Women in Denmark, the National Union of Danish Students, and the Federation of Danish Housewives' Societies—and fourteen local consumer societies. There are also a few individual members. Each of the national organizations appoints two representatives to the council, and each local society appoints one. The council is headed by a chair and an executive committee. As the principal representative for Danish consumers and with recognized "insider" status as far as government is concerned, the Consumer Council provides information to government agencies, trade and industry, and consumers generally; represents consumer interests on official boards and committees; promotes standardization and informative labeling of products; encourages research; and operates a complaint service.

An organization that combines attributes of the interest group and the political party is the People's Movement Against the European Community (Folkebevægelsen mod EF). The movement came into being in 1972 as an umbrella organization for parties (Communist, Left Socialist, Socialist Peoples, and Justice) and organizations opposed to Danish entry into the Common Market. It campaigned for a no vote in the referendum of October 2, 1972, and, though it lost, helped to mobilize against membership 37 percent of those voting. It has had slates of anti-EC candidates in the three elections for the European Parliament since 1979, polling around 20 percent of the votes and electing four members each time. The movement, as an interest group and a political organization in European elections, retains as its goal an end to Danish membership in the EC. This it would replace with forms of broad international cooperation that would not diminish the Danish people's right to self-determination.[9]

THE WOMEN'S MOVEMENT

The battle for women's rights began in the nineteenth century. An 1857 statute on freedom of trade recognized the legal rights of unmarried women, but the status of married women remained quite different. In effect, a husband was his wife's guardian, responsible for all family decisions, even those on jointly owned money and property. Divorce brought the woman alimony only when the man had sought the divorce without legal grounds. "In practice, legal grounds for divorce existed only when the woman could prove that the man threatened her life."[10] She had no political rights. Both girls and boys were required to have seven years of schooling; except for a few girls of wealthy families who attended private schools, this meant for most girls a practical education. Women were first admitted to the university in 1875, but their numbers were small, about 10 a year as compared to 350–400 men.

In 1871 the Danish Women's Society (Danske Kvindesamfund, or DK) was founded by Mathilde and Fredrik Najer to work against these legal, political, and educational inequalities. The society drew its members mainly from the middle class. (Unskilled working-class women were beginning to be organized in their own trade union, the Kvindeligt Arbejderforbund, which formed in 1875.) The society gained access to political decision makers through its members' personal links with leading Liberal politicians and other men of standing, and it opened a public debate on women's rights.

DK was chiefly interested in legal reforms, education, and the opening of professional careers to women. Somewhat hesitant to press for women's suffrage for fear of tarnishing its image of respectability, it did not include the franchise explicitly in its program until 1906. In the meantime the struggle for women's right to vote was already underway. Suffrage extension was debated in the Folketing, with the first bill being passed there in 1887 only to be rejected by the more conservative upper house, the Landsting. Although the Danish women's suffrage movement was never as militant or direct-action oriented as the British, women displeased with the slow pace of DK left that organization and joined with others to establish a new group, the Danish Women's Association Suffrage Federation. The first victory was won in 1903 with passage of a law providing universal suffrage for parish council elections. In 1907 feminists who believed the federation too moderate split off and formed the National League for Women's Suffrage to campaign for voting rights at all levels of government. As the agitation and public debate continued, the suffrage organizations grew rapidly. In 1908 women won the right to vote in local government elections and finally, with the constitutional revision of 1915, in national elections.[11]

Other legislative victories followed: authorization of equal pay for men and women in the public services (1919); equal right of entry into government employment, except in the church and the military (1921); and equality of parental authority between husband and wife (1922). A Social Democrat, Nina Bang, became the first woman cabinet member as minister of education in 1924. In 1937 children of unmarried parents acquired equal status with children of married parents, including rights to name and inheritance. In 1947 the ban on women clergy in the state Church ended. The 1970s saw revisions of the marriage and divorce laws and liberalization of the abortion statute. Changes came not merely because of the increased political power of women (few were elected to local councils or parliament) or the strength of women's organizations, but also because economic development had opened new employment opportunities in varied fields for women workers and had given many of them the chance to attain economic independence. Important as they were, these gains did not mean that equality between the sexes had been achieved.

> It was continually the case at all social levels, but especially among the worse off, that much less was spent on girls' education than on boys'; and for many girls life continued to revolve around marriage and house-

keeping. Women entered the labor market in increasing numbers, but usually in fields that required the poorest education and paid the lowest wages. The number of women who obtained leading positions was modest in all areas.[12]

The suffrage groups have disappeared, but the Danish Women's Society remains one of the principal women's organizations. A widely respected organization that receives favorable coverage in the press and on television, it works for full equality between men and women and serves as a watchdog on government policies affecting women. Recent emphases include demands for more job training for women and for reforms in secondary education to encourage girls to take more science and math.

Another major organization is the National Council of Women in Denmark (Danske Kvinders Nationalråd, or DKN). DKN is an umbrella association of thirty-eight organizations (including the American Women's Club in Denmark, women's committees from the political parties, religious groups, the women's trade union, and organizations of women teachers, nurses, doctors, artists, etc.) that collectively have around a million members. Its goals are "to protect women's rights and interests socially, professionally, economically, and culturally; to aid and inspire women to active work in society; to act as the coordinating body of the member societies to strengthen cooperation among women and to undertake common tasks." The Danish Women's Society belonged to DKN until 1985, when it left the umbrella group in a pique over its failure to receive a separate invitation to the U.N.'s Nairobi Conference on Women. Some observers say that as a more broadly based association, DKN cannot focus on some women's issues as well as DK can, as it must maintain harmony among its numerous member organizations. Of course, nothing prevents its members from working together on an issue outside the DKN framework. Government agencies tend to consider DKN as the women's group to be represented on official boards and committees. It receives some money from the public treasury.

The presence of older organizations like DK and DKN enabled the more radical feminists who appeared in the 1970s to take on specific issues without the need to engage the established political institutions generally. The group that attracted most attention was the Redstockings, formed in 1970. Rather than directing their efforts primarily at government as the older women's organizations had done, the Redstockings focused primarily on women, seeking changes of consciousness, attitudes, and behavior, and did not shun methods of direct action.

During the 1970s many schisms appeared in the women's liberation movement as individuals and factions disagreed on such things as the priorities between the gender struggle and the class struggle. In time, most of these organizations disappeared, and some of their members entered the Danish Women's Society with the avowed aim of revitalizing it and recruiting a younger membership. The various organizations left in their wake numerous independent units and organizations: centers for battered women, feminist research groups, women's culture festivals, lesbian groups, and feminist publishing houses. And the gap between the old and the new has narrowed: Danish Women's Society units now have consciousness-raising groups and self-defense classes. Most Danish political parties now have national or local women's committees or equal-status committees, as do the trade unions.

Women have steadily increased their representation in elective and appointive bodies, though not yet in proportion to their numbers in the population. "There seems to be an iron rule about power which dictates: the more power, the fewer women."[13] After the 1988 parliamentary election women held 30.7 percent of the seats in the Folketing, a percentage that ranks among the highest for the world's parliaments. Following the local elections of 1984 and 1985 they comprised 23.7 percent of the members of local councils and 28.6 percent of the members of county councils.

On the executive side the tradition of male dominance continues but is being weakened by national legislation. In 1989 four women were cabinet ministers—19 percent of the cabinet. No woman has yet served as prime minister. A study of 153 government committees and councils in 1979 showed women in 8 percent of the places, with a tendency for concentration in the social welfare, education, culture, and interior ministries. By 1981 the percentage had risen to 10.4 and in 1985, to 15.7. The passage of a new law in 1985—the Act on Equality of Men and Women in Appointing Members of Public Committees—increased the percentage of women on newly appointed public bodies to 30.7 in 1985–1986, with the percentage on all such committees or councils rising to 15. The law requires that public councils or committees appointed by a minister for preparation of legislation or for planning shall have, to the maximum possible extent, a balanced representation of men and women. Within the public administration only 22 percent of higher civil servants—and only 8 percent of bureau heads—are women.[14]

Much of the governmental effort at attaining equality between the sexes is centered in the Equal Status Council (Ligestillingsrådet), set up in 1975 in the prime minister's office and still housed there administratively, and then established by law in 1978, with a revision in 1988. The council's nine members include a chair appointed by the prime minister (the practice has been to select an M.F.); one member each from LO, DA, FTF, and the Danish Women's Society; three members from the National Council of Women; and one member representing research on women's issues. The council's charge is to promote the equality of men and women in society, at work, in education and training, and in family life. One of its duties is to approve cases of "positive discrimination" permitted by the Equal Opportunities Act, to enable actions to be undertaken to promote the status of women. In its first ten years it dealt with 150 such cases. It is in touch with local governments through an equality consultant in each county. It may examine all matters under its jurisdiction on its own initiative or by request.

Other aspects of equal treatment are enforced by different bodies. The Equal Pay Act of 1976 (amended in 1986) provides that men and women performing the same work for the same employer are entitled to equal pay. Disputes are handled by the industrial courts if there is a collective bargaining agreement, by the regular courts if there is not. The Equal Opportunities Act of 1978 (amended in 1984) states that employers must not treat men and women differently because of their sex. It applies to recruitment, promotions, on-the-job training, transfers, general working conditions, and dismissal. Recourse for claims of violation is the same as in the Equal Pay Act.

Despite all these efforts inequalities remain. The gap in pay between men and women has widened. The traditional jobs for women—child care, social work, teaching, nursing, etc.—pay less than many other kinds of work. Women are slowly entering previously male-dominated professions like engineering, and many are in law and medicine. Some businesses—such as IBM and Scandinavian Airlines (SAS)—have done well with affirmative action programs, but the record of smaller enterprises is poorer—and Denmark is a land of small firms. With increasing numbers of women working outside the home, the provision and costs of child care are crucial items, and though Denmark ranks high among nations in these services, there are problems. But, on the whole:

> Compared with most other countries of the world, women in the Nordic countries are lucky in many respects: the material standard of living is generally high, the economic and social differences and tensions are limited and the values of justice and equality are fairly deep-rooted. So far these societies have also accepted gradual reforms to the benefit of women, if not rapid and profound changes in the relative positions of women and men.[15]

INTEREST GROUPS AND THE POLITICAL SYSTEM

Interest groups play an important role in the Danish political process. By speaking for their members, they provide a form of functional representation that supplements territorial and electoral representation. Promoting or defending the interests of their members, they influence the political parties, the Folketing, and other policy-making bodies. Possessing resources of information and expertise, they bring valuable knowledge to bear upon both the formulation and the implementation of public policies.

Most organizations have professional staffs, sometimes fairly sizable ones, and they are also able to draw upon the practical experiences of their members. The staff members usually have backgrounds similar to those of the civil servants and legislators with whom they are in contact, making for easy communication. It is quite possible that many staff members of private organizations have held government positions at some time, or vice versa. Public authorities gladly receive and use the research of the principal economic organizations, like LO studies on wages and prices or Agricultural Council surveys of farm export problems. The organizations also serve as communications channels between the government and their clienteles, explaining and perhaps making more palatable government policies and decisions. They assume some of the burdens of administration, and through their participation they can share part of the blame if plans miscarry, which undoubtedly seems to the administrator no small advantage.

The modern political system must deal with large numbers of complicated issues. Handling them is facilitated if the interplay and bargaining of political decision makers and interest groups produce compromises that all major participants can support. It becomes natural to incorporate the groups into the governmental process and to move from informal relationships to more formal and organized arrangements. The groups thus become more than seekers for influence over certain policies through the application of "pressure" to parties, legislatures, and government agencies; they become, in Martin Heisler's words, "continuous, structured participants in policymaking." Or, as a Danish political scientist puts it, "organizations are not normally pushing against a wall, trying to be heard in the decision-making process, but rather pushing against an open door."[16]

The only political party and interest organization with formal connections are the Social Democratic party and LO, the trade union federation. The unions, the party, and the urban cooperatives all consider themselves part of the same labor movement, and they have representatives in each other's governing bodies. When the Social Democratic party is in office, a committee made up of the prime minister, some other Social Democratic ministers, the LO president, and several other LO leaders meets regularly to discuss policies and problems. Relations between LO and the party are generally good, but there are occasional periods of coolness, as in 1978 when the LO president roundly condemned the formation of a Social Democratic–Liberal coalition government.

Other organizations have their political sympathies but lack the direct connection with a political party that the trade unions have. Historically, there have been close relations between the Federation of Danish Agricultural Societies and the Liberal party, and over the years many Liberal M.F.s have been employed at some point in their careers as "county agents" by local agricultural societies. Since the formation of the Agricultural Council in 1919, its chairmen have often been Liberal members of parliament. Ordinarily no differences in policy appear between these two major agricultural organizations and the Liberal party. Leaders of commercial and industrial organizations usually support the Conservative party or the Liberal-Conservative alternative to the Social Democrats. But in all these cases the ties are informal, not formal structural links.

Many organizations contribute financially to political parties. National and local unions provide money to special Social Democratic election funds as well as to general party needs. The Conservatives admit that the Employers Confederation and the Federation of Danish Industries contribute to their party, but neither they nor the organizations will comment on the amounts. It is supposed that lesser amounts are given by business groups to the Liberal party. Contributions are made by individual businessmen as well as by organizations.

Groups frequently have a direct representation in the Folketing through an officer or a leading member who is also an M.F. Trade union leaders have often sat in the Folketing as Social Democrats, and some may become ministers. Agricultural organizations have been well represented in parliament. Anders Andersen, president of the Agricultural Council from 1960 to 1973 and a Liberal M.F. for a number of years, held important cabinet posts in the 1970s and 1980s. Members of the local and regional agricultural societies that are included in the Federation of Danish Agricultural Societies have been Liberal M.F.s, and the smallholders' organizations have had some members as Radical M.F.s. In 1989 the minister for agriculture, a Liberal, had been president of the Fishermen's Association, and the minister for industry, a Conservative, had been president of the Federation of Danish Industries. Many other members of the Folketing have had ties with various business groups.

Organizations do not have to rely upon direct representation in the Folketing for presentation of their views on legislation; they play a significant part in the preparation and enactment of bills. As a rule their representatives sit on the commissions whose reports serve as a basis for important measures introduced in the Folketing. In any case, they will be consulted by the appropriate ministry before government bills are introduced. When bills are in the legislative committee stage, interested groups give their views to the committees both orally and in writing. By all accounts these presentations are extremely useful to the committees through their provision of information on matters affecting the organizations. Group leaders may meet with the prime minister or other ministers to make their views known. On particular questions there may be direct negotiations between the government and the principal organizations affected. "Nearly all groups emphasize that their main influence stems from their technical argumentation based on facts, expertise, and experience. Hence, the style of Danish lobbying has been largely determined by the highly technical and specialized nature of most modern policy issues."[17]

Members of the Folketing find a great many advantages in their contacts with interest organizations. First of all, they believe that in a democratic society a lawmaker should listen to affected interests. Beyond that, they agree that such contacts provide information that might otherwise be difficult to obtain. Consultation may save time and effort, may help with the implementation of eventual decisions, and may assure good relations with the groups and help avoid criticisms. The M.F.s agree that there are also disadvantages to contacts with interest organizations: Strong groups may be favored at the expense of the unorganized, special interests may gain too much influence, and solutions may be short-term. The assessment by interest-group representatives of their contacts with legislators gives a somewhat different picture. The only great advantage they can see is the provision of information, and they see a major disadvantage: Decisions are actually made not in parliament but in government departments.[18]

The close relationship between groups and government has often been given the name *corporatism*. This is a word with many meanings but with a common denominator among definitions: "the penetration, incorporation or integration of interest groups into the apparatus of the state, i.e., the executive branches of the state such as cabinet and public bureaucracy."[19] A similar definition stresses the element of direct representation and participation of interest groups in the making of public policy. "Interest groups are not considered as standing outside, competing for access to government. Their access has become institutionalized, and administered as a matter of right by the public authorities concerned."[20]

Danish corporatism developed as the state's role changed during two world wars and the Great Depression of the 1930s. The disruptions of the international economic order during World War I necessitated increased regulation at home, and the government drew the major economic organizations into cooperation with it. For example, the Extraordinary Committee of 1914 that helped to manage many of the wartime controls included representatives from the Federation of Danish Agricultural Societies, the Federation of Danish Industries, and the Copenhagen Chamber of Commerce. When another disruption of the international economy in 1929 and the development of policies of greater state intervention in the 1930s called again for cooperation, the earlier experiences could be drawn upon. One example was the Foreign Exchange Committee (created in 1932 as the Economic Board, or Erhvervsnævn), which the minister of trade had to consult before imposing restrictions on imports. Besides the minister and eight Rigsdag members, it had representatives from many economic organizations, including the Retail Clerks and Office Workers' Union, the Agricultural Council, LO, the Federation of Danish Industries, the Provincial Chamber of Commerce, and the Danish Shipping Association.

Numerous current examples of the role played by private organizations in the making and implementation of public policy can be cited. The trade unions have operated the unemployment insurance system since 1907. Government funds for the expansion of agricultural markets have been administered by the Marketing Committee of the Agricultural Council and the Federation of Danish Smallholder Societies. On the state's Land Law Committee are ten members of the Folketing plus four persons appointed by the minister of agriculture from each of four agricultural and labor organizations. The Tariff Council, established in 1908, draws half of its members from the Folketing and half (appointed by the minister of finance) from representatives of trade and shipping, agriculture, handicrafts, and industry. The Advisory Committee for Industrial Policy, set up in the Ministry of Industry in the 1980s, has four members from the Federation of Danish Industries; six from the Economic Council of the Labor Movement; one from professional associations of engineers; one from associations of supervisors, technicians, and nonunionized white-collar personnel; one from the Danish Chamber of Commerce; and one nonvoting member each from the Danish Federation of Crafts and Smaller Industries and the Agricultural Council. A 1984 publication of the Consumer Council listed 155 commissions, boards, and committees on which the council has representation, and other major organizations can make similar claims.

Another important function performed by interest organizations is that of self-regulation—"to a considerable degree, they have acquired legal authority from the state whereby to regulate, administer, police, or otherwise manage many of their own affairs."[21] A 1912 law on illegal competition was largely written by commercial groups after the failure of voluntary efforts to control misleading advertising and discount stores; it gave such organizations as the Federation of Danish Industries and the Confederation of Danish Retailers' Associations the right to lodge formal complaints with the minister of trade and the courts against firms that use certain unfair practices. The Maritime and Commercial Court in Copenhagen assists businessmen in the settlement of disputes; it is a state court but draws a number of lay judges from experts recommended by such organizations as the Copenhagen Chamber of Commerce, the Retail Clerk and Office Workers' Union, the Confederation of Danish Retailers, and the Danish Shipping Association. The Industrial Court's foundation is a statute drafted in 1910 by LO and the Employers Confederation and enacted by the Rigsdag. The court draws most of its judges from those two organizations and settles cases brought to it under the auspices of one of these organizations.

Stein Rokkan put it succinctly: "Votes count, but resources decide."[22] Of course, not all areas are equally open to corporatist decision making. Erik Damgaard writes that research confirms the importance of interest organizations in policy making for the labor market, agriculture, industry, and commerce, but notes that "almost nobody believes that organizations are more influential than parties in such areas as taxation, justice, and defence." Nevertheless, he sees a rise in the power of interest groups at the expense of parties. "The political parties are less in command than previously. There is more interest representation and less government than there used to be in Danish politics."[23]

But what of the "outsiders," those groups that are too new or too weak to be included in the corporate system or that deliberately seek to remain outside it because they want to challenge the decision-making structure? Some turn to political action, without necessarily giving up their interest group activities. The People's Movement Against the European Community puts up slates of candidates in the elections to the European Parliament and uses the election campaign as a way to bring its views before the public. Other groups may resort to direct action—boycotts, demonstrations, marches, or sit-ins—in an effort to gain attention for their cause, to influence public opinion, or to pressure the authorities to change a policy or adopt a new one. Such tactics have been used, with varying degrees of success, by university students, some consumers' groups, the peace and antinuclear movements, and environmental organizations like Greenpeace. In the 1960s, for example, the Campaign Against Atomic Weapons organized a series of marches from Holbæk to Copenhagen to gain media attention and to mobilize their sympathizers. Also in the 1960s occupation of university buildings by students brought changes in the system of university governance. Recent years have seen an increase in the number and activity of local grassroots organizations involved with planning and development issues, environmental problems, and similar concerns.

Sometimes established organizations have also resorted to the tactics of direct action and confrontation. The labor unions threatened a general strike in the Easter crisis of 1920. In 1961, in the midst of negotiations with the government on a new contract between farm employers and farm workers, the principal organizations involved—the Agricultural Council, the Federation of Danish Agricultural Societies, and the Federation of Danish Smallholder Societies—told their members not to deliver products to processing plants, and some farmers poured their milk down the drains. This farmers' strike was settled by passage of the Agricultural Marketing Act of 1961. In 1979 farmers blocked one of the key bridges in downtown Copenhagen, causing a gigantic traffic jam, to call attention to their demands.

There is a well-established belief in the Danish political culture that all major interests should be consulted and have a say in matters of public policy affecting them. It does not follow from this that interest groups can dictate policy, even to those parties with which they are most closely associated. One Danish researcher revises Rokkan's dictum: The public favors consultation with interest organizations but does not place them on a par with the political parties. "Votes should count and resources should not decide."[24] The situation is a reciprocal one: The trade unions may influence the Social Democratic party, for example, but the party also influences trade union policy, and it is hard to say which organization is the more dominant.

No interest group can guarantee electoral success, and the major parties realize that they must look beyond a single interest if they expect to capture and hold a significant share in political power. In the Danish multiparty framework, a coalition must be formed of several interests and parties to secure the adoption of a policy. This creates a bargaining situation in which both groups and parties have important roles. The parties must concern themselves with a variety of issues that are outside the special knowledge of the individual interest groups, however, and the politicians have to try to strike a balance among the various needs and demands and to find a compromise as acceptable as possible to all of them. If the principal interest organizations are solidly established and responsible, as they are in Denmark, and if they accept and are willing to play by the rules of the game, as they generally do, then, other things being equal, the compromise is likely to be adequate and fairly durable.

7

The Welfare State in Denmark

Denmark seems to me to be quite the most valuable political exhibit in the modern world. . . . Denmark is one of the few countries in the world that is using its political agencies in an intelligent, conscious way for the promotion of the economic well being, the comfort and the cultural life of the people. . . . Denmark shows that the state can control the distribution of wealth and increase its production as well. It can destroy monopoly and privileges of all kinds. It can put an end to poverty. It can make it possible for all people to live easily and comfortably.[1]

So wrote the U.S. reformer Frederic C. Howe in 1921. Though his praise may have been excessive, it was true that during the period from the 1890s through World War I, Denmark had made many social advances. If Howe had been writing a century earlier, however, his conclusions would have been far different, for in the mid-nineteenth century Denmark had instituted a poor-law system as onerous and degrading as that existing in Britain at about the same time.

Prior to the Reformation, care of the poor had rested largely with the Church; but after the religious changes of the sixteenth century, law, rather than voluntary charity, tended increasingly to govern the fate of the needy. Various statutes in the eighteenth and early nineteenth centuries emphasized the responsibility of local governments for the poor. By the 1830s, patterns of relief that had tried to keep the poor in their homes gave way to the "indoor-relief" system of poorhouses and workhouses. The new arrangement was expected to be cheaper than the old, both by bringing the poor together and thereby lowering administrative costs and by deterring people from seeking help: Public assistance should be made available under such conditions that no one would ask for it. Under the 1849 constitution, receipt of poor relief also brought the loss of political rights.

The change in approach to social welfare had several consequences. People did become concerned about the possibility of coming under the poor-law system, and many tried, through private self-help organizations, to prevent this from happening. They established savings banks, sick-benefit associations, and burial societies. Also, as industrialism came to Denmark, people began to wonder whether it was fair to treat in the same way the "deserving" poor—those who were unemployed through no fault of their own or who because of age or illness were no longer able to make a living—and the "undeserving" poor—those without means because of drunkenness, unwillingness to work, and similar causes. It was not surprising that the burgeoning labor movement, as well as small farmers and tradespeople who also felt insecure, should favor a different approach to social legislation.

In 1863 a commission, set up to consider the state's relation to the sick-benefit associations, asked local governments to give association members a reduced rate in their hospitals. Local authorities followed this advice, thus providing an indirect subsidy that enabled the associations to expand their services. The Poor Law of 1891 continued many of the existing arrangements but recognized that in some cases poverty was not the individual's fault; the deaf, the blind, and the sick no longer suffered legal disabilities if they received aid. The Old Age Assistance Law of 1891 removed people over the age of sixty from the poor-law system and gave them a very modest amount of financial assistance without taking away any of their legal rights.

An act of 1892 provided state subsidies that enabled the sick-benefit associations to reduce premiums and increase benefits. They remained private organizations, but with the financial grants came state supervision. Professor Kjeld Philip notes that the 1892 law was significant because "self-help became help for self-help. It can be said that state-regulated social insurance here appeared for the first time in Denmark."[2] Other laws soon followed, including a workmen's compensation act in 1898 and a state subsidy to the trade unions' unemployment funds in 1907.

Despite the new social legislation, laissez-faire continued as the dominant economic philosophy into the 1920s. Th. Madsen-Mygdal's Liberal government, elected in 1926, thought that government should reduce expenditures and ease the tax burden. It cut the costs of social welfare and slashed expenditures for the elderly and subsidies to the sick-benefit associations. Reaction against these moves partly accounted for the electoral gains of the Social Democrats in 1929 and the accession to power of a Social Democratic–Radical coalition, pledged to more state intervention in economic life and to reform of social legislation.

Adopted in a piecemeal fashion over the years, Danish social laws had developed inconsistencies and confusions. As early as 1918 the Interior Ministry called upon K. K. Steincke, a civil servant in the Frederiksberg local government, to prepare a thorough revision of the laws. Nothing could be enacted during the years of Liberal rule (with Conservative backing) in the 1920s; but in 1930, Steincke, then social minister in Stauning's government, could introduce his proposals in the Rigsdag, covering some 900 closely printed pages. Since the government had a majority only in the Folketing, cooperation with either the Liberals or the Conservatives was essential if both houses were to pass the proposals.

The changed economic situation had made that cooperation a real possibility. After the world economic crisis of the 1930s struck Denmark, others besides the socialists had come to accept the need for state intervention. When the Liberals lost ground in the 1933 Folketing election, the stage was set for a compromise (known as *Kanslergadeforliget*) between Social Democrats, Radicals, and Liberals, in which the Liberals got increased aid for agriculture and provisions to maintain farm prices and the Social Democrats gained protection against cuts in workers' wages and the promise of Liberal support for Steincke's social reforms.

Steincke's proposals became law on May 20, 1933. They brought together the scattered social legislation of the past into four statutes, covering labor exchanges and unemployment insurance, social insurance (including sickness and disability insurance and old age pensions), accident insurance, and public welfare (including provisions for child welfare services, general public assistance, and care of the blind, the deaf, and other special groups).

SOCIAL WELFARE TODAY

The Danish welfare state at the end of World War II has been described as "a hybrid combination of liberal insurance principles with public provision of maintenance, of individual member contributions with state financing, of stigmatizing features with a rights' principle, and of strictly defined qualifying conditions with universal entitlement."[3] It was not until the 1960s that the pattern began to undergo basic changes with new laws affecting pensions, health insurance, family allowances, and rehabilitation. The system again needed reorganization and rationalization, and a Social Reform Commission, appointed in 1964, produced reports in 1969 and 1972 that helped accomplish this. Its recommendations formed the basis for the social reforms of the 1970s, a number of broad statutes that supplement each other and provide the foundations for today's welfare state. It is impossible to consider all these measures in detail, but the general nature of the important programs can be summarized, keeping in mind that marginal changes occur from time to time.[4]

Administration and Social Assistance

One of the first changes was a simplification and decentralization of the administrative structure. The Social and Health Insurance Administration Act of 1970 set the principle that a person needing any form of aid should be able to have the case handled by a single local office. The act abolished a variety of state-run agencies and decentralized services to social assistance offices in the municipalities. Some municipalities have further decentralized by establishing district offices. The county assists through institutional services and expert advice, and regional boards make decisions on disability pensions. The national Ministry of Social Affairs is left free to concentrate on overall planning and legislation, with other national responsibilities placed under a social security board and a social assistance board. The Social Appeals Board Act of 1972 simplified the process for the appeal of decisions so that, with few exceptions, an individual can appeal either to a county appeals board or to the national board in Copenhagen.

A key element in the Danish welfare state is the Social Assistance Act of 1974 (with subsequent amendments), described as "the most ambitious and far-reaching of the reforms introduced in the 1970s."[5] Its approach is based on consideration by a social worker of the demands and needs of the entire family. This act replaced earlier entitlement and categorical assistance programs. Because only needs are to be taken into consideration, aid is available to all who require it. A recent amendment provides, however, that financial assistance will generally be granted according to fixed rates, rather than individual evaluations.

Pensions

Previously covered by a variety of laws, most parts of the pension system were revised and consolidated under one statute in October 1984 (there have been later revisions). A pension is payable from age sixty-seven, with the basic amount being adjusted through age sixty-nine in relation to the pensioner's previous income. At age seventy the pensioner receives the full basic amount, with no reference to earlier income. Those in particularly difficult economic circumstances or with no income except the pension may receive supplementary amounts. Pensions are adjusted twice yearly in accordance with changes in the cost-of-living index. An "anticipatory" pension may be granted between the ages of eighteen and sixty-seven if an individual's poor physical or mental health or a combination of health and social reasons have resulted in a reduction in earning capacity by at least 50 percent.

A partial pension plan, introduced in 1987, allows persons between the ages of sixty and sixty-seven with stable employment records to cut their working hours to between fifteen and thirty per week (twenty hours, in the case of a self-employed person) and receive an hourly compensation (the same flat amount for all) for the "pension" hours by which the work week has been reduced. The full costs of basic old age pensions and partial pensions are borne by the national treasury.

A Labor Market Supplementary Pension plan (Arbejdsmarkedets Tillægspension, or ATP) covers wage-earners between the ages of sixteen and sixty-six, with the pension beginning at age sixty-seven. Both employers and employees make obligatory contributions to the pension fund, but in 1988 the state assumed the cost of employers' contributions. The pension amount depends on the number of years of contributions and is in addition to those under the general old age pension system. The ATP fund is managed by a committee with equal representation of employees and employers.

A plan for voluntary early-retirement pay gives older employees (between ages sixty and sixty-seven) an opportunity to cease work before the normal retirement age with an income more gradually reduced than under the regular old-age pension. The plan is financed by employer and employee contributions to the unemployment insurance funds. A person receiving an early-retirement pension can work up to 200 hours a year with no reduction in pension.

Public employees have their own generous retirement plans, based on contributions of certain percentages of their basic salaries and with heavy subsidization from the state. In recent years private pension arrangements, through banks and insurance companies, have flourished, also with state subsidization through the use of tax credits.

Health Care and Help for the Elderly and Others

Until 1971 Denmark's health insurance scheme continued to rest on the sick-benefit associations. The National Health Security Act of 1971 ended all the insurance elements and abolished the associations, transferring their responsibilities to government agencies. The state now pays for practically all the individual's health costs, from doctor's and dentist's bills to hospital stays. There are government subsidies that reduce the cost of medicines, with the state covering on average around 57 percent of the bill. Treatment at public hospitals is free. Most hospitals are operated by county governments and the municipalities of Copenhagen and Frederiksberg; the central government runs only the National Hospital in Copenhagen.

The Daily Cash Benefits Act of 1972 provides for financial aid to replace earnings lost due to sickness, maternity, adoption, and work injuries, payable at 90 percent of the average wages earned in the four weeks prior to eligibility (up to a fixed maximum). The act covers both employees and the self-employed. For the first five weeks, benefits for the wage-earner are paid by the employer, provided that the employee has worked at least forty hours during the preceding four weeks and for a total period of at least three weeks. The government picks up the cost in the sixth week and pays for the first five weeks also if the worker fails to meet the employment criteria. A self-employed person receives benefits after three weeks of sickness, with the amount determined by the individual's earnings. Benefits are intended to be short-term (there is a two-year limit), with the local social and health administration watching the case and determining whether other forms of assistance are more appropriate.

Similar daily cash benefits are paid under this act and the Maternity Leave Act of 1987 for pregnancy, birth, and adoption. During pregnancy an employed or self-employed woman may receive payments for four weeks before the birth (she may receive them for a longer period if incapacitated because of illness that would endanger her or the fetus's health, should she continue working) and for up to twenty-four weeks afterward. The parents can divide the last ten weeks between them, i.e., the father may remain at home with the new baby part of the time and receive benefits while the mother works; and the father can receive benefits along with the mother in the first two weeks after childbirth so that he is able to stay home and help.

Denmark has moved away from a policy of nursing homes as a primary element in the care of its older citizens to a policy of helping to keep them independent in their own homes for as long as possible. In 1987 the Folketing unanimously passed legislation with a variety of provisions aimed at implementing this policy, including an end to the construction of nursing homes and protected or "sheltered" apartments after 1988 and provision for permanent home help, to be free beginning in 1989. Mimi Jakobsen, a former minister of social affairs, has spoken against the old practices: "Now we see the new generation of retired people. They are different from my grandparents. They want to jog, to travel, to read books, to lead their own lives—so you can't put them into a nursing home with a needle to sew, some small pills to keep them quiet and some pocket money."[6] Existing nursing homes continue in operation. Public social agencies cooperate with private organizations to offer a wide range of services to older citizens: meals-on-wheels; vacation and holiday outings; day centers; clubs; educational, cultural, and library arrangements; laundry; and home nursing. Some 160 local governments have introduced evening or around-the-clock home assistance schemes for personal security.

For handicapped persons the trend is also away from large institutions to smaller units and, if possible, to help within one's own home. The state provides aid for the establishment and operation of work clinics, training programs, and sheltered workshops. Special facilities exist for the mentally ill, the blind, the deaf and hard-of-hearing, and others with special problems.

Since the 1950s there has been a national program of allowances for families with children, with coverage and age limits changing from time to time. There are also rent subsidies for large families with low incomes.

Unemployment Insurance and Work Injuries

The foundations of the present unemployment insurance system were laid in 1907 when the government began to subsidize the trade unions' unemployment funds. Subsequent legislation, including the statutes of the 1980s, has continued this pattern. The plan remains in principle a voluntary arrangement, but all union members must belong. Nonunion workers also may join, and practically all wage-earners are covered.

To qualify for unemployment benefits, a person must have been a member of an unemployment fund for the previous twelve months and must have had at least twenty-six weeks of work in the last three years. A second category of workers, receiving somewhat lower benefits (called the "school-leaver rate"), is composed of apprentices, the newly trained, and members admitted while in military service. The maximum period for which an individual may receive benefits is three and a half years; after that, aid can be given under the Social Assistance Act. The maximum benefit is 90 percent of a person's previous earnings, up to a fixed ceiling. Ineligible for benefits are workers who are on strike or locked out, those who are unemployed because of their own misconduct, voluntary leaving of a job without good cause, or illness, persons receiving old age or disability pensions, and those who are not available, able, and willing to work. The unemployment insurance system is financed by contributions from insured persons, employers, and the government. General supervision of the program is by the Ministry of Labor.

Wage-earners have had legally guaranteed vacations since 1938. The first law provided for two weeks. In 1953 this was increased to three weeks, in 1971 (by collective bargaining agreements) to four weeks, in 1981 to four weeks and two days, and in 1982 to five weeks.

Workers have been protected against the loss of earnings through industrial accidents and occupational diseases by a series of laws dating back to 1898. This part of the nation's safety net differs from others in that it is fully financed by the employer, who is required to obtain insurance from an approved private company. The National Social Security Office determines the extent of disability and the amount of compensation in individual cases. If a person cannot resume normal work after a period of recuperation, the Social Assistance Act provides for rehabilitation and/or retraining, as well as for possible assistance to the individual's family. An Employees' Wage Guarantee Fund, financed by employers, covers wages, holiday allowances, and other allotments to workers whose firms have gone bankrupt or suspended payments.

THE WELFARE STATE IN TROUBLE

The implementation of the social reforms of the 1960s and early 1970s set the framework of the Danish welfare state. Most of that legislation represented a general consensus, supported in its basic elements by all the major political parties. The Danish citizen seemed well protected against life's adversities, at least insofar as public programs could afford that protection. "It is very hard to fall through the fine mesh of the income security net, unless one consciously cuts a hole and jumps through to choose the life of the hermit, the prophet, or the aging hippie."[7]

Despite the seemingly general acceptance of the welfare state, troubles were brewing. The programs were costly and social expenditures increased more rapidly than public expenditures as a whole. With the growth of the public sector generally and the social welfare sector particularly, the number of public employees increased apace, from 12 percent of the labor force in 1950 to 21 percent in 1970. Grumblings began to be heard about the size, cost, and power of the bureaucracy. A much-discussed book by Professor Jørgen S. Dich, entitled *The Ruling Class* (*Den Herskende Klasse*) argued provocatively that the bureaucrats, not the people or their governmental representatives or the capitalists, were the real rulers of Denmark. Public opinion polls indicated a growing distrust of government and of politicians.

Increased public expenditures meant a heavier tax burden. Revision of the income tax system brought a sharp increase in 1970, and Danes became one of the most heavily taxed people in the world. A Danish factory worker was paying close to 40 percent of his or her wages in direct taxes and another 20 percent in indirect taxes. Income taxes, the most visible and so perhaps the most painful of the levies, had gone up as a percentage of government revenue from 44 percent in 1965 to 57 percent in 1973.[8] And the overall fairness of the tax system was called into question with the well-publicized revelations of Mogens Glistrup that neither he nor any other intelligent Dane paid any income tax and that he earned a healthy living as a tax lawyer by finding loopholes for his many clients.

When Glistrup's new antitax, antispending, antibureaucracy party took second place among Danish parties in the "political earthquake" election of 1973,[9] newspapers in Denmark and throughout the world were full of stories and editorials about the backlash against the welfare state. Reeling under the unprecedented political shock of the 1973 election, the nation soon found itself in a major economic and fiscal crisis as well. As summarized by Lars Nørby Johansen, its elements included "the oil crisis of 1973/74; the rise in the unemployment rate from 2 to 8 percent in less than two years, which unleashed soaring expenditures on unemployment benefits; the cost of social reforms, planned during the affluent 1960s, and timed to be implemented during this period; and the economic recession itself, which reduced general taxable revenues."[10] In these circumstances social expenditures became a heavier burden, financed as they were mostly from tax revenues. Unemployment benefits, which had been 3.5 percent of social expenditures in 1973, rose to more than 13 percent by the late 1970s.

As budget deficits grew, retrenchment became the watchword. Neither Social Democratic nor nonsocialist governments undertook to alter the basic contours of the welfare state, but both tried to brake its expansion and to institute some changes at the margin. Nevertheless social expenditures continued to increase in the 1970s, as did employment in the public sector. A number of changes in the 1980s, largely under nonsocialist governments, brought some cutbacks without significantly altering expenditures. Included were reduced subsidies for medicines, dental care, and physiotherapist treatment; a change in eligibility for unemployment benefits, in 1980, to require twelve months' membership in an unemployment fund (previously the requirement was six months) and, in 1982, a doubling of contributions from both employers and employees; benefit ceilings for social assistance; and, at various times, a freeze on some benefits through a halt in cost-of-living increases. At the same time some benefits were improved or extended: changes in preretirement pensions, new programs for the unemployed and especially for out-of-work young people, and extensions of maternity leave. In 1988 the state assumed employers' contributions to the unemployment funds, the anticipatory and labor market pensions, and the Employees' Wage Guarantee Fund and levied a special tax on employers instead.

None of these changes represented major attacks on either the concept or the programs of the welfare state. Indeed, it appears doubtful that there was ever the extensive "backlash" that critics of the Scandinavian model had so gleefully hailed. The Progressives' 1973 success has not been repeated, and the party has been largely irrelevant in parliament. It seemed on the rise again in the late 1980s, after polling 9 percent of the votes in 1988, when it was still tapping the veins of antitax and distrust of government sentiments, as well as seeking to make political capital out of antirefugee feelings. But its antiwelfare stands seemed more often general war cries or calls for program modifications than demands for the abolition or substantial reduction of specific programs.

Like citizens everywhere, Danes are against taxes; but at the same time they (or most of them) give substantial backing to social programs. Public opinion polls after 1974 showed sizable increases in support for the welfare state. The nation's economic problems, perhaps because they reminded people that affluence may quickly be threatened or lost, seem to have mobilized increased support for the welfare system. And the organized strength of those with a stake in maintaining that system—pensioners, welfare clients, the unemployed, and civil servants—is a political fact of life that the parties cannot ignore.

The welfare state has been trimmed around the edges, but there is little likelihood of major surgery, barring a major economic collapse. Problems continue, of course. Social expenditures have proved difficult to control (in 1986 about one-third of the national government's expenditures went to the social services), and taxes remain high. Gaps appear in some services that have become increasingly essential. As more and more women work outside the home, for example, provision of child care facilities becomes critical. Yet there are not enough facilities to meet the demand, and often their cost consumes most of the mother's salary. The maternity leave of six months seems generous, but children often cannot be placed in nurseries until they are one year old, thus complicating the problem for employed parents.

The worst cases of poverty are gone, but there are still poor people, as many as 10 percent of the population according to a study by the Low Incomes Commission. Pensioners unfortunate enough to have only their public pensions to live on are hard-pressed. Some demographers and other analysts fear that, with the advances of medical science, there will be more and more pensioners, living longer and longer with ever-greater demands for expensive health care, and that these rising costs must be borne by a diminished working-age population. Others hold that these fears are exaggerated and that pressures on the pension system will be alleviated by reduced expenditures on education and family services for declining numbers in the younger age groups.[11]

HOUSING

Before World War I, homebuilding in Denmark was primarily a responsibility for private enterprise. Public intervention was limited to regulations about such things as fire prevention and health and sanitation provisions and to a few efforts to aid particular groups. The housing shortage of World War I brought more government action through rent controls and a program of loans and subsidies, at first only for "social housing" for low-income groups and then to private homebuilders as well. The State Housing Fund Act of 1922 provided borrowers with state-guaranteed bonds that they had to sell in the private money market. The arrangement was not completely satisfactory, however, as the economic conditions of the 1920s often made it difficult to sell the bonds at reasonable prices.

A number of factors in the 1930s combined to bring about significant changes in the government's housing policies. The Social Democratic–Radical ministry in power after 1929 considered housing an important aspect of its social welfare program and found government-aided construction activities one means of combatting the unemployment of the depression years. Besides, various surveys indicated that many dwellings were obsolete and deficient in modern conveniences and that, although there had been improvement over the years, overcrowding still existed. Bad housing conditions were not limited to the cities and towns but were extensive in rural areas as well.

The Housing Subsidy Act of 1933 returned to the principle of direct government loans for construction and established more public control over housing. A 1938 law continued loan arrangements and added provisions for rent rebates or subsidies for large families. It became a condition of government loans to housing associations that the association build a certain number of units at least three rooms in size and give preference to families with three or more children. The law also permitted loans to local governments for housing construction and to private owner-occupiers but not to other types of private building. By 1937, national legislation had begun the policy of encouraging local governments, through sizable subsidies, to construct dwellings for pensioners. Around the same time special assistance was also provided for housing for agricultural workers.

With the outbreak of the war in 1939 the government instituted strict rent controls as it had done in World War I, and it also took steps to relieve financial pressure on those who had borrowed to build homes. After the war the housing shortage was recognized as one of the most pressing domestic problems, and the government adopted a number of different laws aimed at overcoming it. A 1946 act provided for subsidies and loans for building, following the same general principles in earlier laws. The main emphasis was on social housing for people with limited means, and nonprofit housing associations received especially favorable terms on loans. The programs of rent subsidies for low-income families and of special treatment for pensioners continued.

The hope that rents in new uncontrolled housing would be about the same as in older rent-controlled units was not realized, and new legislation was enacted in 1955. Amendments to the Rent Act accepted the idea of a gradual rise in rents so as to narrow the gap between old and new housing. Moderate increases in the rent level for rent-controlled housing in 1955 and 1958 brought it to 60 percent more than the prewar average, but rental for new housing was more than 100 percent above the prewar level, so the differential continued. In subsequent years controls over older housing were gradually abolished except in the larger towns and in the Copenhagen area, with local governments in medium-size areas given authority to decide on the continuation of controls. New and unsubsidized housing was freed from restrictions.

Housing was a very politicized issue in the post–World War II period, with Conservatives and Liberals calling for a return to a free market as soon as possible and Social Democrats defending public housing and existing policies. Compromise among the "old" parties in 1958 and 1966 brought major changes in direction, albeit at some political cost to the Social Democrats. The party lost ground among renters, many of whom found the new policies disadvantageous, and fears among home owners about Social Democratic proposals for cuts in their tax deductions led in 1973 to the defection of Erhard Jakobsen and the formation of the Center Democratic party. "Once the social democrats took the initiative to attempt a reform of housing policies, renters were pushed heavily to the left, while homeowners were pushed to the right."[12]

The 1958 Housing Act broke with past patterns to give greater scope to financing by private institutions at normal market rates. State guarantees of second mortgages largely replaced government loans, although the national government could still lend for social and experimental projects and slum clearance and in areas with special housing needs. Subsidies were in gradually diminishing amounts and were intended to disappear altogether by 1973. Various regulations covered provision of apartments for large families, nursery schools in apartment projects, and dwellings for pensioners and others in the lowest income groups. Rent subsidies continued, though with changes affecting their coverage. The earlier laws had favored social housing, with an emphasis on units for the larger families; the new act gave an impetus to private building and especially to the construction of smaller apartments. A 1966 law took the same approach and sought to "normalize" the housing market by removing numerous restrictions and phasing out rent control.

Senior citizens' housing, Charlottenlund

Although there have been subsequent modifications, the basic principles of the 1958 and 1966 laws have remained largely unaltered. The end to most government restrictions stimulated homebuilding, especially that of single-family homes. Nearly 70 percent of the population lived in single-family homes in 1985. In social or public housing, the trend has been away from multistory buildings toward smaller projects, and systems of "tenant democracy," in which tenants' representatives and management share responsibility for some decisions, have been introduced.[13]

Public policies on housing remain important even though controls have ended and government expenditures on housing have dropped considerably. Private home buyers receive indirect subsidies through the allowance of generous income tax deductions for mortgage payments. National and local governments continue to subsidize social housing; national law sets an annual quota for construction, and the geographical distribution of the projects is determined by negotiations between the ministry of housing and local governments. Also subsidized are cooperative housing and housing for special groups, including the young and the old. The economic crisis of the 1970s brought the national government more deeply into the housing area with efforts to stimulate employment through loans and subsidies for slum clearance projects and dwelling rehabilitation.

CONSUMER PROTECTION

Protection of the consumer had received some attention before the consumerism of the 1970s arrived in Denmark, but government's role was at first peripheral. The Government Home Economics Council (Statens Husholdningsråd), established in 1935, and the Consumer Council, begun in 1947, tested products and provided information to consumers. The Consumer Council also operated a Complaints Department to take up with sellers the cases of consumers dissatisfied with a product or service. Reorganized in 1960, the Home Economics Council has a statutory basis and is governed by a board of eighteen members, with twelve appointed by the minister of trade on the nomination of interest organizations, two chosen by the minister directly, and four appointed by other government departments. The Consumer Council receives most of its funding from the public treasury but is independent of government in its activities. Legislation affecting the consumer included the Price Supervision Act of 1956 (with changes in 1962), which allowed a Monopoly Control Authority (*monopoltilsynet*) to undertake inquiries on seemingly unreasonable prices or profits upon the request of consumers, manufacturers, or trade organizations, and the Unfair Competition Act of 1959, which banned advertising that was harmful to competition.

The shaky finances of the Consumer Council, questions of overlap among the agencies involved with the consumer, and the realization that some problems were not covered by existing organizations and laws led to the trade minister's appointment of a Consumer Commission in 1969. The commission investigated the position of the consumer under existing laws, the relations between business and consumers (especially in such areas as advertising, information on goods and services, and complaint handling), and the coordination and division of labor among institutions and organizations serving the consumer. Its members represented consumer groups, government departments, business and industry, consumer cooperatives, and labor. The commission's four reports (1971, 1973, 1975, and 1977) furnished the basis for important legislation.

The Marketing Practices Act (*markedsføringsloven*) of 1974 outlaws the use of false, misleading, or incomplete statements to affect the demand or supply of goods or services; requires the provision of accurate information on the nature of goods and services, including durability and risks; prohibits certain marketing practices that disadvantage consumers; provides for adjudication of cases under the law by the Maritime and Commercial Court; and creates the office of Ombudsman for Consumer Affairs. The Consumer Complaint Board Act of 1974 (with later revisions) sets up an agency for consumers to use in disputes about goods or services. The Act on Marking and Displaying of Prices (1977) requires that information on price, tax, and other charges for goods offered for sale be clearly indicated; it also orders the provision of essential information on price, interest, charges, and payment time for installment purchases. The Act on Certain Consumer Agreements (1978) forbids door-to-door and telephone sales (with some exceptions: books, subscriptions, insurance, and direct sales of meat, fish, vegetables, and ice cream and dairy products) and gives the purchaser a right to annul contracts under certain conditions. A 1979 law amending the Sales Act declared that consumers' rights under general law cannot be overriden by contract in cases of late delivery or defects in products. Aspects of some of these laws met opposition from Conservative, Liberal, and Progressive M.F.s who argued that the laws were unnecessary, went too far, or were already being carried out voluntarily by sellers. Not included in the Consumer Commission's package was the Food Act of 1973, prohibiting certain food additives and prescribing the amounts of those permitted.

The two chief institutions created by the 1970s legislation are the Ombudsman for Consumer Affairs (*forbrugerombudsmand*) and the Consumer Complaint Board (*forbrugerklagenævnet*). Appointed by the government for an unspecified term, the ombudsman must possess the same qualifications as a judge. The 1974 act gives him the duty of ensuring that enterprises engage in "proper marketing practices." He receives complaints from individuals and organizations and may also take up cases on his own initiative. He may issue nonbinding advisory opinions and guidelines. In 1987 40 percent of the 1,649 new cases that reached the ombudsman's office came from individuals, and 30 percent came from business people; not quite 10 percent were on his own initiative. The remaining cases were brought by consumer organizations, trade associations, and public institutions, with a handful of anonymous communications.[14]

What kinds of cases reach the Consumer Ombudsman? A used car dealer included in his contracts a statement that the agreements would be valid only with the signature of the firm's owner and that this signature had to be added within six days but in the meantime the contract bound the purchaser. The ombudsman found this contrary to the Marketing Practices Act. An ad says "You save kr. 2000–3000 when buying from us." Ombudsman guidelines say the truth of this claim must be ascertainable through adequate documentation. On the other hand, a slogan like "The Best Shirt Shop in Town" is acceptable as a common form of praise. Dealer bonuses have been found to violate the act because they may affect service to customers and raise prices for consumers.

Settlement by negotiation is preferred, but if no solution can be found, the case is referred to court. In 1987 the Consumer Ombudsman disposed of 1,400 cases, 1,160 (about 80 percent) by negotiation or explanation. Only 18 (less than 2 percent) went to court; 138 were sent on to some other government office; and 84 were dismissed. Decisions by the ombudsman cannot be appealed to any other administrative authority. At first, some business people feared that this new office would interfere with their enterprises or seek to control them, but now the general feeling seems to be that his approach has been even-handed.

The Consumer Complaint Board serves as a kind of small claims court for consumers, although it has no power to enforce its findings. It hears complaints concerning the purchase or rental of goods, their delivery or lack of delivery, service contracts, and so on, up to a value of kr. 20,000 (about $3,000). Problems in certain areas are excluded— real estate, motor vehicles, doctors' and dentists' fees, among others. Four persons—two from consumers' organizations, two from business organizations—decide a case. These adjudicators are drawn from a panel of consumer and business representatives, appointed by the minister of trade on the nomination of the various associations. The board's staff handles many cases, either working out compromises or negotiated settlements or rejecting complaints either as not within the board's jurisdiction or as obviously groundless. Those not settled by the staff go to the four-member hearing.

In most instances the consumer who wins a case finds that the business firm will accept the board's conclusion. If it does not, the Ombudsman for Consumer Affairs will intervene and take the case to court on behalf of the complainant. The board has accepted various nongovernment, often industrywide, panels as alternative sites for consumer complaints, including boards in the insurance, travel agency, laundry, radio and TV equipment, and fur businesses or industries. If the amount involved in the problem is large or if the difficulty falls outside the board's jurisdiction, the consumer may take the case to the Consumer Council's Complaint Department, where a settlement through negotiation will be sought. Of course, the consumer may also choose to seek the aid and advice of an attorney on a lawsuit or other legal action.

ENVIRONMENTAL PROTECTION

As in the United States, the conservation movement in Denmark long preceded broader concerns with environmental quality. The rapid disappearance of Danish forests gave rise to attempts to preserve remaining woodlands; a forestry decree in 1805 was the first effective step toward the creation of protected forest reserves. Later in the nineteenth century the success of the Danish Heath Society in reclaiming the Jutland heathlands led to action by botanists and zoologists to save what was left of the heath. In 1911 the forerunner to what became the major conservation organization, the Nature Conservation Association, was established, and its lobbying efforts began to meet with some success. The first Nature Conservation Act in 1917 set up a system of special courts, the nature conservancy boards, which still exist on the county level. A Superior Conservation Board serves as a court of appeal. Under the 1917 law the conservancy boards were empowered to issue orders to property owners and to facilitate public access where desirable; full compensation was to be paid. A second Nature Conservation Act, in 1937, also covered public access to forests and beaches and, perhaps more importantly, prohibited building within 328 feet (100 meters) of beaches and allowed construction within 984 feet (300 meters) of forests only if a conservancy board approved. As a result, most of Denmark's 4,660-mile (7,500-kilometer) coastline has not been built on and is open to the public.[15] Also in the 1930s came the establishment of county committees to analyze conservation problems and consider them in conjunction with general physical planning.

By the 1960s, as the building boom and suburban development seemed increasingly to threaten the landscape, the time was opportune for an overall examination of conservation needs in the customary Danish way, the appointment of a commission. The Nature Conservancy Commission, after an early failure when four "land laws" it had backed were defeated in a national referendum, produced in 1967 a major report on public access to nature and protection of the countryside and helped inspire passage of new legislation. The Town and Country Zoning Act of 1969 set up additional safeguards against unauthorized building and development and regulated the siting of public projects and some private activities. Later planning acts, in 1973 and 1976, extended government powers for national, regional, and local planning, with national and regional authorities responsible for the framework of physical planning and local governments in charge of local planning and determining utilization of areas within the framework.

A revised Conservation Act, enacted in 1978, reinforces government planning powers and authorizes additional steps to preserve the landscape, flora and fauna and their habitats, and ancient monuments and buildings. Under its provisions certain areas have been set aside as nature reserves, to be preserved and protected because of their scenic beauty or historical significance. These include Denmark's most famous natural monument, the white chalk cliffs of Møn (Møns Klint), as well as the remains of the Jutland heath; the sand dunes of Råbjerg Mile; and "The Highway"

(Hærvejen), a scenic road dating back to 1650 that runs north and south along the ridge that is Jutland's backbone.

By the late 1960s, then, as Danes began to debate seriously and to take action on problems of pollution, the nation had had years of accomplishment in conservation. Rachel Carson's *Silent Spring* focused attention on the dangers in pesticides and herbicides, and awareness grew that there were other perils as well. It was clear, for example, that the waters of Køge Bay, south of Copenhagen and intended as a national recreation reserve, were dirty and unhealthy and that the fish in the bay were diseased and becoming fewer. The first step was to find out the nature and extent of the country's environmental problems, and in 1969 the government appointed a Pollution Control Board (Forureningsråd) for that purpose. The board set up working groups of experts to collect and analyze data and issued twenty-nine reports covering water, air, solid waste, and noise pollution.[16]

The next step was creation of an administrative structure, accomplished without legislation in 1971 when Prime Minister Jens Otto Krag transferred to a new department some of the responsibilities of other ministries and appointed a minister for the environment. The administration and policy framework was completed in 1973 with Folketing passage of the Environmental Protection Act.

The new law had the support of the Social Democrats and the Conservatives, with the other parties abstaining on the final vote in the Folketing. Some environmental groups thought that the law was too weak and that there had been too many concessions to industry. The act sets general principles and procedures and empowers the minister to draw up detailed orders on such things as the quality of surface water and air or the reduction of the noise level. Administrative rules and decisions made under his jurisdiction and some made by county and local authorities can be appealed to the independent Environmental Appeals Board, half of whose expert members are nominated by environmental organizations and half by government.

The act covers any activities that might pollute the air, the lakes and streams, the sea, and the soil. A general principle is that the polluter must pay the costs of antipollution actions. For a number of years after the law's passage, however, enterprises in operation before it went into effect could receive government subsidies to help cover the costs of the new requirements. In 1980 the approach changed, and now subsidies go for the development and application of new technology that is environmentally sound. Factories or enterprises that are likely polluters or emitters of hazardous substances must receive national and/or local government authorization before starting operation.

Within the Environment Ministry the National Agency of Environmental Protection (Miljøstyrelsen) draws up regulations, negotiates them with local and regional governments and with industry, and submits the final form to the minister for approval. The agency advises the minister, prepares draft legislation, sets priorities, and keeps the public informed through pamphlets bearing such titles as "From Garden Refuse to Good Mulch," "Invisible Destroyers: Chemical Pollution," and "Good Drinking Water—Not Inevitable." The names of other units within the Environment Ministry give some idea of its scope: the National Agency of Physical Planning, the National Agency for Forest and Nature Conservation, the National Food Institute, the Geological Survey of Denmark, and the National Agency for the Protection of Nature, Monuments, and Sites.

Together, the national and local governments seek to control, diminish, or eliminate all forms of pollution. Nearly all of Denmark's water supply comes from groundwater so preventing contamination from dumps, oil and chemical waste, and wastewater is essential. The government sets standards for the quality of streams and lakes and regulates the discharge of wastewater by granting permits that are usually conditional on purification processes. The Environment Ministry sets the rules for drinking water and has overall supervision of planning, supply, use, and protection of that resource. Most sewage receives biological treatment; sewage plants run by local authorities are being upgraded to remove nitrogen and phosphorous compounds. The Marine Environment Act prohibits the dumping of waste at sea. The National Agency of Environmental Protection has contingency plans for oil and chemical spills and a fleet of four ships ready to combat them.

Air pollution from the increasing number of motor vehicles and the emissions from oil- and coal-fired heating systems and from factory processes is a serious problem. Limits have been imposed on the sulfur content of fuel oil and coal, heating plants are more carefully checked, and the result has been a reduction in the discharge of sulfur dioxide. The total level of sulfur emissions in 1990 will be only half the level of 1982. Factories have restrictions on the discharge of other pollutants into the air. The Environment Ministry set maximum limits for the lead content of gasoline and then required lead-free gasoline in 1986.

Every Dane produces on average about 1,540 pounds (700 kilos) of waste annually, a grand total of 3.5 million tons a year. About half comes from households and half from industry. The Environmental Protection Act makes local governments responsible for refuse removal. Some of it goes to dumps but most is incinerated, with some of the resulting heat used for homes. Nonprofit facilities for the disposal of hazardous waste are owned and operated jointly by industries and local government, and many experts have considered the system of waste collection treatment, recycling, and disposal the most advanced in the world. Land disposal of untreated hazardous waste is strictly forbidden.

Local collection systems are provided for the recovery and recycling of paper and glass from homes, businesses, factories, and public institutions. The recycling of beer and soda bottles has been described as the most effective in the world: 99 percent of bottles are re-used, with each used 33 times on the average.

Surveys show that half the population claims to be bothered by noise, and authorities have taken steps, albeit rather limited ones, to combat noise pollution. The chief problem is road traffic; alleviating efforts include rerouting, noise-reducing ramparts, and window insulation. Environmental agencies provide guidelines for housing design and insulation against noise and have set maximum limits to noise around airports.

Denmark's geographical location complicates its fight for the environment as pollutants know no national boundaries. The nation cooperates with the antipollution activities of the European Community, the Nordic Council, the OECD, and the United Nations. Denmark and Sweden have worked together to clean up the Øresund (the Sound). In February 1974, the Nordic states signed a Convention on the Protection of the Environment, obligating each of them to consider any environmental harm that its projects might cause to the other states or their citizens. Under the Baltic Sea Convention of 1974 Denmark cooperates with six other Baltic states—Finland, Sweden, East Germany, West Germany, Poland, and the USSR—to control pollution in those waters.[17]

In 1986 the Folketing adopted the most extensive changes to the Environmental Protection Act since its passage in 1973. Along with a clear statement that protection of the environment takes precedence over economic interests (the old law gave both concerns equal status), the revisions introduce stricter time limits for carrying out environmental orders and heavier penalties for violaters, strengthen local and regional supervision of enterprises, and tighten recycling requirements for homes and industries (including imposition of a special tax on waste brought to refuse centers, thus giving an additional incentive to re-use). The changes were backed by all the parties except the Progressives, who warned against environmental terrorists who dominate the debate and undermine the Danish economy.

CRIME

Though protection from consumer exploitation and environmental pollution are relatively new functions of government, protection against the misdeeds and violence of some individuals against others is a very old responsibility of the state. At first, in Denmark as elsewhere, law enforcement was a private matter. Gradually, it became a public charge. By the thirteenth century cities had night patrols or nightwatchmen. In 1682 the king appointed a police chief for Copenhagen, and in 1701 an ordinance listed a number of activities to be regulated: taverns, prostitution, gambling, trade, aliens, and church attendance. Later the police became responsible for investigating crimes, a function previously in the hands of the courts. In the nineteenth century the forces in Copenhagen and other towns were reorganized and their numbers increased, with policing remaining a local government responsibility.

A 1911 statute set up a state police force to assist local departments with difficult crimes and in emergencies. Reorganization under the Police Act of 1937 placed a national police commissioner, accountable to the minister of justice, in charge of central administration, specialized offices (records, fingerprint and other laboratories, etc.), personnel, the police academy, and other units. Fifty-four local police districts, each headed by a chief of police, remain operationally independent.[18]

The police have had to cope with a growing crime problem. From 1960 to 1987 the total number of crimes (offenses registered by the police) rose from 126,367 to 525,969, and the crime rate per 100,000 inhabitants increased about two and a half times. Murders were still relatively few, at least in comparison with the United States, but more numerous in 1987 (47 murders) than in 1960 (8 murders)—the rate per 100,000 inhabitants was 0.6 in 1960, 1.3 in 1987. (In the United States the murder rate per 100,000 inhabitants was more than six times higher, at 8.3 in 1987.)[19] Although the number and rate of assaults grew substantially from 1960 to 1987, the largest increases in reported crime came in theft and robbery, with the rate of robbery nearly five times higher in 1987 than in 1960. Violent crimes comprised less than 2 percent of those reported. In 1985 nearly half of lawbreakers who received a heavier sentence than a fine were under the age of twenty-five, but there was evidence in the mid-1980s of a decline in criminal offenses by young people. In seeking the causes of the increase in crime, Danish studies point to the major changes in Danish society since World War II: exodus from the farms and growth of the urban areas; radically altered business, family, and residential patterns; weaker ties of people to their neighborhoods; and so on.[20]

Drugs have become a more serious problem in recent years. Estimates are that there are about 7,000 addicts on "hard" drugs, with many turning to crime or prostitution to get the money for those drugs. Between 1968 and 1986 about 1,700 deaths were recorded as due to narcotics; because many drug deaths were listed as from other causes, the actual number was probably three to five times greater. As far as marijuana is concerned, the public prosecutor issued a circular in July 1969, finding that a person possessing the drug for his or her own use should receive a warning rather than an arrest and that efforts should be directed at prevention of its smuggling and sale. In May 1985, the Supreme Court upheld a complete ban on growing the plants in Denmark. Several political parties—including the Socialist Peoples and the Left Socialist—have called for total legalization of marijuana.

A number of steps have been taken to try to cope with the growth of criminal activity. The number of police has been increased. A special board awards compensation to the victims of violence if they do not receive payments from the criminal or from the welfare system. Compensation may be paid for pain and suffering, lost work time, disability, maintenance, and medical and dental costs. Since 1971 a Crime Prevention Council has worked to inform and educate the public on protection against crimes like burglary, theft, and vandalism. The council's membership is drawn from more than 40 associations and government agencies and works on the principle that crime control is a responsibility of the community as well as of police and courts. In addition to broader research studies it publishes and circulates widely materials on locks and burglar alarms, safety and security measures at work and at home, drugs, preventing car theft, property identification through photos or engraving of serial numbers, and community planning and cooperation. It works with schools, social workers, and police in special committees to provide activities for young people.

Rising crime rates have not yet altered the national policy (in effect since the Corrections Reform Act of 1973) that emphasizes fines and probation rather than imprisonment. In 1987 about 20 percent of sentences were prison terms, 43 percent were fines, and the remainder were suspended sentences or similar actions. Essentially there are three types of sanctions under Danish criminal law: fines, *hæfte* (one of those difficult-to-translate words, sometimes called "mitigated" or "simple" detention), or imprisonment. *Hæfte* is a milder form of custody, in which the convicted person has more privileges than does a prison inmate and serves the seven days to six months of a sentence in a local jail. Prison sentences may be for life or for periods from thirty days to sixteen years. The life sentence is the penalty for murder. Capital punishment was formally abolished in 1930 but may be applied in time of war to both civilian and military offenders. Except for the execution after World War II of some persons convicted of heinous crimes in aid of the Nazi occupation regime, no one has been executed since 1892. Today's life sentence for murder is technically without parole, but in practice the queen grants a pardon after ten to twelve years have been served. Most prisoners with sentences of less than five months are freed on parole after serving two-thirds of their time; longer term prisoners generally have to serve seven-twelfths of their sentence. For the young, the old, and first-time offenders, parole often comes after half the sentence has been served. The prison population has grown from 2,010 in 1950 to 3,435 in 1988.[21] Danish prison officials agree that the purpose of imprisonment is punishment but believe that loss of liberty is sufficient punishment, with inmates being treated as humanely as possible during their incarceration. The result is a system of "open" prisons in which inmates have a right to frequent furloughs home and to various other amenities.[22]

Some police actions have aroused controversy and criticism in recent years. After many protests against the police practice of photographing participants in legal, peaceful demonstrations, the police in 1982 were forbidden to engage in systematic photography of participants. They can photograph demonstrators only if there are definite grounds to believe that a demonstration could develop into illegal or disorderly behavior. The firing of tear gas and the practice of mass arrests, occasionally used against (mostly) young activists who have occupied a building or blockaded a street, have led to additional restrictions on police behavior. Each of the nation's police districts has a complaints board, made up of representatives of the police and the local government, that hears charges against the police. The basis for the board's finding is an investigation conducted by the police, and about 90 percent of the time the board decides that the complaint is groundless.

8

The State and the Economy

Surveying the Danish economy, one is struck by the nation's poverty in raw materials, especially those essential to industry and manufacturing. The country lacks fuels (though North Sea oil and gas have improved the situation), minerals, metals, and fibers. To maintain its high standard of living, Denmark must make intensive use of what it has: its agricultural resources and the skills of its people. As the domestic market is small, the country has to place a heavy emphasis on exports so that their earnings will pay for the materials that have to be purchased abroad. This means that the Danish economy is greatly affected by international economic conditions over which it has very little control.

Traditionally, Denmark has been a farming country, but in recent years manufacturing has grown so fast that it must now be described as both an agricultural and an industrial land. Still, agriculture remains of utmost importance to the economy. About two-thirds of the total area (nearly 80 percent if forests are included) is devoted to agriculture. The Netherlands is the only other country in Europe with so great a proportion of its land used in farming. Compared to other Scandinavian countries Denmark has better soil and considerably higher productivity both in crops and in livestock.

Until the 1880s Denmark was primarily an exporter of grain. Then harvests from the new lands of the United States and Russia flooded the world market, prices dropped, and Danish farmers found they could no longer compete. To survive, they had to shift from the export of grain to the export of animal products. There was a notable expansion of dairying, cattle and pig farming, and poultry raising and a development of bacon factories, cheese factories, and other processing industries. Feed crops were cultivated intensively, but grain and fodder had to be imported in substantial quantities.

Dominant in dairying and in the bacon factories are the cooperatives, which in these and other fields handle most of the agricultural exports. At the time of the nineteenth-century changes the farmers realized that they could retain individual proprietorships while gaining the advantages of large-scale production by the formation of cooperative societies, which have been fundamental to Danish agriculture ever since. Today these include cooperative dairies, bacon factories, and egg export associations, as well as other producer cooperatives for butter, cheese, cattle, poultry, fish, and fruit. Closely associated with the labor movement are a number of urban consumer cooperatives, bakeries, fuel purchase associations, and building enterprises. In the agricultural field the cooperatives have not only brought economic advantages and strengthened the position of Danish exports in the world market by their emphasis on high quality and uniformity of product, they have also provided their members with practical training in the art of self-government.

Ever since the eighteenth century the government has tried to promote an agricultural economy based upon the individually owned farm and to see that those without land have a chance to acquire it. The results of this policy can be seen in the large number of moderate-size farms in Denmark. The "typical" Danish farm is worked by its owner and his family, without full-time hired help; it is a general farm, producing grain, root crops, and fodder, which are fed to livestock rather than sold; cows and pigs are the main source of the owner's income. Like his fellow farmers he uses machinery much more than his father did before World War II. The productivity of his land is high, not only because of mechanization, better seed and fertilizers, and the information he gets from government advisory services and agricultural societies but also because as an owner-operator he tends to watch carefully over his land and livestock. He realizes that he is one of a diminishing number of Danish farmers. In 1901 the rural population was 1,001,000; in 1981, although the total population had more than doubled, the number of rural dwellers was 827,000.

Since World War II Danish industry has expanded rapidly, and manufacturing now contributes more than agriculture to the national income. Industrialization came late to Denmark, compared to other Western European countries. In the seventeenth century the state attempted to promote factories in accordance with mercantilist theory, but without much success. It was not until the change of direction by Danish agriculture in the last quarter of the nineteenth century that industry really began to develop. The shift in agriculture created a demand for fertilizers, farm implements, and machinery for the dairies and bacon factories, as well as for plants to process the animal products. As farmers gave up the attempt to be self-sufficient, their demand for manufactured goods increased, and Danish enterprises began to meet their needs. By the end of the nineteenth century a number of industrial establishments were thriving: fertilizer and chemical factories, farm machinery plants, sugar refineries, shipyards, distilleries, breweries, and tobacco factories.

Even today, a significant part of Danish industry is concerned with processing agricultural products, though in recent years other manufactures have increased in importance. The metalworking, chemical and pharmaceutical, electrical, and shipbuilding industries all made considerable progress. In 1986 enterprises involved in metal products and machinery employed the largest number of workers and had the highest gross value of production among Danish industries. Ranking second were the food-processing concerns. Much attention is focused on production of specialized quality goods for the world market. Many U.S. consumers are familiar with Danish furniture, glassware, silver, porcelain, beer, cheese, and ham. The nation's economy is characterized by private enterprise (along with the flourishing cooperative movement in agriculture); public enterprise is limited largely to "natural monopolies." Most of the railway service is provided by the Danish State Railways (Danske Statsbaner, or DSB), though some subsidiary lines are privately owned and publicly subsidized. DSB also operates many bus services in urban areas, as do local governments. The national and local governments own a number of harbors; the Port of Copenhagen Authority, with representatives from the central government, the Folketing, the Copenhagen city government, and trade organizations, directs that important facility. The Danish, Norwegian, and Swedish governments jointly own half the share capital in the Scandinavian Airlines System (SAS), and the Danish government owns the Copenhagen airport at Kastrup and the airports in some of the provincial cities. Telephone service is provided partly by private companies under government license and partly by the state through the Directorate of Postal and Telegraphic Services. Radio and television are publicly controlled. A publicly owned insurance company was being privatized in 1990. Local governments generally own water, gas, and electricity facilities.

The state-supervised National Bank has an autonomous position and a considerable degree of independence. Its statutory objectives are maintenance of a safe and secure currency system and regulation of traffic in money and the extension of credit. It is the government's banker; it issues notes, and its monetary policy is relied on by the government in its efforts at economic regulation.

ECONOMIC PROBLEMS AND POLICIES

"A typical feature of Scandinavian economic policy is that it is not conducted according to any single and simple general formula. On the contrary, attacks on the economic problems are made on a number of fronts by means of differentiated measures adapted to the circumstances under which the problems occur."[1] This remains an accurate statement for Danish economic policy. Most people agree that there is a public responsibility to help maintain high employment, promote economic growth, establish prosperity and economic stability, and solve the problems stemming from Denmark's sensitivity to international economic developments.

The nation has been plagued in the post–World War II years by balance of payments crises, inflation, and erratic economic growth. The period from 1950 to 1957 was one of slow development, but more balanced expansion occurred from 1958 to 1960, with a rise in the gross national product (GNP) and especially in industrial production, full employment, expansion of demand at home, and increased investment.

Danes look back on the 1960s as the economic "golden years." In the four-year period from 1958 to 1962 the GNP at fixed prices increased by 26 percent, a rate unequalled either before or since. The incomes of wage-earners, salaried employees, and old-age pensioners grew faster than those of the rest of the population, and the progressive income tax and social welfare programs combined to bring a more equal distribution of disposable income than in earlier years. Not everyone gained, however. Many farmers worked long hours for low incomes. Older workers with health problems fared less well than other wage-earners: They were not old enough to qualify for pensions and not sick enough to receive disability pay but often found it hard to keep factory jobs. Divorced or widowed women with children, frequently without vocational training or skills, ended up in the lowest paid work. Small shopkeepers met increasing competition from new chains of supermarkets. Taxes were getting higher, with the income tax bringing in an ever-larger proportion of government revenue.

Inflationary tendencies had appeared by the early 1960s, and throughout the decade governments introduced various measures to restrict demand and curtail public expenditures. These proved only temporary palliatives for Denmark's economic problems, however. Inflation grew ever higher, and the balance of payments deficit persisted. Political and economic crisis coincided in the early 1970s with the "political earthquake" of 1973, the weak minority governments that followed, and the oil crises of 1973–1974 and 1979–1980 and their devastating effects on the economy. With the sharp increase in oil prices the balance of payments deficit rose to nearly twice what it had been before the Middle East war. The effect of higher oil prices on wage indexes brought a wage rise of 20 percent in 1974, and the inflation rate surpassed the West European average. Competitiveness dropped; purchasing power abroad declined; unemployment grew. The major political parties agreed on the need for an incomes policy to tackle these problems but could not agree on the steps to be taken. In 1982 Anker Jørgensen and his Social Democratic cabinet resigned without an election, opening the way for a nonsocialist government to try new policy directions.

With Poul Schlüter, the Conservative leader, as prime minister, the new minority cabinet—it had only 66 seats in the 179-member Folketing— faced serious difficulties.

> The economic problems were indeed agonizing despite the numerous efforts to cope with them during 8 years. Thus, in 1982 unemployment as well as inflation averaged 10 percent, the interest rate was 20 percent, the balance-of-payment deficit 4 percent of the GNP, and the public deficit almost 10 percent of the GNP. The economic growth rate was 3 percent after two years of negative growth.[2]

The government's policies aimed at restoring the competitiveness of the private sector and cutting inflation by reducing interest rates, holding down wage increases and suspending cost-of-living payments, and curtailing public expenditures, including those for some social programs. Despite the government's stated opposition to tax increases, it resorted to them on a number of occasions, with the tax level reaching a historic peak of 51 percent of GNP.

Unemployment continued to be high, but the balance of payments difficulties and inflationary pressures eased. In June 1983, the OECD could report that Denmark's annual inflation rate was down to about 4 percent, the lowest level in fourteen years. The Schlüter government was quite happy to take credit for all economic improvements, even though international factors—the drops in oil prices and interest rates— were certainly involved in the gains.

The "four-leaf clover" government continued in office after the 1984 election, still without a parliamentary majority but able to proceed with its economic policies with the backing of the Radicals. Every five or six months the cabinet came to the Folketing with a new austerity package, usually some combination of tax increases, restrictions on consumer demand, and cuts in public projects. Support from the Radical party, often after modifications in the original proposals, brought approval of the package. There were occasional compromises with the Social Democrats as well, for example, on a major income tax reform in 1986.

In October 1986 another economic package, dubbed the "potato diet" (kartoffelkuren, so called because an old holiday occurred traditionally at the end of the potato harvest in October), received the support of the government parties and the Radicals and was adopted over the opposition of the Social Democrats, the left-wing socialist parties, and the Progressives. Among other things it tightened up the terms for mortgages, installment loans, and retail credit; imposed a tax of 20 percent on individuals' net interest payments for most consumer loans; and increased taxes on gasoline (except lead-free, which was reduced), diesel and other fuels, coal, and electricity.

The 1987 election brought losses to the Schlüter government, but the coalition clung precariously to office. In December 1987, the government, the Radicals, and the Social Democrats agreed on an export promotion package, aimed at improving industry's competitiveness by 8 or 9 percent and increasing employment by 50,000 to 70,000 over a three- to four-year period. The plan eliminated employers' contributions to the unemployment and several other labor market funds and to the anticipatory and labor market pensions, substituting a tax of 2.5 percent of a company's value-added tax (VAT) liability. There were also tax concessions to encourage companies to increase exports and research.

A new election on May 10, 1988, brought an end to the "four-leaf clover" coalition and replaced it with a Conservative-Liberal-Radical cabinet, also without a parliamentary majority. Attempts to reach agreement between the government parties and the Social Democrats on a medium-range economic policy failed in the fall of 1989.

The economic report of a leading Danish bank described the national economy as leading a "rollercoaster existence" in recent years. "When domestic activity causes overheating, the external deficits soar to unacceptable heights. The politicians immediately slam on the brakes, and the result is low growth and high unemployment."[3] The budget has been balanced, and the inflation rate dropped from its double-digit figures to 3.6 percent in 1986. Unemployment, especially among young people, remains high, however (the overall rate in September 1989 was 9.6 percent), and the balance of payments deficit continues. In 1988 the *Economist*, calling Denmark "the smug debtor," observed:

> The richest people in the EEC are also the most indebted. Each Dane— man, woman and child—is in hock to the rest of the world to the tune of $8,500. At the end of last year Denmark's total foreign debt was equivalent to 40 percent of its annual GDP—exactly as bad as Brazil's, though below Argentina's 70 percent. More happily, as a proportion of its annual exports, Denmark's debt was 130 percent—well below Brazil's 400 percent.

The journal noted that for twenty-five years Denmark has been warned that it cannot continue living beyond its means but that it blithely continues. Foreign investors are eager to lend the nation money, and Denmark has always paid its debts on time. "Denmark's immediate debt problem is not so much that finance might suddenly dry up, but that borrowing is so easy that there is too little pressure on the Danes to tighten their belts."[4] In the summer of 1989 the economic report of a major bank painted a bleak picture of a stagnant economy, likely to grow less than 1 percent in both 1988 and 1989. The major hope was that exports would expand and that the coming of the EC's single European market would be a catalyst for the economy.[5]

Assisting the government in setting policy is the Economic Council (Det økonomiske Råd), which watches the nation's economic development and tries to promote cooperation among its various economic interests. Members of the council are appointed by the minister of economics. A board of three trained economists (who were immediately dubbed the "three wise men") directs its activities, with one of them designated by the minister as chair. They serve for terms up to six years and cannot be members of the Folketing. Others appointed to the council have three-year terms and are drawn from such organizations as the National Bank, the Employers Confederation, LO, the Federation of Danish Industries, the Agricultural Council, the Consumers' Council, and the Finance Ministry, with the economics minister able to appoint some additional members with special competence in economic questions. The council's reports frequently have served as a basis for government action. Also useful to the executive and the Folketing are annual economic surveys, prepared in the Ministry of Economics.

THE TAX SYSTEM

Nearly every economic package has brought some revision of the tax system. Historically the system has evolved from one that relied mainly on land and building taxes and customs duties to one that depends on income taxes, a general VAT, and taxes on specific goods and services. Post–World War II governments used tax measures as a device to speed up or slow down the economy. Especially favored by the system were home owners who, among other advantages, could deduct loans and repair expenses from their taxable income.

By the late 1950s there was a growing demand for reform of the tax system, which was failing to meet the needs of Keynesian policy in many respects. Excise taxes were so high that any increase would reduce consumption and hence revenue. The first basic change occurred in 1960 with the levying of a 9 percent general sales tax on most commodities except food. This was replaced in 1960 by a 10 percent value-added tax (in Danish, *meromsætningsafgift*, abbreviated as *moms*) on all commodities. This was designed both as a revenue-producing measure and as a preliminary step toward Danish entry into the Common Market (whose 6 members had a preference for VAT). *Moms* went up to 15 percent in 1970 and later went even higher—it was 22 percent in 1988.

Income tax reforms came in 1968. The tax's effective rates in the upper income brackets had not been as high as those in many other countries because of the taxpayer's right to deduct the past year's tax from the current year's income. In 1967 the Social Democratic and Socialist Peoples parties secured passage of a law that ended the deduction (considered by socialists a special boon to the upper income groups) and introduced a pay-as-you-go income tax system with payroll deductions, effective January 1, 1969. One effect of the introduction of *moms* and the income tax changes was a growing tax revolt, manifested partly in the 1973 election returns.

The hard times of the 1970s produced changes in tax rates, as well as new imposts like an energy tax. By the 1980s most of the political parties (except for the Socialist Peoples, Left Socialist, and Progressive parties) were ready for another rewriting of the tax laws. In June 1985 they agreed on legislation to take effect in 1987. The changes were detailed and complex; the most important provisions were (1) a division of taxable income into two categories, personal income (wages, salaries, and pensions) and capital income (interest and other returns on capital and investments); (2) taxation of personal income at rates from 50 percent to 68 percent (compared to the previous high of 73 percent) and of capital income at a rate of around 50 percent; and (3) new rules for permissible deductions and calculation of taxable income. A hypothetical example of the new tax law's operation for a single taxpayer with a personal income of kroner 300,000 (about $44,400) and typical deductions showed a tax payment of kroner 94,193 ($13,940) to national and local governments. A married couple with two children under eighteen years of age and combined personal incomes of kroner 400,000 (around $59,200) would pay kroner 134,441 ($19,900), though they would receive a tax-free children's allowance of kroner 10,000 (about $1,480).[6]

The burden of direct taxes (basically the income tax) remains heavier in Denmark than in most other European countries, with direct taxes as a percentage of the gross domestic product (GDP) equal to 16.6 percent in 1987. Indirect taxes (*moms* and excises) amounted to 18.3 percent of GDP. There is also a wealth tax of 2.2 percent on net wealth above a certain threshold.[7] Of the total taxes and duties the national government levies a little less than 70 percent; the counties, about 8 percent; and the municipalities, 22 percent. County and local governments impose no indirect taxes but derive their revenues mainly from income taxes, with much smaller amounts from real property taxes and with about 30 percent of their revenue coming from block grants and reimbursements from the national government. Members of the state Church also pay a church tax.

GOVERNMENT AND BUSINESS

A major step in government regulation of business came in 1937 with passage of a Price Agreements Act that required restrictive agreements on prices, production, transport, and marketing to be reported to a Price Control Council. The law prohibited agreements that unreasonably restricted, or were likely to restrict, freedom of trade, and gave the council authority to ban such agreements either through negotiations or by legal action. During World War II the council's powers were increased to enable it to fix price ceilings and determine maximum profits. It continued its operations in the early postwar years and only began winding down its work in 1948.

In 1949 a Trust Commission began to study the problems of restrictive business practices, and on the basis of its recommendations the Folketing enacted the Monopolies and Restrictive Practices Control Act of 1955. The act covers private enterprises and cooperative associations (including professional groups) within trades where they "exert or may be able to exert an effective influence on price, production, distribution, or transport conditions." Concern is primarily with the control of restrictive practices, rather than their prohibition. The Monopoly Control Authority (*monopoltilsynet*, or MCA) must be notified of any agreements between enterprises or any decisions made by organizations that may be restrictive in nature, and it enters this information in a public register.

Registration does not imply government approval of the practice, and the MCA may still take action on it after registration. Failure to notify the authority of restrictive practices, as well as violations of regulations issued under the act, may result in fines or mitigated imprisonment (*hæfte*). Types of practices registered include such things as production quotas, exclusive dealing, boycotts, price fixing at other than the retail level, discriminatory rebates, division of markets, customer allocation, profit pooling, limitations on free entry into trade or industry, and suggested price schedules. Agreements on minimum resale prices cannot be enforced without the MCA's prior approval. The MCA issues a regular report of its investigations and decisions and of court rulings, and it makes an annual report to the trade minister.

Individual enterprises or combinations that are considered dominant in their particular trade also must register if the MCA so demands. If the authority's investigation shows a restriction of competition that results in unreasonable prices, unreasonable restraint on trade, or unreasonable discrimination in the conditions of trading, it attempts to end the practice through negotiation. A party dissatisfied with an MCA decision may appeal to a special tribunal of three members, appointed by the minister of trade. The chair of the tribunal must have the same qualifications as a Supreme Court judge, one member must be trained in economics, and one member is appointed after consultation with business groups. A decision of the tribunal may be appealed to a high court by either the complainant or the authority.

The MCA consists of a Board and a Directorate. The Board has a chair appointed by the king (i.e., the government) and up to fourteen other members named by the minister of trade. A majority of Board members must be independent of business enterprises and organizations affected by the act; they are lawyers, law professors, economists, civil servants, and representatives of consumer, labor, trade, cooperative, and employer organizations. The Directorate handles the day-to-day business of the Board, including the registration process and preliminary investigations.

The Danish attitude toward monopoly appears clearly in the provisions of the 1955 Act and its later amendments. The approach stresses publicity but allows firms in a dominant position in their industry or trade to be controlled in practices tending to diminish competition. The Danes realize that monopolies may have some advantages in efficiency and savings in costs, and they understand that their economy is a small one in which a few enterprises are likely to dominate a given field. Thus, the attempt is not to outlaw monopolies and cartel arrangements but only to prevent abuse of power.[8]

The state also concerns itself with business activities through laws dealing with trademarks, patents, incorporation, licenses for certain occupations and enterprises, bankruptcy, and aid for research. General regulations affecting many businesses were included in the Trade Act (*næringsloven*) of 1931; its provisions were greatly liberalized in 1967.

Despite a trend toward concentration, Danish industry is still characterized by many small and medium-size enterprises. Nearly half the manufacturing establishments employ fewer than 20 people; somewhat more than half of manufacturing employees work in firms with fewer than 200 people; and enterprises employing 500 or more workers constitute only 1.2 percent of the manufacturing units although they have about one-fourth of the employees.[9] Although capable of adapting to new conditions for production and marketing, small firms have often been handicapped in technological competitiveness because of an inability to spend much for research and development. In recent years Denmark has devoted about 1 percent of GDP for research and development, whereas Sweden, Germany, Japan, and the United States allocate 2 to 2.5 percent.

The government has not provided much aid to industry through direct subsidies for current production. Instead, cabinets since 1982 have stressed macroeconomic policies entailing "lower nominal income growth, lower interest rates, a stable exchange rate and no further growth of the public sector," along with some special assistance.[10] Subsidies for particular programs or projects have been modest in comparison to those in other countries; the ratio of total business subsidies to GDP was around 1 percent in 1984, when the average in other Scandinavian and West European countries was 2.5 to 3 percent.

There are some loans and credit guarantees, as well as a growing emphasis on grants, technical advice, and other aid for industrial modernization, generally through the Council of Technology under the general aegis of the Ministry of Industry. The government also provides assistance for promotional activities in the export trade, offers planning and consultation services by an Export Promotions Council, and has used tax policies to enhance competitiveness in foreign markets.

GOVERNMENT AND LABOR

Although collective bargaining appeared in Denmark shortly after the guild system ended in 1862, it became definitely established only with the confrontation between employers and unions in 1899. An attempt by the Employers Confederation to defeat the Labor Federation by a lock-out ended after three months with a compromise, the "September Agreement," often described as the "labor market's constitution." The agreement set forth the basic rules on negotiating the nationwide collective agreements that characterize Danish labor-management relations. The agreement has been revised from time to time over the years; the current version is the General Agreement of October 31, 1973, with amendments of March 1, 1987. It recognizes labor's right to organize; establishes a "peace obligation" of no work stoppages during the lifetime of a contract; affirms various employer prerogatives, such as the right to direct work and to exclude supervisors from membership in regular trade unions; provides protection for employees against unfair dismissals; and sets procedures for handling disputes.[11]

The collective agreements cover nearly all of the Danish labor market and set forth detailed provisions on wages and working conditions. They ordinarily have been valid for two-year periods, but the agreements in 1987 were for a four-year term, with the opportunity to reopen wage negotiations after two years. The process of working out a new collective contract begins with discussions and decisions by units on both the employers' and employees' sides on what issues or claims they wish to press. These are channeled to the national organizations, DA and LO, each of which puts together its bargaining package. Individual unions with special claims may negotiate them separately with their employers.

The general bargaining is almost always a centralized process, but there have been some attempts in the 1980s to introduce more decentralized procedures. Under the rules negotiations follow a specified series of steps within a set time limit. If an agreement is reached, it goes to the members of both national organizations for approval. If no settlement is arrived at by the deadline, a mediator enters the picture and negotiations continue. If there is still no accord, the organizations may send out strike or lock-out notices, though the mediator may delay any such actions for two fourteen-day periods. If at the end of those postponements both sides still disagree, they are free to take industrial action unless the government steps in to prevent it.

A system of governmental mediation in labor disputes began in 1910. The minister of labor, upon the recommendation of the Industrial Court, appoints all three members of the Mediation Board (and three substitute members) for terms of three years. The recommendation must be supported by at least one court member representing the employers and one member representing the workers; if no recommendation is forthcoming by December 15, the minister makes an appointment independently. Terms are arranged so that one expires each year; reappointment is permissible and frequent. The members choose a chair from their own number. They may mediate as a body, but more often the chair works with the general issues arising out of the negotiations for collective agreements while the other members concentrate on particular problems. The chair frequently has a long tenure of office—from 1910 to 1959 only eight men served in that position, and most of them had been board members before becoming chair—and thus has experience with the problems of collective bargaining and an ability to intervene with knowledge of the historical background. In 1945 assistant mediators were added to the system, after trade union complaints that the mediators' concentration on overall issues had led to neglect of other problems important to particular unions and trades.

Mediation occurs mainly with the expiration of the old collective agreements and the negotiation of new ones. Under the law the mediator may intervene at the request of either of the parties or on his own initiative if the effects and scope of the actual or threatened dispute are deemed to be of public importance. The mediator, with the consent of the parties, may delay for two weeks a work stoppage that would ordinarily begin with an agreement's expiration. The delay may actually be longer as neither party may want to risk the public's blame for a stoppage and both usually hope that the mediator will bring about a settlement. He has been in touch with the negotiations before his official entry on the scene, through informal contacts with the parties and the reports of assistant mediators. He meets with the parties, jointly or separately as seems advisable; he makes preliminary proposals and informs the parties of his views. He may prepare a final draft of his proposals and submit it to both sides for a vote. If he judges the differences between the parties too great to be settled by a proposal from him, he may refrain from submitting one. His proposal is not made public until after all the voting has been concluded; if accepted, it becomes part of the collective agreement.

Disputes over the interpretation of collective agreements or of alleged violations are heard by a special court if they cannot be settled by negotiation. The tribunal, now called the Industrial Court (Arbejdsretten), has a president, three vice-presidents, and twelve regular judges. Judges in varying numbers are chosen by DA; the associations of banks, insurance companies, and agricultural employers; the LO; the finance minister, the local government associations, and the municipalities of Copenhagen and Frederiksberg; and FTF, AC, and the association of supervisors. All serve three-year terms. The twelve judges elect the president and vice-presidents, all of whom must have the same qualifications as judges in the regular courts (in fact, they nearly always hold such judicial posts). Hearings are generally conducted by the president or one of the vice-presidents, three regular judges or alternates from the employer side, and three from the employee side.

The Industrial Court has jurisdiction over alleged breaches of collective agreements and over questions concerning the lawfulness of strikes or lock-outs. Other disputes may be brought before the court with its consent and if there is a general or special agreement covering the matter. Minor cases are handled by special arbitration boards so that the court's time may be spent on major issues. Except for employers who are not members of the Employers Confederation, cases may be brought to the court only by the employers' and workers' organizations; the individual worker must act through his union. Thus, DA and LO largely decide which cases are important enough to be raised, and they try to keep out weak cases, with the employers usually more successful at this than the unions. The party that is found to have violated an agreement may have to pay a fine that is partly a penalty and partly an award of damages. Judgments can be levied against organizations and individuals, including individual workers. The Industrial Court's decisions are final and legally binding; they cannot be appealed to other courts. The tribunal dealt with 690 cases in 1987, some of which were holdovers from 1986. Of these cases, 453 were settled by compromise, 38 by judgments after the failure of one party to appear, and 81 by verdicts after hearings. The remainder were dropped without any court action.[12]

Besides the Industrial Court there exist a number of arbitration boards set up by the various collective agreements. These usually handle detailed matters requiring specialized or technical knowledge. The court sometimes decides that such a board is the appropriate forum to hear a case and sends a dispute to it for settlement. If the losing party fails to carry out an arbitration board's award, the other party may take the case to the court, which acts then as an enforcement agency, not as an appellate tribunal.

If mediation has failed and action by the Industrial Court is inapplicable, or for general economic reasons, the government may decide to intervene through legislation to prevent a work stoppage that might endanger the national economy. It did so in 1975, 1977, and 1979, in each case before strikes and lock-outs began but after it became apparent that talks would probably deadlock.

By the 1980s labor market negotiations had plainly become a three-cornered affair, with government as a direct participant along with the representatives of employers and workers. In 1983 DA and LO were able to reach a two-year agreement that hewed closely to the cabinet's 4 percent guideline for wage increases. When negotiations collapsed in 1985, the Folketing adopted a comprehensive package that determined wage increases, reduced working hours, and made various changes in taxes and fees. In 1987 workers and employers concluded a four-year agreement for wage improvements and a cut in the work week from thirty-nine to thirty-seven hours over the life of the contract. For governments the outcome of the labor market negotiations has too great an economic and social impact to be left solely to the two parties. The collective agreements are perceived as major elements of public policy that must fit into an overall strategy for controlling income increases, curbing inflation, cutting the costs of trade and industry, and encouraging exports.

Labor relations are not purely a matter of conflict, and a network of labor-management cooperation committees exists at the enterprise level. On the basis of a 1986 agreement between DA and LO, more than 3,000 such committees exist in the private sector, and similar bodies are also at work in the public sector. Committee members share information about the enterprise, with the employer obligated to make available information about its financial position and future prospects, the employment outlook, and plans for any major changes or reorganization, including the introduction of new technology. The committee is a forum for discussing and establishing principles for personnel policy, assessing the consequences of new technology and the principles for training and retraining employees to work with it, considering guidelines for production and work, and informing employees about incentive systems of compensation and the establishment of funds for education and welfare purposes. If technological change results in the elimination of jobs, the enterprise agrees to try to transfer employees or to train them for other work. Excluded from a committee's purview are matters covered in collective contracts or local wage agreements. The committees cannot tell the employer how to run the enterprise, but they can promote day-to-day cooperation within it.

The Limited Companies Act of 1974 entitles employees in firms with at least 35 workers to choose representatives to the company's board of directors, up to the number elected by the stockholders' general meeting (this means a minimum of two members and as many as one-third of the board). The decision to have representation requires a favorable vote by at least 50 percent of the employees, and the election of members, who serve four-year terms, takes place outside the trade union machinery. Employee representatives have the same rights and duties as stockholders' representatives; they must resign from the board if they end employment with the company.

The labor force grew steadily from the 1960s on, but full employment was maintained because the labor supply was insufficient to meet the demand. From 1974 on, the situation changed, and the labor market could not absorb all the new entrants. The economic downturn added to the problem.[13] The result was a sharp increase in unemployment, from 22,000 (about 0.9 percent of the labor force) in 1973 to 245,000 (9.2 percent of the labor force) in 1981. Unemployment was especially severe for young people, with the rate among those under twenty-five rising to about 17 percent in 1981. Women were more likely to be unemployed than men.

Besides the general economic policies discussed in earlier pages, governments in office since 1973 have undertaken a variety of special programs to combat unemployment. A series of plans attempted to increase jobs through public spending. An anticipatory pension or early retirement scheme was introduced in 1987. A job offer program entitles an unemployed person to an offer of work or training after the individual has been unemployed for a specified period. Jobs are at regular pay (with government subsidization) and must be of at least seven to nine months duration. About 75 percent of such jobs have been in the public sector, especially in local governments. Measures to combat youth unemployment have had a high priority, mainly through local governments. They have included work projects, wage subsidies to private employers to help cover costs and enable them to hire young workers, and new educational, apprenticeship, and job training courses. At the end of 1989 unemployment remained high. The problem appeared to be long-term, so measures to solve or alleviate it likely will continue to be an important part of Danish economic policy.

Probably the most controversial current issue in worker-employer relations is the question of economic democracy. The Danish labor movement prides itself on its concern with a wide range of questions going beyond higher wages and improved working conditions. Beginning in the late 1960s unions started to advocate a share for workers in the ownership rights of enterprises. A variety of factors were motivating forces: overcoming the economy's chronic savings deficits, providing investment funds so that new jobs could be created, reducing inequalities in wealth and power, creating more democratic control over the economy, and compensating the workers for an incomes policy that restrains wage increases. In 1971 LO adopted a proposal for economic democracy, and in 1973 the Social Democratic minority government presented it to the Folketing.

The plan called for an annual contribution from employers that would in time amount to 5 percent of total wages paid in each enterprise. Two-thirds of the tax would remain in the company as capital, and one-third would go into a central fund for investment. A board composed of representatives of employees' organizations and the government would administer the central fund, which would eventually own 50 percent of Danish industry. Representatives of blue- and white-collar workers would vote the fund's shares at stockholders' meetings. In firms contributing to the central fund, all employees would receive equal shares in the fund, regardless of differing wages or salaries. The shares would be the individual's personal property but could not be sold or used as collateral for loans; they could be cashed in after seven years.[14]

The LO–Social Democratic proposal for economic democracy met instant opposition from the nonsocialist parties, the employers' organizations, and even the left-wing socialist parties, and public opinion polls indicated that only a minority of trade unionists viewed it favorably. Some of the nonsocialist parties proposed voluntary schemes of profit-sharing as alternatives. Lacking a parliamentary majority, the Social Democrats had to drop the plan but presented new versions of it in subsequent years. There is very little chance that any compulsory arrangement can be adopted through labor-management bargaining, so the advent of economic democracy will depend on legislation, which, in turn, depends upon finding a parliamentary majority for an acceptable plan. The Conservative, Liberal, Center Democratic, Christian Peoples, and Progressive parties continue to oppose a compulsory scheme; the Social Democratic, Socialist Peoples, and Radical parties favor it but are not in complete agreement. The debate continues.

GOVERNMENT AND AGRICULTURE

Historically Danish farmers have been proud of their independence and their ability to manage their own affairs without government intervention. Until the post–World War II period the principal area of government activity in agriculture was land policy. Aside from emergency aid in the depression years of the 1930s, it was not until the late 1950s that the state began to take an active role in the support of farm prices and the maintenance of farm income. Land policy since the eighteenth century had aimed at establishing numerous independent farms by dividing up larger holdings and by reclaiming new land. Under a 1919 law the state acquired land and sold or leased it for new smallholdings or to provide supplementary plots for existing ones. About 30,000 new farms were established with government aid in this century.

The 1960s brought an easing of strict statutory regulation of the size of holdings and the sale and purchase of land. Policy changes encouraged the development of larger units through the merger of smaller farms. The Agricultural Property Act of 1986 divides farm holdings into three categories. Those of less than about 37 acres (15 hectares) can be bought or sold freely by citizens of Denmark and the other European Community nations. A buyer of land between 37 and 74 acres (15 and 30 hectares) in area must live on the land and use it himself. Purchase of land of more than 74 acres (30 hectares) requires the buyer to live on the holding, operate it, and have an appropriate agricultural education, manifested by possession of the so-called "green certificate" (grønne bevis). Additional rules cover the amalgamation of farms and the ownership of more than one farm.

In the 1950s agricultural prices and farm profits declined, while operating costs rose. Exports suffered because of increased agricultural production elsewhere and trade restrictions adopted by other countries. Farmers kept production high despite lower prices in hope that Denmark would soon join the European Community and benefit from the higher prices of the Common Agricultural Policy.

As long as Denmark remained outside the EC, its agriculture was bound to suffer. Farmers demanded government assistance, and the cabinets in office agreed both that the country needed an efficient and productive agriculture whenever entry into the Common Market became possible and that in the meantime subsidization of agriculture would be necessary. In 1958 the Folketing passed a Grain Act designed to guarantee minimum prices for bread grains and to set minimum prices for imported feed grains, with the government required to buy bread grains when prices fell below the level fixed by the law. Other legislation set minimum prices for domestic sales of pork, veal, beef, eggs, and poultry.

In the spring of 1961, in negotiations between Danish agriculture and the government on a new contract between farm employers and farm workers, agricultural employers demanded full compensation from the state for the higher wages they expected to have to pay their employees, as well as compensation to cover the decline in farm income. To back up their demands, their principal organizations—the Agricultural Council, the Federation of Danish Agricultural Societies, and the Federation of Danish Smallholder Societies—told their members not to deliver products to processing plants. The Folketing ended this farmers' strike by passing the Agricultural Marketing Act of 1961. An extensive program of farm subsidies set up a Rationalization Fund, from which additional cash payments were made to farmers.

The 1961 act also furnished Danish agriculture with yearly grants for the promotion of exports. The government gave refunds to farmers to cover fertilizer purchases, and under the Grain Act of 1958 it refunded to small farmers fees collected on imported feed grains. The "package" economic solution of 1963 continued the existing farm subsidies with little change, and in 1965 the Folketing approved by an overwhelming vote an Agricultural Products Marketing Act that extended the subsidy provisions.

The agricultural organizations had pressed for Danish entry into the Common Market. With membership approved in the October 1972 referendum, Denmark became subject to the EC's farm policies and regulations. These aim at both a reasonable income to agricultural producers (an income comparable to that gained in trade and industry) and an adequate supply of farm products at reasonable prices for consumers. As a consequence of entry, government subsidies to Danish agriculture came to an end, and the Ministry of Agriculture's budget shrank by about two-thirds in the 1973/74 fiscal year, compared to 1972/73.

For Denmark membership in the European Community meant an expansion of export opportunities, including recovery of markets lost or diminished during the time the nation had remained outside the EC. It meant access to a free market of 270 million consumers who wanted the kind of farm products that Denmark sold. Danish agriculture made good use of this opportunity.

In terms of quantity, the industry's total sales production has risen 30 percent when comparing the averages of 1970–74 and 1981–84. During the last decade, home consumption has risen only slightly so that the bulk of the increase has been exported. As a result, export quantities rose from 1972 to 1984 by no less than 55 percent, leading to an increase in foreign currency earnings from 12.4 billion kroner in 1972 to 43.5 billion kroner in 1984—an impressive 250 percent boost.[15]

Great Britain remained the most important single customer, buying about 20 percent of total farm exports, principally pork and bacon, canned meat, butter, and cheese. West Germany was second, taking a wide range of products, including mink and fox pelts. Outside the EC the United States is the best market (and third best customer overall), with 11 percent of the exports, mainly canned meats but also pork, cheese, and mink. Japan is the fifth best customer, with about 8 percent of Danish farm exports. Denmark receives financial help from the EC for such things as export aid, denaturing of grain, and support of oilseed production, and its farmers are guaranteed EC prices for all their major products.

But times have not been entirely happy and prosperous for farmers since EC membership became a reality. In its 1987/88 report, the Agricultural Council declared: "Danish agriculture is in crisis. . . . The situation has created widespread pessimism in the industry. Many are about to lose faith that they have a future ahead of them as farmers. Production and investment are falling, and the entry of young people into agricultural education has now dropped below a critical minimum."[16] As farming in Denmark is a capital-intensive industry, farms are often mortgaged up to 40 percent of their sales value, a figure that is about twice the debt level in neighboring countries. In the late 1970s and early 1980s very high rates of interest became a heavy burden for many farmers, increasing, from the period 1970–1974 to 1986, from 29 percent to 54 percent of gross farm income. Rates dropped later in the 1980s, but this helped new borrowers and not those who had taken long-term loans earlier. The government makes loans at low interest rates to young farmers for first time purchases of farms, as well as loans for certain other activities, including farm modernization.

Another concern is the effect on agriculture of the increasingly stricter efforts at environmental protection. Laws and regulations on land planning and zoning, conservation of nature, waste disposal, and contamination of residential areas all may impact on farmers. For example, some proprietors of poultry, pig, and fur farms have been forced to limit or end production because of possible harmful effects on residential neighborhoods. Laws restrict the use of pesticides and fertilizers and of antibiotics in animal production. The Social Democratic, Radical, and Socialist Peoples parties—representing a so-called green majority in the Folketing—have agreed that marginal land should be taken from agricultural use and put into forests or parks.

Danish farmers were incensed when EC agriculture ministers agreed in 1987 on cuts in farm production. To them reductions in acreage meant loss of income, and a protest meeting of 5,000 farmers in Herning in April 1987 expressed loud opposition to EC policy changes, more restrictive environmental laws, and the elimination of marginal land. Sensitive to the farmers' protests and perhaps noting that the most enthusiastic applause at the Herning conclave went to speakers from the right-wing Progressives, the government parties in the spring of 1988 joined with the Progressives and the Center Democrats to provide help for some 17,000 debt-ridden farmers through state refinancing and guarantees of loans. A concession to the Progressives liberalized some of the rules on farm size and amalgamation.

The government continues to aid agricultural exporters to promote and publicize their products and works closely with farm organizations and individual firms. An Export Promotion Council includes representatives of government and the major commercial, agricultural, and industrial organizations. The Export Credit Council guarantees exporters against losses on foreign export debts and affords surety for loans for export purposes. Exporters assume 10 percent of any loss and pay a premium for the guarantees.

Government also directs or finances a large share of agricultural research, with a focus on practical problems. The Royal Veterinary and Agricultural University, a public institution under the jurisdiction of the minister of education, offers courses and degrees in the forestry, agricultural, horticultural, veterinary, and dairy sciences and conducts research in these fields. Many research institutes are housed in the Ministry of Agriculture, and a few may be found in other departments as well. The government pays about 25 percent of the cost of advisory services for the farmer, carried out largely through the agricultural organizations.[17]

Laws also establish a framework for the farmer's education and the acquisition of the coveted "green certificate," which is essential if the farmer wants financial help for purchasing a farm. After completing a general education, the would-be farmer must attend a basic five-month course at an agricultural college, acquire three years of farming experience, and then pursue a nine-month farm management course. The green certificate is issued at the successful completion of this program.

GOVERNMENT AND FISHERIES

Although less important than agricultural exports, sales abroad of fish and fish products accounted for about 6 percent of Danish exports in 1987. Some 11,000 full-time commercial fishermen search the waters for cod, plaice, shrimp, lobsters, eels, herring, and other fish. The EC countries are the most important market; West Germany traditionally has been the largest single customer.

Commercial fishing is regulated by the EC's Common Fisheries Policy (CFP), established by agreement in 1983 for a ten-year period. The Danish government has a variety of schemes intended to benefit the fishing industry without exceeding the CFP quotas. It offers financial aid for development or rationalization of processing plants and modernization of fishing vessels, and it allocates grants to promote experimental fisheries. A state-guaranteed Royal Danish Fisheries Bank makes loans to cover part of the construction cost of new fishing boats and part of the purchase price of second-hand ones. About three-quarters of the owners of fishing vessels belong to the Danish Fishermen Producers Organization, set up under EC rules. Its members are guaranteed a minimum price for their fish.

Nevertheless, the fishermen consider themselves beset by a host of problems: quotas that are too low, prices that have fallen, and intensive competition in their principal markets. They point out that because of lower prices they must stay at sea sixty days a year longer than they used to. These difficulties, plus the feeling that the other EC nations do not understand the plight of the fishing industry, have led to demonstrations by fishermen, including attempted blockades of the Copenhagen harbor with their vessels and efforts to pressure the government to give them more financial aid and loan guarantees.

9

Government and Culture

Americans think of cultural activities as organized and financed mainly by private individuals or families and foundations. Public institutions that help support arts and letters, like the National Endowment for the Humanities, the National Endowment for the Arts, and similar state government agencies, are often suspect in the eyes of many people, including the legislators who must vote public monies for such institutions. Views are far different in Denmark, where cultural policy is widely debated, a minister for cultural affairs sits in the cabinet, and public funding is significant. Concern with enlightenment and enjoyment, with the "production" and "consumption" of culture, extends to many areas— art, music, film and theatre, libraries and museums, church, schools, the mass media—as well as to individuals involved in these areas.

As in other European countries the Catholic Church was the first benefactor of the pictorial arts and music in Denmark. After the Reformation that role fell to the monarch and the royal court, which, especially during the reign of Christian IV (1588–1648), became known as one of the most musically active in Europe. One of the first royal stipends for artists came in 1549 with a grant to a young painter for four years of study in Germany and Italy. To ensure a steady supply of artistic talent the Academy of Art was established in 1754. Prince Christian Frederik, the academy's chairman from 1808 to 1839, encouraged state aid to artists. During a period of economic distress in the early years of the nineteenth century he emphasized the importance of the nation's cultural life: "Now we are poor and destitute. If we also become stupid, we can stop being a nation."[1]

In return for grants from the crown that enabled them to study abroad (sometimes for lengthy periods), artists were expected to contribute paintings and sculptures for public buildings. After his study tour to Rome and Paris, for example, C. W. Eckersberg, often called the father of Danish painting, returned to Denmark in 1816 and painted pictures on historical themes to decorate the royal palace of Christiansborg,

143

although he became better known for his nature scenes. Writers also received aid. Authors of "merit," such as Hans Christian Andersen, could receive support from public funds for considerable lengths of time.

When the period of royal absolutism ended in 1849, the crown largely relinquished its responsibility for support of the arts and literature to a cabinet officer, the minister for church and education, and to parliament. The minister had to rely on the legislature's generosity in the national budget, and the finance committee often found itself discussing the merits of particular authors or artists before voting an appropriation. To eliminate these public discussions, the minister convinced parliament in 1902 to give him the responsibility for selecting those to receive public grants. Parliament still could discuss the minister's proposals and often did, sometimes with quite critical debates on individual authors and artists and their work. A further move from parliamentary to administrative decision came in 1931 with creation of an Advisory Panel for Literature, a professional body outside the direct authority of both minister and legislators.

After World War II parliament continued its support for the arts through a series of yearly grants, with financial action often still preceded by discussion of particular artists rather than of cultural policy generally. A Cultural Fund, set up in 1935, allocated money for the encouragement of music, especially for performances at the Royal Theatre. Various ministers who dealt with cultural affairs, and notably the Social Democrat Julius Bomholt, pressed for development of a national policy and for transfer of the grant-making procedure from parliament to a more professional body. The associations of composers and drama and fiction writers showed their backing for such a move by a joint demonstration in Copenhagen in 1952. After the establishment of the State Science Fund in 1952, Bomholt and the artists' and writers' organizations sought a similar fund for the arts. As a consequence of a commission's study, parliament set up the State Art Foundation and created funds to support "the artistic decoration of public buildings" and to aid "artists in financial need." Backing for this move came from the Social Democrats, Radicals, and Conservatives; opposing it were the Liberal and Justice parties, which argued for less public involvement in cultural activities. (In recent years the Progressives have been virtually the only party to stand against public support.) By 1964 parliamentary opposition to the government's role had virtually disappeared, and the law establishing a National Endowment for the Arts passed with only six dissenting votes in the Folketing. That act was followed by a statute creating a Film Foundation, the Theatres Act of 1970, and the Music Act of 1976.

The Ministry for Cultural Affairs had been established as a government department in its own right in 1961. The responsibilities of its various bureaus and offices indicate its broad scope today: art education, library education, libraries, archives, museums, zoos, music and music conservatories, the school of architecture, theatre and the theatre school, aid to artists, film, the circus, radio and television, and sports. Of course, not every aspect of all these fields falls exclusively within the Culture Ministry's purview.[2] After the minister's annual report has been submitted to the Folketing, the parliamentarians engage in a general debate on cultural policy.

GOVERNMENT AND THE ARTS

The National Endowment for the Arts

Until the establishment of the National Endowment for the Arts, government aid, under the State Art Foundation, consisted largely of commissions to artists for the decoration of public buildings and distribution of information about the availability of grants. The endowment struck off in a different direction. Its concerns were broader: Literature and music had joined the pictorial arts in 1964, handicrafts were added in 1969, and architecture, in 1979. It undertook a program of direct grants to artists, and the near unanimity in the parliamentary vote creating the endowment disappeared with publication of its first list of grantees in January 1965. There was controversy in the press, in public meetings, and in the Folketing. Some people argued that grants should be given only to artists in real need. Others objected to grants to those who produced esoteric or "elitist" works—they believed that aid should go only to those whose products the ordinary person could understand or appreciate. And some thought that government expenditures, already too high, should not extend to this kind of assistance. The storm eventually subsided, although rumblings of the same types of criticism are still heard.

The endowment makes grants, generally for three-year periods, to young and talented painters, sculptors, writers, craftsmen, architects, and musicians who need help while they are developing their abilities. It awards some grants for shorter periods and some travel stipends. It also provides a small number of lifetime grants to artists considered outstanding in their fields. The amount of such awards varies with the other income of the recipient but ranges from a minimum of kroner 32,000 (about $4,700) a year to a high of kroner 102,000 ($15,100). In 1988 the public treasury spent about kroner 8.1 million ($1.2 million) for lifetime awards to 207 artists.

Concerned also with the dissemination of art, the endowment purchases paintings and sculptures and places them in museums and public and private buildings. It makes grants directly to composers and to performers, including orchestras and ensembles as well as individuals. It provides financial aid for books and musical works that have not had the sales that their merit warrants. It may commission new musical works, recordings, and performances. It buys handicrafts for display in exhibitions, study collections, and museums.

Decisions on grants in the endowment's five fields are made by six grants committees (two in the visual arts and one each for literature, music, handicrafts, and architecture). The members of each committee, who are experts in the art form with which it deals, are appointed by the minister of culture for three-year terms. The minister selects the endowment's directing board, but a majority of its members are nominated by the various associations representing writers, pictorial artists, composers, performing artists, and related groups.

Theatre

Outside the National Endowment for the Arts is the public support given to the Royal Theatre, three regional theatres, a regional opera, and various other aspects of the drama. The Royal Theatre in Copenhagen is Denmark's national theatre, founded in 1748 and financed by private funds until 1935. Then a parliamentary statute gave the Theatre complete public financing, with any deficit covered by the government. As a national institution it is required to offer a varied program of the best drama, opera, and ballet by Danish writers and composers, both traditional and modern. The Theatre comprises two large theatres, a small one, and a touring company. The internationally famous Royal Danish Ballet, with its Bournonville tradition, is part of the Theatre, as are a ballet school and the Royal Orchestra, which plays for opera and ballet and gives concerts. In 1988 Boel Jørgensen, previously rector at Roskilde University Center, became the first woman to head the Royal Theatre. One writer described her mission as saving the institution from "the illness that has affected many famous European theatres—bureaucracy and artistic stagnation." "We must strive to be the best," said Jørgensen, emphasizing that artistic decisions would be made by the Theatre's four artistic directors.[3]

All other national subsidies to the theatre fall under the Theatre Act of 1970 and its later amendments. National and county governments underwrite the costs of the regional theatres in Århus, Odense, and Ålborg, with deficits covered equally by the two jurisdictions. Theatres in the Copenhagen metropolitan area cooperate as the Greater Copenhagen Regional Theatre; the national government and the area's county and municipal authorities share any deficits. Children's theatres are subsidized, and there is some financial aid for amateur theatre, drama training, construction of new theatres and modernization of old ones, and purchase of technical equipment. Subsidies from central and local governments make possible reduced ticket prices for children and students.

The national government's administrative unit is the Theatre Council, reporting directly to the minister of culture and with all its members appointed by the minister. Nearly 40 percent of national expenditures for theatres go to the Royal Theatre, and experimental drama organizations often complain that too much of the money is spent on safe or traditional stagings and not enough on pioneering efforts.

Music

Public support for music was complicated by the belief of jazz and popular musicians that they received inadequate assistance from the National Endowment for the Arts. The minister of culture advised them informally to develop an organization to promote their interests, and they did so in 1981. In 1983 two board members of the State Music Council were chosen to give specific representation to jazz and popular music.

The State Music Council aids festivals, concerts, and musical organizations like orchestras, choirs, and ensembles. It has an "instrument bank" that lends rare or expensive musical instruments to orchestras or for educational purposes. It helps support five regional orchestras, with any deficit for these autonomous, semipublic institutions shared equally by national and local governments. The council's nine-member board, appointed by and reporting directly to the minister of culture, has a majority of its members nominated by associations of professional musicians. Its concerns extend to classical music, jazz, rock, folk, and other popular forms, as well as to amateur efforts. Transferred administratively to the Music Council, the Cultural Fund continues to direct a major part of its own spending toward music. Excluded from coverage under the Music Act are the Royal Orchestra, Radio Denmark's symphony orchestra and light orchestra, the five conservatories of music, and military bands, all of which receive public support in other ways.

Film

Danish cinema has a long and distinguished history. In 1981 Nordisk Films Kompagni celebrated its seventy-fifth anniversary. The oldest active film company in the world, its founding followed by three years the making of the first Danish feature film in 1903. Between 1906 and 1910 the company produced an average of 125 films a year, and the time between 1910 and World War I has been called the "golden age of

Danish film." Danish movies were seen—and copied—throughout the world. The war years brought the cinema into the doldrums, however, although there were individual achievements, especially the career of the internationally famous director, Carl Th. Dreyer. Film-making faced a host of problems: a small domestic market, increasing production costs, difficulties of finance, and the dominance of Hollywood. It was not until the 1960s that the industry once more began to display signs of real life, with talented new directors and notable films and with government help to overcome some of the problems.

Government aid came first through the Film and Cinema Act of 1965. A 1972 revision created the Danish Film Institute, superseding the earlier Film Foundation. The institute receives its funds directly from the public treasury and uses them to finance the production of feature films, to secure the importation of children's films and foreign films of artistic merit, to promote knowledge of Danish films and advance their sales abroad, and to operate the National Film School.

Film-making in Denmark has become largely a publicly financed enterprise. Costs of production, though low by international standards (most films are made with a budget of less than a million dollars; *Pelle the Conqueror*, the most expensive film ever made in Denmark, cost about $3.5 million), are too high to make purely private initiatives an attractive investment. Seldom does a film recoup its investment. So government support is essential if there is to be a Danish film industry, and the state becomes virtually a partner in any production.

The Film Institute makes grants for the preparation of scripts, subsidizes production through guaranteed bank loans, and helps cover the losses of films judged to have artistic merit. Until the passage of the 1989 law, subsidies covered about 80 percent of production costs for films displaying artistic merit. This meant preference for "serious" films over "popular" ones. Recent revisions in the law may make it easier for private companies to make lighter films: They are guaranteed subsidies of up to 50 percent of the costs if they can themselves raise the rest. Many feature films have been shot in a government-owned film studio in the Copenhagen suburb of Lyngby. Its facilities are primarily rented to private production companies, but very occasionally the institute may itself produce a film that would not otherwise be made.

A recommendation on whether a script has "artistic merit" and hence is worthy of financial support is made by one of three film consultants, appointed by the Film Board for a maximum term of three years. One writer calls the consultants "absolute monarchs" over film production: "The Danish Film Institute has become a monopoly. A director or producer who doesn't find favor in the film consultants' eyes has nowhere else to go."[4] One consultant deals exclusively with the production and importation of children's films. A consultant's recommendation goes to the Film Institute's autonomous governing board. The minister of culture appoints the board's five members, two of whom have been nominated by organizations representing film producers, directors, technicians, cinema owners, and film distributors, and two nominated by a representative body selected by organizations associated with film-making. Only one board member is the minister's free choice. In 1987 the institute had a budget of kroner 79 million ($11.7 million) and spent 57 million ($8.4 million) of this on feature films. In the same year it released a dozen films (compared with more than 400 in the United States and 150 in France). It also arranges and helps pay for the import of foreign films (more than 200 in 1987), many of which would not otherwise have been seen in Denmark.

The institute runs the National Film School, which offers degree and short-term courses in directing, cinematography, editing, sound, and production. Highly selective, it admits about 25 students out of 200 to 250 applicants. Most of the present crop of directors and technicians received their training in the School. The Film Act also provided for the Danish Film Museum, which, as one of the world's oldest film archives, preserves films, still photos, and other materials; maintains a library of books and pamphlets about film; and endeavors to make the public aware of the history and art of the cinema. The producer of any Danish film must deposit copies with the museum, which also secures foreign films for its collection.

In the late 1980s talk began to be heard—and not merely in Denmark—about a second "golden age" for Danish cinema. In 1988 *Babette's Feast* (based on a story by Isak Dinesen) won an Oscar for the best foreign film, and *Pelle the Conqueror* (based on a novel by Martin Andersen Nexø, the Danish social realist) repeated the honor in 1989. The reputations of a number of talented moviemakers—Lars von Trier, Gabriel Axel, Jon Bang Carlsen, Erik Clausen, and Jørgen Leth—have been growing, and there has been greater diversity in Danish films. Extensive use of coproductions helped with costs and made Danish films more available throughout the world.[5]

Also involved in the movie industry is the Government Film Office, set up in 1939 to purchase and distribute educational films and documentaries. Today it buys or produces short films for informational and educational purposes and distributes them to schools, libraries, trade unions, and other organizations. The Film Office and the Film Institute cooperate in producing children's films under a legal requirement that each spend at least 25 percent of its funds for that purpose. Recommendations on films come from a Children's Film Council.

Movie theatres are regulated by local governments within the framework of the Film and Cinema Act. Most movie houses are privately owned—one firm owns 80 percent of all Copenhagen cinemas and 40 percent of those throughout Denmark—but local governments license them, subsidize some of them, and even own and operate a few. As in other countries, ticket sales have dropped and the number of cinemas has been shrinking; at the end of 1987, nearly half the municipalities had no movie theatre.

Film censorship existed from 1913 to 1969, with censors particularly concerned about violence and pornography. General censorship now has ended, but a rating system restricts attendance by children. The state's film censor determines whether a particular movie should be forbidden to children under sixteen or to children under twelve or permitted to those under seven only with a warning to their parents.

Museums and Libraries

Most of the principal art museums—the Royal Museum of Fine Arts, the New Carlsberg Glyptotek, the Hirschsprung Collection, and the Ordrupgård Collection—are funded and operated by the national government, as are a number of general history and natural history museums, including the National Museum. Local governments, art societies, businesses, foundations, and private owners assist other museums and galleries, and there is financial aid from the national government for the purchase of works of art, cultural events, conservation, and the maintenance of collections. Most national grants are conditional upon the museum's meeting certain standards or providing some of the financing. The overall national administrative agency is the State Arts Museum Board in the Ministry of Culture; a State Inspectorate of Local Museums also provides professional supervision and consultation.

Outside of government, significant help to cultural and scientific activities began in 1876 when the brewer J. C. Jacobsen set up the Carlsberg Foundation to finance the Carlsberg Laboratory. Today, under a board appointed by the Royal Danish Academy of Science, the foundation owns and operates the Carlsberg Breweries and over the years has given much financial aid both to science and, through the New Carlsberg Foundation, to museums, art, ballet, and many other cultural endeavors. Often, when a Dane downs a bottle of Carlsberg beer, he declares that he is supporting the culture.

Public libraries exist in every municipality, supported by local governments with some financial help from the national government. A revision of the library law in 1983 provided for block grants from the national treasury to libraries that meet certain requirements, including provision of services to the sick and handicapped who are homebound. Libraries cannot charge to circulate books, but imposition of fees for tapes, videos, and records has become a matter of some controversy. Authors frequently complained that their books were bought by the public libraries and circulated to thousands of borrowers, with no royalties accruing to the writers. Since 1946 the Danish Authors' Fund, financed from the national budget, has made yearly payments to writers of books owned by the libraries.

A national research library of some two million volumes, the Royal Library in Copenhagen, and six university libraries fall under the jurisdiction of and are financed by the central government. The School of Librarianship provides a four-year program for aspiring librarians and researchers. Under the 1983 law the directors of public libraries appointed after January 1, 1984, must be trained librarians.

Problems and Controversies

Government is extensively involved in cultural affairs, with the Ministry of Culture and the various boards associated with it serving as the center for decision making. Because decisions on grants and awards to individuals and groups are made by professionals in the various fields, they are in large measure insulated from partisan politics or government dictation, although they are not immune from controversy. The allocation of grants is never an easy task, and the criteria are often in dispute, even among nonpolitical experts. The controversy involves "well-documented quality versus less certain experiments, young versus old, professional versus nonprofessional art."[6] Sometimes there are charges that the same people receive awards time after time and that this smacks of elitism. Such criticism is probably inevitable in a small country where there is only a limited number of persons eligible for awards. "There has to be a choice between equality (support to many artists of varying quality) and quality (support to a few artists who definitely have demonstrated high artistic talents and standards)."[7] The solution has usually been to award relatively large grants to fewer people, on the grounds that it is better to give some artists longer periods for concentrated work than to provide many with short-term aid. Economic hard times have imposed additional restraints, with the Culture Ministry's budget suffering cuts in recent years. Nevertheless, the principle that government has a definite responsibility to promote and help finance artistic and cultural endeavors seems firmly established.

SPORTS

It may seem something of an anomaly to include sports under the rubric of culture, though one can cite the "sound mind in a sound body" goal as justification. Sports and culture are linked financially because since 1948 a proportion of the national government's take from legalized gambling on football (soccer) has been allocated to the activities of both. The 1948 statute created the Danish Football Pools Company and provided for distribution of funds to amateur sports, recreation for young people, cultural activities, and charity and general welfare functions. Four national ministries—culture, education, environment, and finance—make yearly recommendations on allocations to the Folketing's finance committee.

The bulk of the government share from the football pools goes to sports and leisure time activities and organizations, for such things as construction of sports halls, clubhouses, and swimming pools; aid to organizations with special concerns (students, the handicapped, etc.); and education, research, or publicity that help develop sports at the local level. The Ministry of Culture gets some of the money for allocations to pictorial art, literature, cultural organizations, museums and archives, and theatres and films.

In 1976 general national responsibility for sports moved from the Interior Ministry to the Culture Ministry, but despite an increasing national role in sports finance, the overwhelming proportion of public aid—about 85 percent—comes from local governments. Most of the total financing still comes from private sources, however. Local authorities build football fields, stadiums, sports arenas, tennis courts, swimming pools, skating rinks, and other facilities and help with sports and athletics in many other ways. Estimates suggest that around half of all adults take part in sports of some kind, whether in organized teams or on an individual basis. There are many athletic organizations and facilities throughout Denmark. Local clubs, which are voluntary, self-governing associations, are joined in national federations.

RELIGION

For centuries the Church was an important bearer of culture in Denmark through its efforts and encouragement in music, art, literature, and education. After the Reformation and the establishment of absolute monarchy those cultural responsibilities shifted more and more to secular society and to kings, legislators, and bureaucrats. Today the churches have been left mainly with spiritual functions although interest and concern with many public policies necessarily remain.

Denmark continues to have an established Church, though Danish writers make a distinction between a "state church," defined as a Church directed by the state and representing some kind of official religion, and a "national church," one meriting the support and aid of the state because a vast majority of citizens are members. They conclude that the Danish Church fits the latter description. The constitution uses the term "national church" (*folkekirke*) rather than "state church" (*statskirke*) in its religious references.

Most Danes—nearly 91 percent according to 1986 figures—belong at least nominally to the Evangelical Lutheran Church. Slightly more women than men, and proportionally more rural citizens than urban ones, are members. Formal membership is not equivalent to active membership, and Danish writers often complain of a decline in religious interest. Church attendance is low—it is estimated that only about 5 percent of the membership may be found in church on a normal Sunday. Some 81 percent of one-year-olds are baptized (but only 51.5 percent in Copenhagen). Doctrinally the Church recognizes Martin Luther's Short Catechism and the Augsburg Confession as basic documents. In the nineteenth century, revivalist movements—Grundtvigianism and the Inner (or Home) Mission—influenced the Church and still have some importance today.

Government involvement in the affairs of the established Church takes the form of provision for religious training in the schools, a role in the appointment of clergy and bishops, a special church tax based on income and paid by church members only, and legislation pertaining to Church organization. In the public schools "Christian Studies" is a compulsory subject for nine years. A student may be exempted from this requirement if a parent promises, in writing, to take personal responsibility for instructing the child in religion. There must also be school instruction about non-Christian religions, though this is usually provided in conjunction with other subjects rather than in a specific course. The national budget covered about 15 percent of the Church's net expenses in 1987; the rest of the money came from contributions and the church tax.

No Church constitution has ever been developed so the Folketing remains the final authority on organization. A cabinet department handles general administration for the government. The king appoints bishops after nomination by the clergy and church councils, and he appoints clergy upon nomination by the cabinet minister, who has acted on the basis of recommendations from parochial councils. These are *pro forma* appointments, with the actual decisions being made by the appropriate bodies within the Church. The government does not interfere with religious matters and makes no attempt to impose a rigid orthodoxy, and the clergy and their congregations carry on their activities with extensive freedom. Special legal provisions allow individuals to join together, choose their own pastor, and be recognized as a "free congregation" within the Church. The whole arrangement was once described by Professor Hal Koch as "a fairly well-organized anarchy that has proved its ability to function."[8]

Some 2,100 parish councils (*menighedsråd*) direct local affairs. In 1984, about 17,000 persons (43.8 percent women) were elected as council members, in a voting turnout of 16.8 percent. A council recommends candidates for clerical posts when vacancies occur, participates in the election of bishops, appoints nonclerical parish personnel, and supervises generally the administration of the parish church. The nation is divided into ten dioceses, each headed by a bishop who ordains and supervises the lesser clergy, performs a number of administrative duties, and is considered an adviser in ecclesiastical matters both to the clergy and to the government. Except for the monarch, whose role is symbolic and nominal, there is no overall head of the established Church, and bishops may frequently disagree, as they did in 1989 on a Folketing statute recognizing homosexual "marriages." Clergy receive their education in the theological faculties of Copenhagen and Århus universities. Many organizations work in close cooperation with the Danish Church, including the Blue Cross (a temperance group), various youth and student organizations, the YMCA and YWCA, and a number of welfare and mission societies.[9]

Eleven other religious congregations are legally recognized, which means that their clergy can perform baptisms, weddings, and other ceremonies that are legally valid and that they can maintain registers of births, deaths, and marriages and issue the appropriate certificates. Many of these organizations receive some financial aid from the state for their education and welfare activities. They determine their own organizational forms, and their members are exempt from the church tax. In 1986 less than 1 percent of the population belonged to religious congregations other than the established Church.

In 1982 Denmark and the Vatican agreed for the first time to the establishment of full diplomatic relations and an exchange of ambassadors. Danish Roman Catholics, who number about 27,000, had hoped for an increase in their ranks as a result of the first-ever papal visit to Denmark in June 1989, but a public opinion survey a month after Pope John Paul II's departure indicated that there had been few converts. The meeting between the pope and the Lutheran bishops was described as "tense."[10]

EDUCATION

From 1916 to 1961 administration of most of the national government's cultural programs fell under the Ministry of Education. In 1961 the new Ministry of Culture assumed almost all these responsibilities, including general direction of specialized artistic, musical, and cultural education: the schools of the Art Academy, music conservatories, the librarians' school. The other tasks of education remain under the overall jurisdiction of the Ministry of Education, with much involvement by local authorities and with many opportunities for flexibility and experimentation at various levels.

From 1814 to 1972 the law required seven years of education. Today nine years are compulsory, from the ages of seven to sixteen. Most people attend the public schools, but parents may teach their children at home or send them to private schools. In any case there will be governmental supervision to ensure that certain standards are met. About 9 percent of students in the first to tenth years (the tenth year is optional) go to nonpublic schools. Education is free in the public schools; other schools charge fees, but the national government provides subsidies that cover up to 85 percent of operating costs. Local governments must provide kindergartens, and a high proportion of children attend in the preschool years.

The basic public school is the *folkeskole* (literally translated as the "people's school" and in official literature as the "primary and lower secondary school"), which provides education for grades one through ten. The chief statute, the Folkeskole Act of 1975 with subsequent amendments, declares the purposes of the schools to be acquisition of knowledge and skills, all-around development of the individual, expansion of the imagination, promotion of a capacity for independent evaluation, and preparation for active participation in life and decision making in a democratic society. School life should therefore be based on intellectual liberty and democracy.

Required subjects in all nine years are Danish, mathematics, physical education, and Christian studies. Other subjects required for lesser periods are creative art (five years), music (five years), history (seven years), geography (five years), biology (five years), needlework (one year), woodwork (one year), English (five years), home economics (one year), physics/chemistry (three years), and contemporary studies (two years). Schools must offer three years of German as an elective. Topics required in the basic curriculum include traffic safety, sex education, Norwegian and Swedish, other religions and philosophies of life, educational and vocational guidance, and health education, including drug awareness. Many elective courses are available in the eighth, ninth, and tenth years.

The organization and direction of the public schools involve a number of national and local institutions. The Folketing enacts the school law that sets the basic structures and requirements, and it appropriates funds and decides on their distribution among the various types of education. The Ministry of Education exercises general supervision over the national school system; determines overall aims and objectives; issues guidelines and often detailed regulations on the curriculum and other matters; allocates monies within the framework enacted by the Folketing; and settles educational disputes. The local government fixes the number of hours to be spent on each subject and issues curriculum regulations for the schools in its area. The individual school, through its board and its teachers' council, develops an educational plan (subject to local council approval) and decides which topics will be included in each subject in each class year. The teacher decides when a given topic will be taken up during the year, how much time will be allotted to it, and how it will be taught.

Nor are these the only actors in the educational process. County governments have supervisory functions and are responsible for educational units at the upper secondary level. Since 1970 each public school has had a school board with five or seven members who are elected every fourth year by and from parents with children in the school. The principal, two teachers' representatives, and (except on individual personnel matters) two pupils' representatives may attend board meetings, as may a municipal council member if the local government wishes; none of these individuals has the right to vote.

The school board has much to say about texts and teaching materials and school operations and may influence the appointment of principals and teachers. There are also teachers' councils and pupils' councils for representational purposes. Each local government has an education committee of thirteen members (drawn from the local council, school board members, and the youth school board) that is responsible for ensuring that all eligible children get a good education. It expresses its opinion on school budgets, helps develop the local government's school plan, and participates in the appointment of teachers.

Denmark has always used school-leaving examinations to determine the successful completion of a course of study. The old system of a single comprehensive examination gave way under the 1975 Folkeskole Act to a choice by students of the courses in which they wish to be tested. A Leaving Examination at the end of the ninth or tenth year of education may be taken in any or all of eleven subjects: Danish, mathematics, English, physics/chemistry, German, Latin, French, creative art, woodwork, home economics, or typing. An Advanced Leaving Examination, after the tenth year, may be taken in any or all of the first five subjects.

After completing the compulsory nine years of education, the continuing student has a number of options. He or she may attend a *gymnasium* or enroll in Higher Preparatory Examination (*højere forberedelseseksamen*, or HF) courses. If most immediately interested in a job, the student may choose among apprenticeship training, basic vocational education (*erhvervsfaglige grunduddanelser*, or EFG), technical or commercial examination courses, and other types of vocational training. Possibilities also include various continuing education courses or attendance at one of the famous folk high schools. Danes worry because, despite this plenitude of opportunities, about 20 percent of those who complete their required schooling fail to pursue any further education or training. Those who do not go on are more likely to be girls than boys and very much more likely to be children of unskilled workers than from middle-class families.

A *gymnasium* education or its equivalent is essential for those who plan to attend a university or other institution of higher learning. Admission to a *gymnasium* depends on a statement of satisfactory performance from the *folkeskole*, passing certain subjects in the Leaving Examination, and completion of some other specified subjects. In a three-year course of study the student pursues one of two lines, mathematics or languages, each of which has a number of subdivisions. In either line there will be courses in religion, Danish, German, French, classical culture, history and civics, mathematics, and computer science. Capping the education is the student examination (*studentereksamen*), a government-directed oral and written examination. The certificate acquired by the successful completion of the student examination is the passport to a university education.

Gymnasier are run by county and local governments, by the national government (only one, Sorø Akademi), and as private institutions. They are much more centrally controlled than is the *folkeskole*. A directorate in the Ministry of Education provides general supervision of both public and private *gymnasier*, sets goals in the various subjects, issues detailed regulations on their scope and content, and approves the examination syllabuses. Administration of the individual schools is by a headmaster, assisted by various representative bodies. Private *gymnasier* that meet required standards receive public subsidies for 85 percent of their operating costs. The number of *gymnasium* students has increased greatly in recent years. In 1950 only about 6 percent of all school-leavers were admitted; in 1982 the proportion was 38 percent (this included also the HF students). In prosperous cities a good 50 percent of school-leavers go on to a *gymnasium*, but in poorer areas only 10 percent may do so.

An alternative to the *gymnasium*, introduced in 1967, is the Higher Preparatory Examination (HF), a set of written and oral examinations open to anyone over the age of eighteen. Most of those who choose this route need additional academic preparation, and *gymnasier*, teachers' colleges, and other institutions provide courses and a two-year full-time program for this purpose. The HF curriculum has a common core of subjects and a number of electives. The examination may be taken one subject at a time over a three- or four-year period; successful completion of all parts enables a student to go on to higher education. The Ministry of Education regulates both the curriculum and the examinations. HF has proved a successful and popular innovation, with its students increasing from 500 in 1967 to 12,700 full-time and 42,000 part-time in 1982/83. The program has a special appeal to persons who have been out of school and working for a number of years.

Passing the student examination, the HF examination, or the higher commercial examination (equivalent to the student examination but more vocationally oriented) makes one eligible for admission to a university or other institution of higher education. Until 1977 there was little question that a student who had successfully completed one of these examinations would be admitted, but the number of applicants has increased so greatly that entry into certain programs has been restricted. A 1976 statute authorized the establishment of quotas, fixing the maximum number of entrants for each field. In 1965 about 12,000 were admitted to the universities, engineering schools, teachers' colleges, and other specialized units of higher education. By 1975 the number of applicants had grown to more than 20,000, and not all could be accommodated, despite the establishment of a new university (Odense in 1964) and two university centers (Roskilde, 1970, and Ålborg, 1974). For centuries Copenhagen University, founded in 1479, had been the only university in Denmark. It was joined by Århus University in 1928. After 1977 free access to technical and scientific study continued but not to such fields as medicine, the social sciences, and the humanities. In 1989, 44,000 applied for university admission; 15,000 were rejected, the highest number ever. Courses of study follow the general European pattern, usually requiring up to six years. Major examinations come at the end of two years and four years, with the culmination in the M.A. or M.Sc. examination.

Besides pressures on the universities to expand enrollments and to revise and modernize the curriculum and teaching methods, there were demands of students for a share in the power of governance. A student revolt began in Copenhagen on March 21, 1968, led by psychology students proclaiming the slogans "End professor rule" and "Co-determination now." Others joined the demonstrations, buildings were occupied, and negotiations commenced between the university administration, professors, and students. After much dispute tentative agreements were reached, not entirely acceptable to any side, and the Folketing followed them up on May 28, 1970, with a new law for the governance of all universities and other institutions of higher education. Students gained one-third of the seats on the university governing board and faculty councils and half the seats on study councils. In 1973 parliament revised the law to give the faculty half the membership on administrative councils and to allot students and the technical-administrative staff each 25 percent of the seats. Disagreements continue about the new arrangement. Some students argue that it is not sufficiently democratic, and some professors believe that students and administrative staff lack the insight needed for policy making.

As state institutions, the higher education units fall within the general purview of the Ministry of Education, save for those few schools that come under the Ministry of Culture. Within the framework set by the Folketing the Ministry of Education sets the rules for admissions, degrees, courses of study, and the employment of teachers and research staff. Each institution is headed by a rector who is aided by various boards and committees.

For those heading for a job rather than advanced academic training, Basic Vocational Education courses (EFG), a new route that combines work and classes, has become a popular alternative to the traditional apprenticeship program. Other educational opportunities include vocational training in technical and commercial schools, municipal youth schools, home economics schools, agricultural schools, and other institutions. Continuing education courses—free until 1983 when fees were imposed—are given through the *folkeskole* and *gymnasium*. Nongovernment organizations, which receive state subsidies, also offer a great variety of courses for adults.

Attracting large numbers of students every year are the folk high schools, called by a former cabinet minister "the most important (some say the only) original Danish cultural product."[11] The folk high schools had their origin in the ideas of N.F.S. Grundtvig, the clergyman, historian, poet, and educator who in the 1830s and 1840s began to advocate their creation. Grundtvig saw the need for a new type of school to educate the peasantry who were on the way to gaining political power, a school that would be based not on lectures and book-learning but on a dialogue, a "living exchange," among pupils and teachers. He also wanted to promote "Danishness" and to strengthen the national culture by emphasizing the "fellowship of the Danish people" and the values that united them. By 1870 there were 52 folk high schools, catering in the nineteenth century largely to the rural population, but in the twentieth century drawing upon people from all parts of the nation.

The folk high school is a boarding school where students not only study together but also live and work together. It is, as a former principal wrote, "a community concentrating on learning, not on teaching."[12] Attendance is voluntary; there are no entrance or final examinations and no grades, though a student may receive a statement of course completion if desired. The schools are generally nonvocational, although some may stress a single subject (athletics and gymnastics or prenursing education) or preparation for the HF examinations. They are self-governing, nonprofit institutions.

Many students take short courses of one to two weeks, some stay four to six months, and others enroll in courses that are ten months in duration. The subjects most commonly offered are Danish literature, history, social affairs, international relations, psychology, foreign languages, and music appreciation. There has always been diversity among the folk high schools, and the variety has increased in recent years. Today, besides those offering a general curriculum and the gymnastics and nursing ones (disappearing with changes in nurses' training), there are schools emphasizing religion or philosophy (Inner Mission, charismatic Christian, transcendental meditation); socialism; labor unions; women's studies; art; and the interests of old-age pensioners. Youth folk high schools were established in the 1960s for seventeen- to nineteen-year-olds who want to continue with some studies after finishing the *folkeskole.* The number of schools has been increasing (from 55 in 1950 to 104 in 1985) as have enrollments, and a sizable proportion of the population takes at least one folk high school course.

The national government began helping the folk high schools with grants as early as the 1840s. Today the Ministry of Education approves buildings, school regulations, curriculum, and headmasters, and sets some conditions on course duration. High schools meeting those requirements and having a certain minimum enrollment receive grants for teachers' salaries, building maintenance, staff costs, educational materials, taxes and interest, and so on. Additional revenue comes mainly from student fees. The national government may also make long-term, low interest loans for building construction. Students may receive direct grants with the amount depending on need; a low-income student can obtain up to half the total cost. Student grants may also be available from counties and municipalities.

For education generally, student grants had first come from a Youth Education Fund, with aid going only for college or university education. Now, under the State's Education Assistance Plan, grants may go to students over the age of eighteen in any acceptable programs. Stipends are based on financial need and do not have to be repaid. Government loans to needy students are interest-free during the years of school but with interest at 2 percent above the National Bank's rate after completion of education. Private banks offer government-guaranteed loans to all student applicants, regardless of their financial circumstances.

To sum up, education in Denmark is largely a blend of national and local government responsibilities. All of the educational network is supervised in one way or another, sometimes through very detailed regulations, by the national Ministry of Education. The national government subsidizes all county, municipal, and private schools; pays for most of the operating costs of engineering and teachers' colleges and technical and commercial schools; and provides students with direct grants and guaranteed loans. The national parliament enacts the basic laws governing the whole educational structure.

THE PRESS, RADIO, AND TELEVISION

The constitution guarantees to every person the right to "publish his thoughts in printing, in writing, and in speech, provided he may be held answerable in a court of justice." Press censorship existed under the absolute monarchy; it was abandoned for a time in 1770, but limitations again appeared in 1771 and censorship was reinstituted during the Napoleonic wars and lasted until the time of the 1849 constitution. An individual may have to answer in court to charges of libel or slander, but the permissible scope of "fair comment" is rather broad. The government's role concerning the press is a very limited one; its role in the newer mass media of radio and television is much more extensive.

Newspapers have existed in Denmark since the seventeenth century; the four oldest papers still in existence—*Berlingske Tidende* and the *Stiftstidende* of Ålborg, Århus, and Odense—date from the eighteenth century. The press began a rapid development after censorship ended. The first newspapers were politically conservative, but as party competition developed, Liberal journals began to appear in the 1860s and 1870s, and socialist newspapers soon joined them. After the split in the Liberal party in the early twentieth century newspapers speaking for the Radical party also came into being. Even fairly small towns had four newspapers, each speaking for one of the "four old parties." They covered local and national political events and general news and served as the voice for their party in the local area. The four-party system was paralleled by the four-newspaper system.

By 1913 there were 143 dailies, with 3 or 4 representing different party views in 30 towns. The period since World War I has seen the disappearance of many newspapers, however, as competition from other media, technical developments, increasing costs, and changes in reader interest took their toll. In 1988 there were 46 daily, general-interest newspapers with an average daily circulation of 1,851,000 copies, figures that have remained fairly constant in recent years. Danes seem to be avid newspaper readers although proportionally fewer buy papers than do the citizens of other Scandinavian countries.

The dominant newspapers are the Copenhagen dailies, which have a nationwide circulation. These include *Berlingske Tidende* (independent conservative in political views, weekday circulation 130,000, Sundays 167,000)—"one of Europe's best serious, responsible, interesting and relevant elite newspapers"[13]—and its mid-day tabloid *B.T.* (circulation 227,000 weekdays); *Politiken* (founded 1884, independent Radical, 152,000 weekdays, 192,000 Sundays) and its mid-day paper *Ekstrabladet* (224,000 weekdays); and *Aktuelt* (owned by the trade unions and pro–Social Democrat, 61,000 weekdays, 65,000 Sundays). Smaller but important Copenhagen dailies are *Information* (a nonparty newspaper that developed out of the World War II Resistance press and devotes much space to national politics); *Kristeligt Dagblad* (independent, religious); *Børsen* (a commercial-financial paper, 49 percent owned by a Swedish publisher); *Land og Folk* (the organ of the Communist party); and *Minavisen* (Socialist Peoples party). The morning papers have tended to decline in circulation, while the mid-day tabloids have grown. The only important non-Copenhagen daily that is national in its outlook and sales is *Jyllands-Posten* of Århus.

"The charms of the Danish people and their history seem to exude from their newspapers. . . . Danish papers do entertain, but the overriding tone is one of responsibility, seriousness, open-mindedness and tolerance."[14] Most newspapers have moved away from stridently political comments and have weakened or ended their historical partisan connections. Often they have a regular political feature in which the views of all political parties are presented. Thriving in recent years has been a host of local weekly "giveaway" papers, sent free of charge to households and financed completely by advertising. Many are printed by the daily newspapers.

Ownership of most of the larger newspapers has been transferred for legal and financial reasons from companies and individuals to independent trusts or foundations. The change often gives the editorial and technical staff of the paper representation on its board of directors. The major dailies jointly own Ritzaus Bureau, which covers foreign news for them, and they also have a common purchasing agency and cooperative distribution facilities. Most papers belong to the Danish Newspaper Publishers Association.

Working journalists—including those in newspapers, radio and television, periodicals, publishing houses, and other communications media—belong to the Danish Union of Journalists (Dansk Journalistforbund, or DJ), established in 1961. The union concludes separate agreements with a majority of the companies employing its members. Most of the publishers belong to the Employers Confederation, but DJ is independent and not affiliated with LO, AC, or FTF. The government operates a school for journalists in Århus, which graduates about 200 students yearly after a program of eighteen months of study, eighteen months of practical experience, and a further year of study. Newspaper strikes, involving mainly the typographers' union, have sometimes been costly for all involved. A major strike shut down *Berlingske Tidende* and two other papers for six months in 1977, and one lasting from March to mid-June in 1980 closed 35 dailies and for three weeks in April the entire Danish press.

Government involvement with the press is very limited. Despite problems of cost and income, publishers have been adamantly opposed to direct financial aid from the government, even though their Norwegian and Swedish counterparts accept such help. Indirectly they receive assistance through reduced postal charges for newspaper delivery, payments for government advertising and for printing the results of the national lottery, and the absence of a value-added tax on newspapers. The government's mediation machinery may be used in labor disputes. A special national agency (*berigtigelsesnævnet*, literally "corrections board") hears complaints about a newspaper's failure or refusal to print a correction of factual items that have been incorrectly or wrongfully printed and may impose a fine if it holds the paper liable.

Government's role with the newer media of communications, radio and television, has been much more extensive, with Radio Denmark (Danmarks Radio, or DR) occupying a monopolistic position until fairly recently. Through this public but independent agency radio broadcasting began on April 1, 1925, with the government taking over the airwaves from the radio amateurs and their organizations. The organizations continue in existence as listeners' and viewers' associations that retain a significant influence over the media. All of them are joined in a national federation.

Radio Denmark today provides three nationwide radio services, along with nine regional broadcasting stations (five in Jutland, two in Zealand, one in Funen, and one in Bornholm). A majority of their programs are music and light entertainment, with sizable segments devoted to news and current events. The government monopoly on radio and TV broadcasting was broken in 1983 when the Folketing enacted a temporary statute (made permanent in 1987) allowing local and private radio and television stations to operate. Permission to operate comes from a board appointed by the municipal government. The stations cannot be controlled by commercial or economic interests or newspapers, although they may make agreements with newspapers to supply some of their news programs. They can sell time to political parties and religious movements.

Black-and-white television transmissions began on an experimental basis on a government channel in 1951, and regular programming started in 1954, with color television coming along fifteen years later. Until October 1988 there was only one channel (except for a few local stations), though viewers in the right locations could pick up Swedish, West German, or East German broadcasts. A second television channel, called appropriately TV-2, began broadcasting on October 1, 1988, operating as an independent, advertising-financed alternative to the previous one-channel monopoly. For the first time commercials appeared on Danish national television but only at the start or end of a program. No advertising for medicines, beer, wine, spirits, or tobacco is permitted, nor can there be ads for interest organizations, political parties, or religious groups. TV-2 is run by a government-appointed board of five members.

Until May 1987 Radio Denmark was governed by a Radio Council (*radiorådet*) appointed by cabinet ministers, listeners' and viewers' associations, the principal parties in the Folketing (M.F.s were eligible to serve), and DR personnel. A Program Committee, drawn from the council but also including representatives of different fields of cultural life, supervised program content. Day-to-day management rested with a director-general responsible only to the council. In 1987 the Folketing adopted legislation replacing the Radio Council with a new governing board of eleven members. The minister of communications appoints the chair; the political parties in the Folketing select nine members, with M.F.s now ineligible to serve; and DR personnel choose one member. The board has overall responsibility for DR's operations and appoints the director-general. A program committee of twenty-one members (one-third chosen by listeners' and viewers' associations, two-thirds chosen by organizations representing business, labor, education, religion, art, sports, and consumers) advises the board. Complaints about DR and its programs are heard by a three-member independent agency. Aside from advertising revenues generated by TV-2, radio and television continue to be financed from license fees required of radio and TV set owners. Faroese Radio and Greenland Radio are outside the jurisdiction of Radio Denmark but cooperate closely with it.

10

Denmark and the World

In seeking to attain its goals in foreign policy and in its choice of methods to achieve them, any Danish government must recognize certain "given" factors that determine the confines within which it must work. Geographically, culturally, and politically, Denmark is part of Norden; it has close ties to the other Nordic nations and shares many interests with them. The attitudes and concerns of these nations must be considered in foreign policy decisions, and it is assumed that, when possible, actions should be taken in concert. That unity became more difficult upon Denmark's entry into NATO and the European Community, but it remains important.

Denmark's location at the entrance to the Baltic has always been a significant factor for its foreign policy. Its waterways—the Belts and the Sound—are vital to any state wanting access to or exit from the Baltic. For centuries Denmark has been affected by the distribution of power in the Baltic region and, since the eighteenth century, especially by the power and policies of Great Britain, Germany, and Russia. From the nineteenth century until after World War II, Danish governments hoped to escape the dangers of involvement by "contracting out" of the Great Powers' politics. The nation's strategic importance in world politics is not limited to its location between the Baltic and the North seas. Its sovereignty over the Faroe Islands and Greenland is also of significance, as both territories are actual or potential bases for the defense of Great Britain and the North American continent and thus are likely targets for any power hostile to the United Kingdom or the United States.

Another vital fact for Danish foreign policy is that its only land frontier is with a stronger neighbor, Germany. No natural barriers separate the two states, and events since the nineteenth century have shown Denmark to be unable to defend itself against a German military threat. Relations with Germany have necessarily been one of the most important problems in the history of Danish foreign policy. The creation of the German Federal Republic and its entry into NATO made West Germany and Denmark partners in the Western alliance, but the Danes are still aware of the power south of their border. Also, the division of Germany brought the Soviet Union, through its domination of East Germany, to within six miles of the Danish coast. With the reunification of Germany in 1990, that particular threat has ended.

An essential factor in Denmark's foreign policy choices is the country's economic situation. Maintenance of a productive and expanding economy and a high standard of living depends on the import of raw materials and semifinished products and the export of manufactured goods and agricultural commodities. Denmark's export trade, though worldwide, is concentrated in Europe—in 1987, 25 percent of its total exports went to the countries of the European Free Trade Association and 48 percent to the European Community members. The nation is vitally concerned, therefore, with economic developments in Europe, as well as with the promotion of general international economic cooperation.

Denmark is a democratic country and a Western country, sharing with the other North Atlantic democracies a community of political interest and belief and a deep concern for the maintenance of a democratic value system. As democrats the Danes almost instinctively reject colonialism and take considerable interest in the problems of the underdeveloped world.

Denmark is a small country with little international political and military influence. The Danes have long understood that by themselves they cannot provide defenses sufficient to deter a stronger state aiming at their domination. After the defeat by Prussia and Austria in 1864 the best solution seemed complete neutrality, plus assurances to the major powers that Denmark would not allow use of its territory against any of them. Following World War I the new League of Nations offered another solution to the problem of defense. Supporting the idea of collective security though chary of the possible use of sanctions, Denmark became a member of the international body but grew increasingly disillusioned. By 1938, after the failure of League action against Italy and with the rise of Nazi Germany, Denmark had reaffirmed its position of neutrality. But World War II brought home the lesson that neutrality was not enough. As a military vacuum Denmark presented a standing temptation to major international rivals, and neither the nation's own unaided efforts nor reliance upon the United Nations seemed likely to provide adequate security.

EUROPEAN SECURITY PROBLEMS

When in the early postwar years the world began to lose confidence in the United Nations as a collective security system, some Danes started thinking of other arrangements for Denmark. Cabinets at first opposed any partial solution that would involve Denmark in Great Power politics. But several events—discussions among Western leaders about an Atlantic alliance, the Communist coup in Czechoslovakia, the signing of a nonaggression pact between the Soviet Union and Finland—forced the Scandinavian countries to make some hard choices.

The three governments—Denmark, Norway, and Sweden—first considered a mutual defense alliance that would promote their security and yet allow them to stand aside from the bloc politics of the powers. After these negotiations failed and Norway cast its lot with the Western alliance, the Danish government decided that national security required membership in the Atlantic Pact. Following heated debate the Folketing voted in 1949 to approve Danish membership in NATO, with 119 members in favor (Social Democrats, Liberals, Conservatives, and 1 Justice party member) and 23 opposed (Radicals, Communists, 1 Liberal, and 4 Justice M.F.s). The Landsting gave its backing the next day, and on May 14, 1949, the foreign minister signed the treaty on behalf of Denmark.

Through NATO the country was no longer on the sidelines but a participant in the Cold War. Its evaluation of international problems was now to be affected not only by its own immediate interests but also by the concerns and goals of its NATO partners. If the government compromised or appeared to yield to its allies, its critics could always accuse it of subservience to others and neglect of Danish interests. For a people accustomed to neutrality and noninvolvement the alliance presented a need for adjustments in thinking about international issues.

Denmark was lukewarm about expansion of NATO in 1951 to include Greece and Turkey but went along because the other alliance members wanted it. The Danes found it difficult to agree to West German rearmament—their memories of the war and occupation years were still vivid, as were their recollections of the uses to which German military power had been put in the more remote past. The Germans were hardly on the list of the Danes' most favorite foreigners. Nevertheless, despite some controversy and misgivings, Denmark agreed with other NATO states in 1954 to accept West Germany as a full and equal member of the alliance. In the ensuing years relations between the two states have been harmonious. The Danes continue to be interested in their compatriots across the border in South Slesvig, but the separation seems no longer a significant problem.

In recent years the most important controversies on Danish security policy have turned upon questions of nuclear weapons and disarmament. On questions of nuclear arms within the alliance, Denmark has been cautious and conservative. It refuses to allow such weapons on its territory and has been restrained in its attitude toward the spread of nuclear weapons within NATO. All this is part of what is usually called the "Nordic balance": a skein of relationships (Denmark, Norway, and Iceland as NATO members; Sweden as neutral; and Finland in a special arrangement with the Soviet Union) regarded as "a stable and beneficial pattern in Northern Europe" and "a delicate situation that demands care and attention in order to be maintained."[1]

In the 1980s restraint began to give way to outright opposition to some NATO policies, and some of Denmark's allies expressed concern over its reliability as a member of the alliance. When in office, the Social Democratic party had accepted NATO's two-track policy on the deployment of U.S. intermediate-range missiles in Europe, although it had hoped for a longer time for negotiations to gain a favorable Soviet response. As an opposition party the Social Democrats moved from this position, and their votes, joined with those of the Socialist Peoples and Radical parties, frequently left the government without majority support on foreign policy questions. All in all, the "four-leaf clover" government met twenty-two parliamentary defeats on foreign policy and national security issues during the five-and-a-half years of its existence. Issues included the deployment of cruise missiles, EC trade sanctions against the Soviet Union because of the situation in Poland, the U.S. "star wars" program, a freeze on nuclear weapons, a Nordic nuclear-free zone, and the Luxembourg Agreement on EC reforms. None of the defeats were interpreted as votes of no-confidence—no major party was anxious to have a new election—so the government continued in office. Within NATO Denmark increasingly gained a reputation for "footnote diplomacy," as alliance statements often had to include a note recording Denmark's reservation on a particular decision.[2]

The government's twenty-third defeat came in April 1988, when a Folketing resolution demanded specific notification of the no-nuclear-arms policy to captains of foreign ships visiting Danish ports. The coalition parties opposed a change, arguing that all Danish cabinets since 1963, including Social Democratic ones, had found satisfactory the existing procedure of general notification and tacit assumption of the policy's observance. Denmark's NATO partners warned that adoption of the resolution would strain Denmark's relations with its allies. U.S. and British spokesmen said that if the resolution passed, their warships would no longer call at Danish ports, and the United Kingdom indicated that it would be unable to carry out maneuvers to back up its commitment to reinforce Denmark in time of war.

Nevertheless, the Folketing majority approved the resolution. Declaring that the resolution placed Denmark's position in NATO in jeopardy, Prime Minister Schlüter immediately called a Folketing election. In the campaign the coalition parties sought to make the vote a referendum on NATO membership; the Social Democrats and Radicals argued that NATO affiliation was not at stake, as the government knew full well that they and a majority of Danes favored continued membership. The outcome of the voting in May 1988 was somewhat confusing. The prime minister called the results a victory for the pro-NATO parties, but they had elected only eighty-six members as against eighty-nine for the parties that had voted for the April resolution. The government that emerged from the post-election negotiations was a Conservative-Liberal-Radical minority coalition, with Schlüter continuing as prime minister; and the Radicals changed course and accepted the former government's position on the antinuclear resolution. With the Radicals now in the cabinet and with support from the Progressives generally to be expected, the government once more had a majority for its international policies; and the period of "footnote diplomacy" seemed over.

The controversies about NATO policy should not overshadow the fact of general support over the years for Danish membership in the alliance. Public opinion polls from 1949 to the present have always indicated a large plurality of Danes in favor of participation in NATO, and since 1977 a majority. Never have the negative responses exceeded 28 percent. According to a 1988 poll, a substantial majority of the voters of all political parties except SF approved membership—58 percent of Social Democrats and 62 percent of Radicals were in favor. The programs of only SF, Common Course, and the Left Socialists demand that Denmark leave the alliance.

DENMARK AND THE UNITED NATIONS

The idea of a new international collective security organization after World War II met with much approval in Denmark. As the wartime community of interest between the powers vanished in postwar bickerings and as the USSR began to use its veto extensively, faith in the United Nations as an organization that would protect small states began to wane. Danish governments began to stress the importance of the international organization as a promoter of the peaceful settlement of disputes, rather than as an enforcer through sanctions and collective military action. In some international crises the U.N. has used military forces to separate belligerents, police ceasefires, and keep the peace; and the Scandinavian countries have frequently been called upon to provide troops. Denmark furnished men for the U.N. peacekeeping forces in the Congo, the Middle East, and Cyprus, and members of observer teams in Kashmir, Palestine, Lebanon, and Yemen. A former prime minister, Poul Hartling, served as the U.N. High Commissioner for Refugees from

1978 to 1986. Denmark has been three times a member of the Security Council, most recently in 1985–1986. The Danish navy sent a corvette to help with the blockade of Iraq after the imposition of U.N. sanctions in 1990. Besides its membership in the U.N. Denmark also belongs to the Organization for Economic Cooperation and Development (OECD) (whose first secretary-general was a former Danish finance minister, Thorkil Kristensen) and to the Council of Europe; it is a signatory to the European Council's Convention on Human Rights.

In Danish opinion the U.N.'s successful performance of its role as mediator requires universality of membership, and Danish governments have tended to favor entry into the world organization of all those states that desire it. The principal exception to this position was the Danish attitude toward Franco-ruled Spain, condemned as the last remnant of fascism, in the early years of the U.N.

In 1970 the General Assembly called on its members to devote 0.7 percent of their gross national product as aid to underdeveloped countries. Denmark accepted the appeal and has provided approximately that amount or more every year since 1979. In 1985 the Folketing decided that assistance to the third world should rise by 0.03 percent a year until 1992 when it would reach 1 percent of GNP. In 1985 assistance amounted to 0.77 percent of GNP; only three other nations—Norway, the Netherlands, and Sweden—gave a greater percentage, and the average for Western industrial countries was 0.36 percent. In 1988 Denmark's figure was 0.88 percent. A little less than half the aid is multilateral, through international organizations and the European Community; the rest is direct. The greatest amounts in technical assistance and advice, loans, and grants go to Tanzania, Kenya, India, and Bangladesh.

In recent years colonial issues have dominated the agenda of the U.N., and Danish representatives have had a prominent role in the discussions. Denmark's colonial past is far behind it, ending with the sale of the Danish West Indies to the United States in 1916. The Danes never really considered Greenland a colony, though the government reported on the administration of the territory to the U.N. until it became an integral part of the realm in 1953. Even before the postwar anticolonial surge there had been in Denmark a sympathetic attitude toward desires for independence, perhaps stemming in part from the nation's support for the principle of self-determination that had developed out of its own concern with South Slesvig.

Among issues relating to colonialism the problem of race relations in the Union of South Africa has drawn much Danish attention. Involved has been not only distaste for the white supremacy doctrine that apartheid policies embody and disapproval of the police-state methods used to uphold them, but also the fear that a continuation of those policies would lead to bloody violence. A General Assembly resolution in 1962 asked U.N. members to break off diplomatic and economic relations with South Africa. Denmark did not support the resolution because it considered the recommended actions as sanctions falling under the jurisdiction of the Security Council. When the council called in 1963 for an embargo on the shipment of arms to South Africa, Denmark readily complied and continued to support U.N. attempts to bring about change in the region during the 1960s and 1970s.

In May 1986, the Folketing approved two laws that in effect ended all Danish trade with South Africa. Support for this embargo came from the Social Democratic, Radical, Socialist Peoples, and Left Socialist parties. The then-government parties—Conservative, Liberal, Center Democratic, and Christian Peoples—opposed the legislation, not because they approved South African policies but because they preferred either a voluntary boycott or action through the U.N., or both. Only the Progressive party took the position that trade with South Africa should be treated in the same way as trade with any other country. When Nelson Mandela was released in 1990, the Danish government began to consider returning an ambassador to South Africa.

THE MAKING OF FOREIGN POLICY

According to the constitution the king acts "on behalf of the Realm in international affairs," but in practice, of course, it is the government that acts. The foreign minister is the cabinet member most concerned with international relations, but he must share his responsibilities with the prime minister, who often acts as national spokesman and who represents Denmark in such international conclaves as the regular meetings of EC leaders. The ministers for defense, finance, economics, Nordic affairs, and agriculture are also involved in various aspects of foreign policy.

Along with the prime minister the foreign minister takes the lead for the government in foreign policy debates in the Folketing; he is the point of contact between the Danish state and foreign governments; and he spends a great deal of time attending the meetings of international bodies and paying visits to the capitals of other states for discussions with their leaders. Major foreign policy issues are discussed by the cabinet, and decisions are approved by it.

The legislature played only a small part in foreign policy until after World War I, although matters of defense policy did occupy its attention a great deal in the years after 1870. Legislative participation in the formulation of foreign policy has increased since 1945. The Folketing debates policy issues; approves treaties and international agreements; considers a small number of bills sponsored each session by the foreign minister; and enacts the appropriations needed for the conduct of foreign and defense policy.

Party leaders may use interpellations to secure information from the foreign minister and the defense minister and to provide the opportunity for discussion of a particular subject. Often such a question is phrased in general terms and is sponsored by the leaders of all the Folketing parties. Infrequently, a motion may be presented at the end of the debate to commit the government to a particular policy line. Members of the Folketing may use the regular question time to ask the prime minister or the foreign minister for information on international affairs. The legislature also has an opportunity to influence Danish foreign policy through its powers to appoint investigating committees, to elect members to other committees that work in the international area, and to choose representatives to some of the international bodies to which Denmark belongs, including the Nordic Council and the Council of Europe.

Of special importance as a link between the legislature and the executive is the Foreign Affairs Committee. Before 1914 the Rigsdag only rarely discussed international agreements or debated issues of external policy, but during World War I the government maintained closer contact with the legislature. After the war parliament became increasingly interested in the executive's conduct of foreign affairs and in 1923 established a Foreign Affairs Committee. The committee was not used as much as some parliamentarians had hoped, and it seemed more an adviser to the cabinet than to the legislature. In secret meetings it discussed the instructions issued for Danish delegations to international conferences; it considered treaty drafts before their submission to other governments and the treaties themselves before signature; at intervals it received and discussed reports from the foreign minister on international questions. Its activities sometimes laid the groundwork for Rigsdag debates on treaties; and it was able on occasion to iron out disagreements before they became partisan issues.

The drafters of the 1953 constitution gave the committee a constitutional status, and a 1954 law provides the rules for its organization. It consists of seventeen members, elected by the Folketing on the basis of proportional representation at the beginning of each legislative year or after each Folketing election. Through the committee the government provides information to the Folketing leaders about its plans in foreign policy. Because of the secrecy to which the committee members are pledged, the government can avoid publicity where it is undesirable and yet keep responsible legislative leaders aware of developments and problems. Although there has been criticism of the committee's lack of staff and of an alleged government tendency to present members with *faits accomplis,* there seems to be general agreement on the body's value both to the legislature and the executive. The Folketing also has a regular standing committee on foreign affairs that handles a very small number of bills and resolutions.

The positions of the political parties on a number of major international issues have already been indicated. The "four old parties" had reached a general consensus on foreign policy in the mid-1950s although some difference remained and seemed to increase in the 1980s. The Radical, Communist, and Justice parties had opposed NATO membership; but the Radicals became formally committed to it when they joined a coalition cabinet with the Social Democrats in 1957. The Communists continued their opposition and were later joined by the Socialist Peoples and the Left Socialist parties. Disagreements on defense spending have generally been resolved by compromises among the major parties. Danish membership in the European Community was and remains a divisive issue. The Liberals and Conservatives wholeheartedly approved it; the Social Democrats and Radicals were officially in favor but with sizable numbers of opponents in their ranks; SF, the Communists, the Left Socialists, and Justice opposed Danish entry.

All the major economic organizations have international interests and seek to influence government decisions in their fields of concern. For policymaking on EC matters, the greatest involvement comes from organizations whose members feel most directly the consequences of those policies. Thus nearly 40 percent of interest organizations in agriculture and fisheries reported contacts with the public authorities concerning the EC, and almost one-third of blue-collar unions had such contacts.[3] Older organizations in the international field include the Norden Association, which seeks to promote cooperation among the Northern countries, and the Danish U.N. Association, which has been especially concerned with policies toward the third world. The peace movement, dormant from the demise of the Campaign Against Nuclear Weapons in the 1960s until the 1980s, has spawned a number of groups: the Cooperation Committee for Peace and Security (an umbrella organization of peace and other groups, trade unions, and individuals, accused by some of being too close to the Communists), No to Nuclear Weapons, and Women for Peace.[4] The People's Movement Against the European Community remains active in its opposition to Danish membership in the EC.

NATIONAL DEFENSE

Denmark's membership in NATO meant acceptance of an increased military effort, even though this might be at the expense of social welfare, housing, and other domestic requirements. Military aid came in the early years from the United States and Canada, but there was still need for more Danish spending on defense than ever before in the country's history.

After the signing of the North Atlantic pact new negotiations resulted in 1951 in a treaty for joint U.S.-Danish defense of Greenland and for continuation of U.S. bases there. In 1951 also the Rigsdag approved the decision of the North Atlantic Council to build an integrated European force under a U.S. commander. The Supreme Headquarters Allied Powers Europe (SHAPE) was established, with four subordinate commands, including the Northern Europe Command covering Denmark, Norway, and the approaches to the Baltic. Under the regional commander, a British general, is COMBALTAP, the commander of the unified forces for the southern part of the region who is always a Dane, supported by a West German deputy and a Danish chief of staff. Since 1960 there have been NATO depots on Danish territory for storage of weapons, ammunition, spare parts, fuel, and medicines for use by alliance warplanes. In 1982 Denmark accepted a NATO plan covering reinforcements— planes and support forces and eventually troops—in time of war or international crisis.

Denmark's major contribution to NATO is its strategic location. Its limited national military strength is insufficient for the country's own defense and so adds little to the deterrent power of the alliance. Denmark had no armed forces at the end of World War II except for the Resistance units and a brigade trained in Sweden during the war. Early postwar governments delayed action on defense until the unlikelihood of an international force under the U.N. became clear. In 1951 the Rigsdag enacted statutes that set a new branch of the armed services, the air force, beside the army and navy. A Defense Ministry replaced the separate war and navy departments, and a new Defense Board was created to direct and supervise national defense. The board's members include the Chief of Defense, who is the defense minister's principal military adviser, the heads of the three armed services, and the chief of the defense staff.

Compulsory military service for men has existed since 1950. In 1973 the general term of service was cut from sixteen months to nine (a reduction opposed by both the Danish and the NATO military staffs). Personnel with special training or qualifications may be retained for longer periods, up to twenty-seven months. The military budget does not allow for calling all men into service when they become eligible so fewer than half (about 6,800 a year) are drafted, and many volunteer to serve their time. A very small number of conscientious objectors refuse military duties and are given civilian assignments for nine months.

Danish armed strength totalled about 37,000 personnel in 1987. In addition there is a Home Guard of 73,500 men and women volunteers, with the men having weapons at home so that they may be available at short notice for local defense. Naval units consist of a small number of frigates, corvettes, minelayers and minesweepers, torpedo boats, submarines, and various other craft. The air force has four squadrons of F-16s and two of F-35s, plus a number of transport planes and helicopters. Denmark has one of the lowest defense budgets in NATO and has often been criticized as a foot-dragger when it comes to paying the costs of security. In 1987 defense expenditures were 2.1 percent of the GNP (comparable figures for the United States, United Kingdom, and Norway were 6.6, 4.9, and 3.2—the average for NATO's European members was 3.4 percent) and about 13 percent of the national budget. Among NATO countries only Luxembourg spent a smaller percentage of its GNP on defense.[5]

How much Denmark should spend for defense has been a controversial issue throughout the twentieth century, and "defense compromise" is a standard term in the Danish political lexicon. After often lengthy negotiations the major political parties (with the Socialist Peoples and Progressive parties excluded), or most of them, arrive at an accord, usually covering a three-year period. In recent years the Radicals have frequently been left out because of their insistence on defense cuts. As part of the coalition bargaining after the 1984 election the Radicals persuaded the Liberals and Conservatives to accept a freeze on defense spending until 1990. In 1989 a more general compromise covering the years until 1992 was reached by the Conservative, Radical, Liberal, Social Democratic, and Christian Peoples parties. Recent defense compromises have tended to maintain military expenditures at existing levels with adjustments for inflation while providing for modernization of some elements of the armed forces. A 1985 public opinion survey indicated that a majority of the population approved such an arrangement: 56.8 percent said that Denmark had no need for a stronger defense, only 26.1 percent that it should be strengthened.[6] It remains to be seen how German reunification and the apparent disappearance of the Soviet threat in Europe will affect public opinion and government policies.

DENMARK AND THE EUROPEAN COMMUNITY

Questions of European unity became a significant issue for Denmark in the 1950s when the movement toward Western European integration began to affect the nation's vital interests. In 1957 six states—the Benelux countries, France, West Germany, and Italy—signed the Treaty of Rome for a European Economic Community or Common Market; but negotiations to include other states with them in a broader free trade area failed. In 1959 the governments of Britain, Austria, Denmark, Norway, Portugal, Sweden, and Switzerland agreed to form a European Free Trade Association (EFTA).

Denmark felt very keenly the economic division of Europe between the Six and the Seven. Of her two best customers, one—Great Britain—was a member of EFTA, and the other—West Germany—belonged to the EEC. With a shrinking of traditional markets for Danish farm products in the Common Market states, it was small wonder that Denmark longed for a solution that would include both Britain and West Germany in a broad market area. British policy was seen as the key, not only for economic reasons but also because of the political balance that the United Kingdom would add to an EEC dominated by countries with more limited or shakier democratic experiences.

So when Britain applied for EEC membership in 1961, Denmark immediately followed suit. Foreign Minister Jens Otto Krag presented the Danish case to the EEC Council of Ministers, pointing out that Danish entry depended on Britain's, that the ties of Scandinavian unity should be maintained, and that there should be interim safeguards for Danish agriculture until attainment of full membership. A period of hard negotiations ended in January 1963, when President de Gaulle abruptly vetoed British entry. Denmark at once suspended its own application for membership.

When the United Kingdom again sought to join the Common Market in June 1970, Denmark renewed its application. This time negotiations, though difficult, went more smoothly, and in January 1972 Denmark signed the Treaties of Accession. Entry depended on the outcome of a national referendum on October 2, 1972; and after a spirited and divisive campaign, 64 percent of the voters endorsed membership. On January 1, 1973, Denmark officially became a member of the European Economic Community.

With its membership Denmark accepted the Treaty of Rome as binding law and became a participant in the organizations it set up. The decision-making body of the European Community is the Council, made up of ministers from the member states. The Council considers proposals from the commission and decides whether to adopt them as Community law or policy. Besides drafting proposals for the Council, the Commission as guardian of the treaty brings violations of it to the Court of Justice. The EC states appoint the commission's members for four-year terms; Denmark has one out of seventeen. The European Parliament is mainly a consultative body, but by a two-thirds vote it may dismiss the entire commission (not individual members) or reject the Community budget. Since 1974 a European Council, not provided for in the treaty, has held several meetings a year, bringing together the heads of state or government of the member countries for a general exchange of views and the development of broad guidelines.

Membership in the EC has introduced a new dimension into Danish policymaking as important decisions affecting Denmark are now made not in Copenhagen but by EC institutions in Brussels, Luxembourg, and Strasbourg. Determination of the nation's position on an ever-increasing volume of EC business is complicated because issues cross the boundaries of a number of ministries with sometimes differing views. Cabinets lack parliamentary majorities so that the attitude of the Folketing is crucial, and parties and public opinion are divided both on particular matters and even on EC membership itself. Out of this complex of attitudes and interests must emerge a consensus that Denmark's representatives can present in the various Community forums.

Scrutiny of proposals from the EC begins in one of twenty-seven special committees (agriculture, finance, etc.), each composed of top civil servants from the ministries affected. A committee gives thorough study to EC proposals and items on the agenda of the Council of Ministers, examining their costs and benefits for Denmark and considering whether amendments are desirable. Its recommendations go to the Senior Officials Committee (also called the EC Committee), a group of ten high-level civil servants from the ministries most involved in Community affairs. This committee prepares recommendations for Denmark's position on items on the Council agenda; it is also responsible for supervising the implementation of agreed policies.

Above the Senior Officials Committee is a cabinet-level Common Market Committee, with the foreign minister in the chair and with the ministers of the interior, finance, economics, industry, fisheries, energy, environment, justice, and agriculture as regular members. The civil servant who chairs the Senior Officials Committee serves as secretary, thus providing important continuity in the process. As he also attends Council of Ministers meetings and sessions of the Folketing's Market Relations Committee, he follows a question through from the Senior Officials Committee to its adoption or rejection in Brussels. The results of the cabinet committee's discussions become Denmark's official position for negotiations in Council meetings, unless the Folketing requires a modification.

The Market Relations Committee (*Markedsudvalget*, or MRC) of the Folketing plays a crucial role in Danish decisions on Community matters. Now a regular standing committee with seventeen members chosen by proportional representation, it can act like any other parliamentary committee but in fact rarely has legislative proposals to consider. The act of accession to the Community, the Folketing's rules, and the MRC's

1973 and 1974 reports impose upon the government the obligation to consult with the committee on EC matters of major importance and to give the MRC an oral explanation of its initial stance prior to any important negotiations. If a majority of the MRC does not oppose the government's position, it can proceed to negotiate on that basis at Council meetings.

The foreign minister is the link between the cabinet and the MRC. The government supplies the MRC with a great deal of information and answers its questions on specific topics; after a Council of Ministers meeting the minister who has represented Denmark reports back to the MRC. For the government the committee provides a useful forum for discussion of Community affairs, and committee discussions reveal to the government before it makes an important decision whether a Folketing majority will support it.

The MRC takes its role seriously, and both M.F.s and the media consider that it has helped ensure good working relations between the cabinet and parliament. A minister can expect a searching examination from the MRC; he may be sent off to do his home work and come back with a better presentation, or he may be told that the committee expects him to consult with it during the negotiations. Or the committee, if a majority opposes the cabinet's position, may require it to rethink its negotiating plans. When government and MRC agree, Community decisions can be quickly translated into national legislation.

Denmark's principal reasons for joining the European Community were economic, and it has continued to emphasize the economic objectives while remaining more restrained in its attitude toward greater integration or a European union. "Cautious," "down-to-earth," "pragmatic" are adjectives often used to describe the Danish outlook. Given the importance of agricultural exports Denmark entered the EC generally satisfied with its Common Agricultural Policy (CAP). In recent years CAP has proved an expensive proposition, as agricultural productivity has increased with no concomitant rise in consumption and foreign sales have diminished. The EC has been forced to adopt drastic measures to reduce surpluses, cutting milk production in 1984 and dairy and beef production in 1986, much to the displeasure of Danish farmers. Most of the political parties continue to support the Common Agricultural Policy, however. On the industrial side free trade in manufactured goods has given Danish enterprises the opportunity to compete in the European market on an equal footing with the firms of other member states. Denmark gains from this and opposes any return to protection of national markets.

Various policies and actions of the Community have been controversial in Denmark. Objections by farmers and fishermen have already been noted.[7] In several instances Denmark has insisted on stricter

standards than required by the EC for labeling substances as dangerous
to the health of workers; and there have been threats of action against
Denmark in the EC Court. The Commission's push for equal treatment
for women has posed no great problem for Denmark except that it took
a judicial decision to allow women to serve in the navy. The Commission's
Equal Treatment Directive allows EC states to exclude from its protection
occupational activities for which by their nature or context "the sex of
the worker constitutes a determining factor." Denmark has interpreted
this to permit continuation of laws under which only women can sell
women's underwear and jobs involving foreign travel may legally be
restricted to men.[8] The labor movement was pleased when the EC Court
in 1989 upheld the Danish laws on equal pay for equal work. In the
fall of 1989 the EC Commission brought to the Court a case concerning
construction contracts for the new Great Belt bridge. Those contracts
provided for the greatest possible use of Danish materials and labor;
and the Commission found this contrary to the Rome Treaty's requirements
of free competition. In a compromise settlement Denmark was allowed
to proceed with the bridge, upon its agreement to compensate firms
that could prove they had suffered losses from the rejection of their
bids.

      Broader issues of European cooperation and integration have proved
even more controversial. Various proponents of European Union have
sought to commit EC members to that goal; and in 1983 the European
Parliament adopted the Spinelli Report, including a draft treaty for a
Union to replace the EC and its treaties. In 1984 a parliamentary
resolution called for preservation of the right of veto in the EC and
rejected the draft treaty. Among the parties only the Center Democrats
are on record today in favor of a European union.

      More division among the parties appeared when the Folketing
turned to consideration of modifications in the EC's structure and policies,
proposed in an effort to formalize European Political Cooperation (EPC).
With foreign and security policies not covered by the Treaty of Rome,
cooperation among the member states had to be outside the general EC
framework. Foreign ministers or heads of government developed EPC
through conferences that discussed and tried to reach common ground
on such issues as East-West relations, disarmament, the Middle East,
South Africa, Afghanistan, Central America, and terrorism. After months
of negotiation EC members agreed in 1985 on a Single European Act—
called in Denmark the EC Package—and submitted it to the governments
for ratification.

      According to the act members would strive to formulate and
implement a European foreign policy; and each would consult with the
others before making a decision on a question of general interest, thus

seeking to avoid any negotiations or positions harmful to the Community. The act also enhanced the power of the European Parliament to some extent, giving it more opportunity to discuss proposals from the Commission; and it extended the use of a qualified majority vote (two-thirds) in the Council of Ministers, though retaining a unanimity rule on the most important matters. It provided for the establishment of the internal market—without barriers to the free movement of people, goods, services, and capital—by the end of 1992; and the Commission worked out about three hundred proposals to harmonize laws and regulations of member states so as to meet this goal. It added to the Commission's powers under the Treaty of Rome by giving it authority to harmonize the laws of EC members on environmental protection and health and safety in the workplace, setting minimum standards but allowing individual states to adopt more stringent rules.

In January 1986, Anker Jørgensen, the Social Democratic leader, informed Prime Minister Poul Schlüter that the Social Democrats would vote against the EC Package. The party expressed a fear that the Package was a first step toward a European Union in which more and more decisions affecting Denmark's vital interests would be made in Brussels. It was also apprehensive that with changes in the unanimity rule for decisions, the EC might be able to nullify tough Danish rules on environmental protection and health and safety in the workplace, with Denmark unable to use a veto to maintain them. As the Radical and the Socialist Peoples parties had already announced their intent to vote against the act, the Schlüter minority government found itself in a precarious political position. Defeat in the Folketing would mean serious embarrassment for the government, probably entailing its resignation and new parliamentary elections. The Social Democratic stand "marked the breakdown of fourteen years of carefully nurtured agreement on Community policy. There was still a parliamentary and electoral majority in support of Danish membership in the Community, but it was also opposed to further integration, supranationality and political union."[9]

Seeking a way out the government referred the issue to the voters in a consultative referendum. Both the Social Democrats and the Radicals declared that they would be bound by the voters' judgment, however; and the government parties also agreed to accept the outcome. At first there were expectations of a negative vote, the more so because in a December 1985 public opinion survey only 38 percent of the electorate had said they would vote for EC membership if there were a new referendum (44 percent said they would vote no and 18 percent were undecided). But in early 1986 the polls indicated that, faced with an actual decision rather than a hypothetical question, voters were shifting to a more favorable view of the Community. Some leading Social

Democrats broke ranks and called for approval of the Package; LO and most of its member unions stood neutral; a number of business and industrial organizations urged a Yes vote; the Radical party did not push for a No vote but left its members free to vote as they pleased. The government parties, arguing that the act made only minor adjustments to the EC system, suggested that rejection, after other members had made concessions to Denmark in the EPC negotiations, would leave the nation in a difficult situation within the Community.

In February 1986, the voters endorsed the Single European Act, with 56.2 percent of them voting yes. The Folketing then ratified the Package by a large majority, with the Social Democrats and Radicals joining the government parties and the Progressives to approve it.

Although the referendum on the Single European Act was not a second vote on Denmark's membership in the European Community, the outcome seemed a reaffirmation of the decision to join. Public opinion polls from 1973 to 1986 had tended to show similar patterns: a plurality (40 to 45 percent) saying they would vote no in a new referendum, a smaller proportion (35 to 41 percent) saying they would vote yes, and 15 to 20 percent undecided. The referendum on the EC Package brought a temporary shift in attitudes, but after the vote the numbers returned to the pre-referendum pattern. It appeared, nevertheless, that when the chips were down and the voters' choice was real rather than hypothetical, a majority would stick with the EC.

Opinions remained divided, however, and the issue of membership is far from dead. Officially, all the parties except SF, Justice, and the small left-wing socialist groups favor continued membership, though many dissenters remain within Social Democratic and Radical ranks. Results of the elections for Denmark's representatives to the European Parliament offer another indication of the continued strength of Community opponents: In the 1979, 1984, and 1989 voting, the Peoples Movement Against the European Community and the anti-EC parties polled 31, 33, and 28 percent of the votes. Although proponents of the European Community might take heart from the diminishing proportion of negative votes, the returns underrepresented the number of opponents as the elections brought out half or less of the eligible voters.

DENMARK AND NORDIC COOPERATION

Both official and unofficial ties joined the peoples of the North in many ways before World War II; but the shared injuries of the war—especially the Soviet attack on Finland and the Nazi occupation of Denmark and Norway—helped enhance feelings of solidarity. After the war the forms and processes of Nordic cooperation burgeoned as new committees and more regular ministerial meetings supplemented the prewar private and public activity.

The most important of the new organs of cooperation is the Nordic Council (*Det Nordiske Råd*), established in 1952 when the parliaments of Denmark, Norway, Sweden, and Iceland approved its basic statute. (Because of its special situation vis-à-vis the USSR, Finland was unable to join until 1955.) In 1962 the Treaty of Helsinki provided an expanded legal basis for the states' joint activities.

Although the Council is composed of representatives of both legislatures and executives, it is largely the parliamentarians who have dominated its proceedings. It has eighty-seven members (plus an equal number of alternates), with twenty each from Denmark, Norway, Sweden, and Finland and seven from Iceland; Denmark's delegation includes two representatives from Greenland and two from the Faroes. The national parliaments elect delegates from among their members, using proportional representation with each party filling the places allotted to it. The term of office is one year; reelection is customary. The parliamentary delegations ordinarily include the principal party leaders, as well as legislative specialists in such fields as education, taxes, labor, and social policy. A certain prestige attaches to service on the Council, and there are practical legislative advantages as well. The body deals with some of the major questions that face each national legislature, and so the delegates discuss problems that interest them and that appear in their national legislative work. They can help shape policy matters that will subsequently be submitted to their parliaments as Council recommendations. The government representatives may join in the Council's deliberations but have no vote on its resolutions.

The Council meets annually in one of the five national capitals. A ten-member presidium—two from each country—meets four or five times a year to coordinate the organization's activities, to review the governments' efforts to carry out its recommendations, and to plan for the coming session. The Council's five standing committees—economics, legal affairs, communications, culture, social and environmental affairs—meet five to eight times a year to discuss proposals from Council members or governments and reports from Nordic institutions and ministers. Each committee makes a written report to the general session of the Council. A budget committee works with members of the Nordic Council of Ministers to scrutinize the Nordic Budget and priorities for expenditures. The contribution of each state to the budget is based on its proportion of the total Nordic gross national products; Denmark's share in 1989 was 20.9 percent.

The annual session opens with a general debate on the Council's activities, reports from governments, and Nordic problems. Both governments and delegates may present matters to the Council. After brief consideration in plenary meeting, a resolution goes to the appropriate committee and then back to the full Council for a vote, with a majority necessary for adoption. Most resolutions are not very controversial, and unanimous or near-unanimous approval is common. Recommendations adopted by the Council are distributed to the member governments, with each taking responsibility for coordinating the work on a number of them. These are recommendations, binding only if the member states choose to make them so, though they are under pressure to accept them. The Council adopts thirty or more recommendations each year. Because the states have different foreign and defense policies (Denmark, Norway, and Iceland are members of NATO; Sweden and Finland are neutral), the Council avoids recommendations on those topics, although it has discussed aspects of them.

In recent years the political parties represented in the Council have begun to cooperate in committee work, to cosponsor proposals, and to vote together. Some observers have expressed fear that the Council's work is becoming too politicized, but others believe that a stronger party role would help the Council by making its debates more lively and interesting. At present, the best way to secure approval of a proposal by all the Nordic governments still is to have broad multiparty support.[10]

In 1971 came the establishment of the Nordic Council of Ministers as a coordinating body at the executive level. Each government appoints a minister of Nordic affairs, and those ministers, or the ones responsible for the subjects under consideration, constitute the Council. Its unanimous decisions are binding on the individual states, although national laws or constitutions may require parliamentary approval in some cases. The Council of Ministers agrees on proposals to submit to the Nordic Council, follows up on Council recommendations and reports to it on outcomes, and directs Nordic cooperation in various fields.

A great many instances of Nordic collaboration antedate creation of the Nordic Council; and many of them have grown out of nongovernment contacts beginning in the nineteenth century. Cultural cooperation, for example, was organized mostly by private bodies and is still largely carried on by them, with occasional small financial grants from governments. In 1956 the Nordic Council set up a Nordic Cultural Fund to promote cultural cooperation; and the Council itself awards prizes for literature and music. There are also bilateral cultural funds, as well as assistance for guest performances, translations of Nordic literature, and the distribution of Nordic films in the region.

In 1946 ministers of education established an advisory Nordic Cultural Commission to consider academic, scientific, educational, and artistic matters. Cooperation in education has centered on exchanges, the development of teaching materials and courses, and various joint projects. Collaboration in research takes place through the circulation of information, the operations of some twenty joint Nordic institutes or committees (including the Nordic Institute for Theoretical Atomic Physics in Copenhagen), and the sharing of costly scientific equipment. Since 1983 a Research Policy Council has helped develop projects and training in scientific research. The Nordic television companies have worked together in NORDVISION to exchange and co-produce programs. Much of this cooperation takes place under the aegis of the Nordic Cultural Agreement of 1971; a great many activities are sponsored by the Norden Associations and other voluntary organizations, professional societies, and individuals.

Extensive cooperation exists in legal matters, and uniformity in law goes far back into Nordic history. Inevitably, as the countries underwent different experiences, divergent trends appeared in their laws; and the Scandinavian Movement of the 1840s and 1850s set legal unity as one of its goals. Progress toward this end began later in the century, as regular conferences of law professors, attorneys, judges, and other officials tried to develop as much uniformity as possible in legislation. In May 1880, identical statutes adopted in Denmark, Norway, and Sweden achieved this goal in bill-of-exchange legislation.

Since then, most progress has come in the fields of commercial law, citizenship, and the law of domestic relations. A number of conventions among the Nordic states have made judgments handed down by the courts of one country enforceable in the others. In 1946 the ministers of justice established a permanent Nordic Committee for Legislative Cooperation whose members scrutinize current legislation in the individual states in the light of regional cooperation, propose new collaborative efforts, and make recommendations to their governments on the priority to be given to the various projects. The Nordic Council encourages these efforts toward legal uniformity and passes its own recommendations for consideration by the governments. In recent years it has discussed such things as patent laws, extradition laws, and some aspects of criminal law. The Council also has urged greater administrative cooperation; and now nearly every contact between national administrative authorities, and even between local governments, is direct rather than through foreign ministries and diplomatic representatives.

The principle of reciprocity in social welfare provisions was well established before the Nordic Council came on the scene, but the Council has aided in its further expansion and development. In 1953 it recommended the consolidation of sixteen existing reciprocity agreements into one general social security pact; the governments agreed and established the 1955 Nordic Social Security Convention (revised in 1981).

It provides for the extension of all social security benefits enjoyed by the citizens of one country to the citizens of other Nordic states residing there. After World War II the Nordic nations became interested in developing a common labor market, and in 1954 signed an international convention that ended the necessity for work permits for wage earners in all the signatory lands. Similar but separate agreements have been reached for many professions—doctors, dentists, nurses, opticians, veterinarians, psychologists—but others—lawyers, architects, accountants, for example—are not covered.

Cooperation in communications and transportation goes back to the establishment of a postal union among Denmark, Sweden, and Norway in 1869. The original agreements were replaced in 1919 by a common postal convention that was broadened by the inclusion of Finland in 1922 and Iceland in 1928 and that became the Nordic Postal Association in 1946. An organization to foster cooperation among the officials of the Danish, Norwegian, and Swedish railway systems has existed since 1874 and was joined by Finland in 1924. (Iceland has no railroads.) The Scandinavian Airlines System, SAS, came out of the merger of the Danish, Norwegian, and Swedish national airlines in 1946. Road traffic regulations are largely uniform, with agreement on such safety measures as the compulsory use of seatbelts and of helmets by motorcyclists. Since 1952 (1955, in the case of Iceland), no passports have been necessary for citizens travelling from one Nordic land to another; and following a recommendation of the Nordic Council the member states agreed to make their region a single passport area even for those who are not citizens of the Northern countries.

In 1863 businessmen, economists, and political leaders gathered in the first Nordic economic conference; and from other such gatherings in 1866 and 1872 emerged a monetary convention and currency union. Nineteenth-century discussion of a customs union proved fruitless, but after World War II the idea reappeared and was considered seriously on various occasions but without results.[11] Further efforts at economic unity were complicated by Danish entry into the European Community, although negotiations within EFTA and between individual countries and the EC have greatly reduced tariff barriers for industrial products. Among the Northern countries there is much joint technical research and development for industry; and a Nordic Investment Bank offers loans for production and exports. The 1976 Nordic Environmental Protection Convention points to the mutual responsibility of the countries to safeguard the environment in the Nordic region and sets some rules for crossnational liabilities and compensations. The Nordic states bordering on the Baltic have signed a convention to protect the marine environment, and Denmark and Sweden have agreed to combat pollution in the Sound.

Because the Nordic Council avoids making recommendations on foreign or defense policies, cooperation in those areas must be advanced through other channels. The foreign ministers meet regularly twice a year, and the Nordic delegations to the various international organizations keep in close touch with each other and generally find themselves in agreement on a large number of issues. Yet there are some different interests and attitudes that hamper development of a common Nordic policy in all international matters—the split on security arrangements, for one example, with Denmark, Iceland, and Norway in NATO, Sweden neutral, and Finland linked to some extent with the USSR by a 1948 treaty of "friendship, cooperation, and mutual assistance" and having to become accustomed to life in the Soviet shadow; and the Danish membership in the EC while other states remained in EFTA. The Nordic states place a great value on foreign policy cooperation, however, and see eye to eye on most issues, even if a common stand cannot always be the result.

Danish political leaders and others have often spoken of Denmark as a bridge between the North and the European Community. Yet the nation's role as bridge or bridge builder is considerably restricted by the fact that on many issues Denmark's first obligation is to the EC and not to the Nordic community. Sometimes it can juggle its obligations; often it cannot. The common Nordic labor market is modified by the eighteen-day rule giving EC citizens preference on job openings in Denmark, for example, although the free movement of Nordic workers has not seemed adversely affected. Denmark signed and ratified the Nordic Convention on the Protection of the Environment even though some Danish administrators thought the government should wait for the development of an EC environment policy. Denmark delayed for several years its ratification of the convention for protecting the Baltic environment until it was clear that the Community did not object. Denmark supported the establishment of the Nordic Investment Bank despite the existence of a similar EC bank. Generally, problems of cooperation stemming from Denmark's EC membership have been solved pragmatically. "Most likely, the Nordic achievements of the past can be retained without EC interference. An expansion of Nordic cooperation into new areas where the EC is also active might prove more difficult."[12] Denmark must continue to juggle its Nordic and its European Community roles, maintaining its ties of values, culture, history, and mutual interests with its Northern friends while reaping the economic benefits and assuming the obligations of an EC member. For a small state whose security and livelihood are affected so deeply and in so many ways by decisions and events outside the Northern region, Nordic cooperation can be only one of the pillars upon which its foreign policy rests.

Notes

Chapter 2

1. Statistical information in this chapter is drawn mainly from the Nordic Statistical Secretariat's *Yearbook of Nordic Statistics 1989/90* (Stockholm: Norstedt, 1990) and from *Denmark: An Official Handbook* (Copenhagen: Danish Ministry of Foreign Affairs, 1974).

2. The terms *Norden* (the North) and *Nordic* are now standard usage in the Northern countries to cover all five of them: Denmark, Norway, Sweden, Iceland, and Finland. *Scandinavia* and *Scandinavian* are used in English, sometimes with reference to all five states, sometimes with reference to all except Finland because of that nation's different language and racial backgrounds, and sometimes with reference to all except Finland and Iceland. I will follow the Northern countries' usage.

3. Dansk Olie og Naturgas, *Energy Facts and Figures* (Horsholm, Denmark: H. C. Jensen, 1987), and Danish Ministry of Energy, *Energy in Denmark: Status Report on Energy Planning, 1987* (Copenhagen: Danish Ministry of Energy, 1987).

4. "Consensual Unions in Denmark" (factsheet, Danish Ministry of Foreign Affairs, 1984).

5. In 1975 Denmark introduced abortion on demand during the first twelve weeks of pregnancy.

6. Herbert Hendin, *Suicide and Scandinavia* (New York: Green and Stratton, 1964), and Donald S. Connery, *The Scandinavians* (New York: Simon and Schuster, 1966), pp. 49–61.

7. United Nations, Department of International Economic and Social Affairs, Statistical Office, *Statistical Yearbook 1983/84* (New York: United Nations, 1986), pp. 454–457, 459–461, 1068–1071; and George Thomas Kurian, *The New Book of World Rankings* (New York: Facts on File, 1984), pp. 98, 102.

8. Kaare Svalastoga, *Prestige, Class, and Mobility* (Copenhagen: Gyldendal, 1959), p. 201.

9. Ibid., p. 68.

10. Erik Jørgen Hansen, *Socialgrupper i Danmark*, study 48 (Copenhagen: Socialforskningsinstituttet, 1984).

187

11. Madeleine Gustafsson, "The Silences of the North," *Dædalus*, 113:2 (Spring 1984), pp. 98–99.

12. "Nordic Voices," *Dædalus*, 113:2 (Spring 1984), p. 8.

13. Arne Melchior, *There Is Something Wonderful in the State of Denmark* (Secaucus, N.J.: Lyle Stuart, 1987), pp. 45, 51.

Chapter 3

1. Palle Lauring, *A History of the Kingdom of Denmark*, 3rd ed. (Copenhagen: Høst & Søn, 1968), pp. 155–156.

2. *Venstre* means "Left," but because this connotes a radicalism that is not characteristic of the present party, I will follow a widely accepted usage and refer to it as the Liberal party.

3. In 1944 Iceland's voters overwhelmingly endorsed the establishment of a republic, and the Icelandic parliament at once took the formal steps to institute that republic, despite a clause in the treaty of union with Denmark that provided for mutual negotiations on such a change. The Danes resented Iceland's unilateral act but accepted it nonetheless.

4. Hannah Arendt, *Eichmann in Jerusalem* (New York: Viking, 1964), p. 171.

5. The text of the 1953 constitution can be found in Albert P. Blaustein and Gisbert H. Flanz, eds., *Constitutions of the Countries of the World* (Dobbs Ferry, N.Y.: Oceana, 1986), vol. 4, pp. 1–99; and in Amos J. Peaslee, ed., *Constitutions of Nations* (The Hague: Martinus Nijhoff, 1956), vol. 1, pp. 730–746.

Chapter 4

1. The Constitution of the Kingdom of Denmark, sections 13 and 15.

2. Because the constitution refers to the monarch as the king, that usage will be followed unless the reference is to the present ruler, Queen Margrethe II.

3. Lord David Cecil, "The Reigning Royalty of Europe," *Life*, August 5, 1957, p. 60.

4. Brief discussions of the monarchy may be found in the factsheets published by the Danish Ministry of Foreign Affairs: "Queen Margrethe II" (1981), "Ten Years on the Throne" (1982), and "Prince Henrik" (1984).

5. Gert Andersen, *The Danish Parliament* (Copenhagen: Schultz, 1988), p. 10.

6. Arne Marquard, *Folketingsårbog 1984-85* (Copenhagen: Schultz, 1985), p. 4.

7. On the use of the referendum, see Kenneth E. Miller, "Policy-making by Referendum: The Danish Experience," *West European Politics*, 5:1 (January 1982), pp. 54–67; and Palle Svensson, "Class, Party and Ideology: A Danish Case Study of Electoral Behaviour in Referendums," *Scandinavian Political Studies*, 7:3 (September 1984), pp. 175–196.

8. Nils Andrén, *Government and Politics in the Nordic Countries* (Stockholm: Almqvist and Wiksell, 1964), p. 46.

9. Quoted in Bent Christensen, "The Danish Ombudsman," *University of Pennsylvania Law Review*, 109 (June 1961), p. 1101.

10. *Folketingets Ombudsmans Beretning for Året 1988* (Copenhagen: Schultz Grafisk, 1989), pp. 11–16.

11. On the ombudsman, see Stephan Hurwitz, *The Ombudsman: Denmark's Parliamentary Commissioner for Civil and Military Administration* (Copenhagen: Det Danske Selskab, 1961); Mogens Lerhard, ed., *The Danish Ombudsman 1955–1969: Seventy-five Cases from the Ombudsman's Reports* (Copenhagen: Schultz, 1972); I. M. Pedersen, "Denmark's Ombudsman," in Donald C. Rowat, ed., *The Ombudsman: Citizen's Defender* (London: Allen & Unwin, 1968), pp. 75–94; and Danish Ministry of Foreign Affairs, "The Ombudsman," factsheet (Copenhagen: Schultz, 1983).

12. Professor Arne Bertelsen, M.F., quoted in *Liberal Debat*, November 20, 1961, p. 8.

13. For brief surveys of Danish law, see N. V. Boeg, ed., *Danish and Norwegian Law: A General Survey* (Copenhagen: G.E.C. Gad, 1963); Nils Herlitz, *Elements of Nordic Public Law* (Stockholm: P. A. Norstedt & Söner, 1969); and Lester Bernhardt Orfield, *The Growth of Scandinavian Law* (Philadelphia: University of Pennsylvania Press, 1953). Useful articles on various aspects of Danish law can be found in the annual publication *Scandinavian Studies in Law* (Stockholm: Almqvist & Wiksell, 1957–).

14. Kenneth E. Miller, "Parliament and Local Government Reform in Denmark," *Parliamentary Affairs*, 24:4 (Autumn 1971), pp. 321–337.

15. On local government, see Jens Christian Birch and Henrik Christoffersen, *Citizen Participation and Local Government in America and Scandinavia* (Gentofte, Denmark: Erling Olsen, 1981); National Association of Local Authorities in Denmark, *Economic and Political Trends in Danish Local Government* (Copenhagen: National Association of Local Authorities in Denmark, 1981); National Association of Local Authorities in Denmark, *Local Government in Denmark* (Copenhagen: National Association of Local Authorities in Denmark, 1983); and Association of County Councils in Denmark, *Regional Self-Government* (Copenhagen: Amtsrådsforeningen i Danmark, 1986).

Chapter 5

1. For fuller descriptions of the electoral system, see Kenneth E. Miller, "The Danish Electoral System," *Parliamentary Affairs*, 18:1 (Winter 1964/65), pp. 71–81; L. N. Johansen, "Denmark," in Geoffrey Hand, ed., *European Electoral Systems Handbook* (London: Butterworth, 1979), pp. 29–57; and Mogens N. Pedersen, "Electing the Folketing," factsheet (Copenhagen: Danish Ministry of Foreign Affairs, 1984).

2. See chapter 3, pp. 26–27. The best sources on the histories of the individual parties are in Danish. Useful though now somewhat outdated discussions of the parties in English may be found in Kenneth E. Miller, *Government and Politics in Denmark* (Boston: Houghton Mifflin, 1968), pp. 57–126, and in

John Fitzmaurice, *Politics in Denmark* (New York: St. Martin's, 1981), pp. 102–126. There are brief accounts in Mogens N. Pedersen, "The Political Parties in Denmark," factsheet (Copenhagen: Danish Ministry of Foreign Affairs, 1982), and Tage Kaarsted, "Danish Politics After 1945," factsheet (Copenhagen: Danish Ministry of Foreign Affairs, 1982).

3. See chapter 3, p. 34.

4. See chapter 3, p. 35.

5. *Economist*, May 28, 1988, p. 50.

6. Poll by Århus University researchers, cited in *Udenrigsministeriets Nyhedsoversigt*, March 15, 1989, p. 3; survey by Institut for Samfundsfag, Copenhagen University, in cooperation with Gallup, reported in *Udenrigsministeriets Nyhedsoversigt*, May 1, 1984, and *Nordisk Kontakt*, no. 9 (1984), p. 652; and Ole Borre, "Some Results from the Danish 1987 Election," *Scandinavian Political Studies*, 10:4 (1987), p. 350.

7. Borre, "Some Results from the Danish 1987 Election," pp. 348–349.

8. The study by Lise Togeby was reported in *Udenrigsministeriets Nyhedsoversigt*, November 7, 1989, p. 6.

9. Survey by Observainstituttet, reported in *Udenrigsministeriets Nyhedsoversigt*, May 30, 1988, p. 3.

Chapter 6

1. Jacob A. Buksti, "Interesseorganisationer i Politik," in Erik Damgaard, ed., *Dansk Demokrati under Forandring* (Copenhagen: Schultz, 1984), p. 53.

2. On the Danish trade unions, see *The Trade Union Movement in Denmark* (Brussels: European Trade Union Institute, 1987) and the pamphlet *LO–A Central Organisation in Denmark* (Copenhagen: LO, 1989). An excellent older study of Danish labor relations is Walter Galenson, *The Danish System of Labor Relations: A Study in Industrial Peace* (Cambridge: Harvard University Press, 1952).

3. Both FTF and AC provide brief summaries in English of their organization and functions: *FTF: Facts, Tasks, Figures* (Copenhagen: FTF, 1982) and *AC: The Danish Confederation of Professional Associations* (Copenhagen: AC, 1987).

4. A good summary of the principal agricultural organizations may be found in P. H. Knudsen and Hans Vedholm, *Farmers' Organisations and the Cooperative Movement* (Copenhagen: Agricultural Council of Denmark, n.d.).

5. Jacob A. Buksti and Lars Nørby Johansen, "Variations in Organizational Participation in Government: The Case of Denmark," *Scandinavian Political Studies*, 2:3 (1979), p. 208.

6. Svend Bichel, president of the association, in its annual report, *Danmarks Naturfredningsforenings Årsberetning 1987*, p. 2.

7. OOA stands for Organisation til Oplysning om Atomkraft (Organization for Information on Nuclear Power).

8. "Fakta om Forbrugerrådet," pamphlet (Copenhagen: Forbrugerrådet, March 1984), p. 3.

9. Ole Borre, Jørgen Elklit, and Ole Tonsgaard, "The Danish Election to the European Parliament in June 1979: A New Referendum?" *Scandinavian Political Studies*, 2:3 (1979), pp. 299–310; Torben Worre, "The 1979 European

Election in Denmark: An Analysis of Participation, Choice of Party, and Attitude Towards Europe," *Cooperation and Conflict*, 16:2 (May 1981), pp. 73–89; and Torben Worre, "The Danish Euro-Party System," *Scandinavian Political Studies*, 10:1 (1987), pp. 79–95.

10. Harry Haue, Jørgen Olsen, and Jørn Aarup-Kristensen, *Det Ny Danmark 1890–1985: Udviklingslinjer og Tendens*, 3rd ed. (Copenhagen: Munksgaard, 1985), p. 59.

11. On the women's suffrage movement in Denmark, see Drude Dahlerup, "Women's Entry into Politics: The Experience of the Danish Local and General Elections 1908–1920," *Scandinavian Political Studies*, 1:2–3 (1978), pp. 141–146; and Joni Lovenduski, *Women and European Politics: Contemporary Feminism and Public Policy* (Amherst: University of Massachusetts Press, 1986), pp. 49–50.

12. Haue, Olsen, and Aarup-Kristensen, *Det Ny Danmark*, p. 61.

13. Torild Skard and Elina Haavio-Mannila, "Women in Parliament," in Elina Haavio-Mannila et al., eds., *Unfinished Democracy: Women in Nordic Politics* (Oxford: Pergamon Press, 1985), p. 79.

14. Louise Wolfson, "Embedsmanden Er en Mand," *Lige Nu*, no. 26 (June 1988), p. 9. On women in public life in Denmark and in Scandinavia generally, see the special issue of *Scandinavian Review*, 65:3 (1977), edited by Carol Gold and Merete Ries.

15. Skard and Haavio-Mannila, "Women in Parliament," p. 5.

16. Martin Heisler, "Corporate Pluralism Revisited: Where Is the Theory?" *Scandinavian Political Studies*, 2:3 (1979), p. 278; and Buksti, "Interesseorganisationer i Politik," p. 52.

17. William E. Laux, *Interest Groups in Danish Politics* (Ann Arbor, Mich.: University Microfilms, 1963), p. 215.

18. Erik Damgaard, "The Importance and Limits of Party Government: Problems of Governance in Denmark," *Scandinavian Political Studies*, 7:2 (June 1984), pp. 101–103.

19. Lars Nørby Johansen and Ole P. Kristensen, "Corporatist Traits in Denmark, 1946–1976," in Gerhard Lehmbruch and Philippe C. Schmitter, eds., *Patterns of Corporatist Policy-Making* (London and Beverly Hills: Sage, 1982), p. 191. On the debate over the definitions of corporatism, see Heisler, "Corporate Pluralism Revisited."

20. Buksti and Johansen, "Variations in Organizational Participation in Government," p. 199.

21. Laux, *Interest Groups in Danish Politics*, p. 311.

22. Stein Rokkan, "Norway: Numerical Democracy and Corporate Pluralism," in Robert A. Dahl, ed., *Political Oppositions in Western Democracies* (New Haven, Conn., and London: Yale University Press, 1966), p. 105.

23. Erik Damgaard, "Causes, Forms, and Consequences of Sectoral Policymaking: Some Danish Evidence," *European Journal of Political Research*, 14 (1986), p. 284; and Erik Damgaard, "The Importance and Limits of Party Government," p. 108.

24. Hans Jørgen Nielsen, "Ambiguities in Attitudes Towards Interest Group Influence," *Scandinavian Political Studies*, 8:1–2 (June 1985), p. 79.

Chapter 7

1. Frederic C. Howe, *Denmark: A Cooperative Commonwealth* (New York: Harcourt Brace, 1921), pp. iii–iv.

2. Kjeld Philip, *Staten og Fattigdommen* (Copenhagen: Jul. Gjellerups Forlag, 1947), pp. 67–68.

3. Lars Nørby Johansen, "Denmark," in Peter Flora, ed., *Growth to Limits: The Western European Welfare States Since World War II* (Berlin and New York: Walter de Gruyter, 1986), vol. 1, p. 300.

4. General summaries can be found in the *Report of the Government of Denmark* to the U.N. Interregional Consultation on Developmental Social Welfare Policies and Programmes, Vienna, September 7–15, 1987; "Social Security, Danish-style," factsheet (Copenhagen: Danish Ministry of Foreign Affairs, 1979); and Danish Employers Confederation, *Social Benefits and Employer Contributions* (Copenhagen: DA, 1987). Mimeographed summaries of particular programs, in English, can usually be obtained from the appropriate government department, generally the Ministry of Social Affairs but for some programs the Ministry of Labor.

5. Johansen, "Denmark," p. 303.

6. Quoted in Tad Szulc, "How We Can Help Ourselves Age with Dignity," *Parade Magazine*, May 29, 1988, p. 5.

7. John Logue, "The Welfare State: Victim of Its Success," *Dædalus*, 108:4 (Fall 1979), p. 75.

8. See the table in Eric Einhorn and John Logue, *Welfare States in Hard Times: Denmark and Sweden in the 1970s* (Kent, Ohio: Kent Popular Press, 1980), p. 12.

9. See chapter 3, pp. 35–36. A good analysis of factors in the 1973 election may be found in Mogens N. Pedersen, *The Defeat of All Parties: The Danish Folketing Election of 1973*, Occasional Paper no. 10 (Odense, Denmark: Odense University, Institut for Offentlig Økonomi og Politik, 1983).

10. Johansen, "Denmark," p. 317.

11. For good summaries of criticisms of the welfare state and answers to them, see Logue, "The Welfare State: Victim of Its Success"; and Jacob Vedel-Petersen, "The Experience of the Danish Welfare State," in S. N. Eisenstadt and Ora Ahimeir, *The Welfare State and Its Aftermath* (London and Sydney: Croom Helm, 1985), pp. 229–236.

12. Gøsta Esping-Andersen, *Politics Against Markets: The Social Democratic Road to Power* (Princeton, N.J.: Princeton University Press, 1985), p. 269.

13. Niels Salicath, *Danish Social Housing Corporations* (Copenhagen: Danish Ministry of Housing and Building, 1987), vol. 1, pp. 8, 17.

14. *Forbrugerombudsmanden Beretning 1987* (Copenhagen: Forbrugerombudsmanden, 1988), p. 9.

15. "Nature Conservation in Denmark," factsheet (Copenhagen: Danish Ministry of Foreign Affairs, 1983), p. 2.

16. For the first steps toward environmental protection, see Joanne Stone Wyman, *The Impact of Issues on Political Relationships: A Case Study of Denmark's Environmental Policy* (Ph.D. dissertation, Brandeis University, 1977).

17. Lennart J. Lundqvist, "Saving the Baltic," *Scandinavian Review*, 64:4 (December 1976), pp. 46–53.

18. For a brief history of the Danish police, see E. O. Hjellemo, "History of the Nordic Police Systems—The Evolution of Policing in Denmark and Norway," in Johannes Knutsson, Eckart Kuhlhorn, and Albert Reiss, Jr., *Police and the Social Order: Contemporary Research Perspectives*, Report No. 6, National Swedish Council for Crime Prevention (Stockholm: Kristianstad, 1979), pp. 14–29.

19. Figures are from Nordic Statistical Secretariat, *Yearbook of Nordic Statistics 1989/90* (Stockholm: Norstedt, 1990), pp. 332–334. The murder rate in the United States is taken from *Crime in the United States, Uniform Crime Reports* (Washington, D.C.: FBI, Department of Justice, August 1989), p. 47.

20. *Crime Prevention Considerations in Local Planning* (Copenhagen: Det Kriminalpræventive Råd, 1984), pp. 3–14.

21. Nordic Statistical Secretariat, *Yearbook of Nordic Statistics 1989/90*, p. 336. The rate per 100,000 inhabitants went from 174 in 1950 to 205 in 1988.

22. Michael S. Serrill, "A Microcosm of Society," *Scandinavian Review*, 67:3 (September 1979), p. 43.

Chapter 8

1. Petter Jakob Bjerve, "Government Economic Planning and Control," in Henning Friis, ed., *Scandinavia Between East and West* (Ithaca, N.Y.: Cornell University Press, 1950), p. 52.

2. Erik Damgaard, *Crisis Politics in Denmark, 1974–86* (Aarhus, Denmark: University of Aarhus, Institute of Political Science, 1986), p. 10.

3. Copenhagen HandelsBank, in *Denmark Quarterly Review*, February 1988, p. 2.

4. "Denmark: The Smug Debtor," *Economist*, September 3, 1988, p. 68.

5. Copenhagen HandelsBank, in *Denmark Quarterly Review*, August 1989, pp. 14–15.

6. *The Danish Tax Reform* (Copenhagen: Danish Ministry of Taxes and Duties, June 1986); OECD, *Economic Survey: Denmark, 1985/1986* (Paris: OECD, 1986); and Ib Garodkin, *Håndbog i Dansk Politik, 1988* (Copenhagen: Munksgaard, 1988), p. 236. The dollar equivalents are calculated at the exchange rate of 1 kroner = $0.148.

7. On the national tax system today, see OECD, *Economic Survey: Denmark, 1987/1988* (Paris: OECD, 1988), pp. 47–50. In 1989 the OECD found Denmark to have the second heaviest tax burden among industrial nations. Sweden ranked first.

8. Ernest Goldstein, *American Enterprise and Scandinavian Antitrust Law* (Austin: University of Texas Press, 1963); OECD, *Restrictive Business Practices: Comparative Summary of Legislations* [sic] *in Europe and America* (Paris: OECD, 1964); and OECD, *Guide to Legislation on Restrictive Business Practices: Europe and North America* (Paris: OECD, 1964), II.

9. Nordic Statistical Secretariat, *Yearbook of Nordic Statistics 1989/90* (Stockholm: Norstedt, 1990), p. 136. These are 1987 figures.

10. OECD, *Economic Survey: Denmark, 1986*, p. 45.

11. The text of the September Agreement is found in Walter Galenson, *The Danish System of Labor Relations: A Study in Industrial Peace* (Cambridge, Mass.: Harvard University Press, 1952), pp. 291–293, and that of the current General Agreement may be found in a pamphlet published by DA and LO.

12. *Arbejdsretligt Tidsskrift 1987* (Copenhagen: Jurist og Økononomforbundets Forlag, 1988), p. 9. These yearly volumes summarize the court's work and findings. An English translation of the statute is available in a pamphlet from DA.

13. Jacob A. Buksti, "Policy-making and Unemployment in Denmark," in Jeremy Richardson and Roger Henning, eds., *Unemployment: Policy Responses of Western Democracies* (London: Sage, 1984), p. 219.

14. Mogens Lykketoft, "Toward Economic Democracy: Wage Earners' Funds," *Scandinavian Review*, no. 2 (1977), pp. 40–45; and Gøsta Esping-Andersen, *Politics Against Markets: The Social Democratic Road to Power* (Princeton, N.J.: Princeton University Press, 1985), pp. 291–313.

15. Kjeld Ejler, "The Marketing of Farm Products," in *Agricultural Production and Marketing* (Copenhagen: Agricultural Council of Denmark, 1987), p. 27.

16. Agricultural Council of Denmark, *Landbrugsraadet 1987/88* (Copenhagen: Agricultural Council of Denmark, 1988), p. 1.

17. *Research, Advisory Services, Education* (Agricultural Council of Denmark, 1987).

Chapter 9

1. Quoted in Marit Bakke, "Government and the Arts in Denmark," in Milton C. Cummings, Jr., and Richard S. Katz, eds., *The Patron State: Government and the Arts in Europe, North America, and Japan* (New York and Oxford: Oxford University Press, 1987), p. 138.

2. The history of Danish aid to the arts and literature is summarized in ibid., pp. 136–156.

3. *Udenrigsministeriets Nyhedsoversigt*, October 25, 1988, pp. 6–7.

4. Claes Kastholm Hansen, "Dansk filmer blomstrer, men . . . ," *Nordisk Kontakt*, no. 5 (1988), p. 76. Hansen was himself one of the film consultants from 1984 to 1987.

5. For more information on Danish movie-making, see the brief summary in "Danish Film," factsheet (Copenhagen: Danish Ministry of Foreign Affairs, 1983); *Denmark: An Official Handbook* (Copenhagen: Danish Ministry of Foreign Affairs, 1974), pp. 795–815; and, especially, the annual illustrated report (in English) of the Film Institute, *Danish Films*.

6. Bakke, "Government and the Arts in Denmark," p. 144.

7. Ibid., p. 155.

8. *Denmark: An Official Handbook*, p. 226.

9. On the established Church generally, see Poul Hartling, ed., *The Danish Church* (Copenhagen: Det Danske Selskab, 1965).

10. *Bien*, July 27, 1989, p. 1; and *New York Times*, June 11, 1989, p. 3.

11. Arne Melchior, *There Is Something Wonderful in the State of Denmark* (Secaucus, N.J.: Lyle Stuart, 1987), p. 64.

12. Poul Dam, "A 'Typical' Danish Folk High School," in Arne Andresén, ed., *The Danish Folk High School To-day: A Description of Residential Education in Denmark* (Esbjerg, Denmark: Arnold Thomsen, 1985), p. 9.

13. John C. Merrill and Harold A. Fisher, *The World's Great Dailies: Profiles of Fifty Newspapers* (New York: Hastings House, 1980), p. 81. Circulation figures for this and other papers are for the first half of 1989 [Nordic Statistical Secretariat, *Yearbook of Nordic Statistics 1989/90* (Stockholm: Norstedt, 1990), p. 353].

14. Merrill and Fisher, *The World's Great Dailies*, pp. 81–82.

Chapter 10

1. Nils Andrén, "Changing Strategic Perspectives in Northern Europe," and Krister Wahlback, "The Nordic Region in Twentieth-Century European Politics," in Bengt Sundelius, ed., *Foreign Policies of Northern Europe* (Boulder, Colo.: Westview, 1982), pp. 26, 79.

2. A typical example was the sentence in the NATO Nuclear Planning Group Communique of October 22, 1986: "Denmark reserved its position on INF and space and defence systems" [*NATO Review*, 34:5 (October 1986), p. 33].

3. Jacob A. Buksti, "Corporate Structures in Danish EC Policy: Patterns of Organizational Participation and Adaptation," *Journal of Common Market Studies*, 19:2 (December 1980), p. 144.

4. Michael Krasner and Nikolaj Petersen, "Peace and Politics: The Danish Peace Movement and Its Impact on National Security Policy," *Journal of Peace Research*, 23:2 (June 1986), p. 160.

5. Forsvarsministeriet, *Årlig Redegørelse 1987* (Copenhagen: Forsvarsministeriet, 1988), pp. 89–91, and statistics in *NATO Review*, 35:6 (December 1987), pp. 29–30.

6. Forsvarskommandoen, *Forsvarets Rolle* (Copenhagen: Forsvarskommandoen, 1987), p. 45.

7. See chapter 8, pp. 141, 142.

8. Sonia Mazey, "European Community Action on Behalf of Women: The Limits of Legislation," *Journal of Common Market Studies*, 27:1 (September 1988), p. 73.

9. Torben Worre, "Denmark at the Crossroads: The Danish Referendum of 28 February 1986 on the EC Reform Package," *Journal of Common Market Studies*, 26:4 (June 1988), p. 361.

10. Claes Wiklund and Bengt Sundelius, "Nordic Cooperation in the Seventies: Trends and Patterns," *Scandinavian Political Studies*, 2:2 (1979), pp. 106–109.

11. Carl-Einar Stålvant, "Nordic Policies Toward International Economic Cooperation," in Bengt Sundelius, ed., *Foreign Policies of Northern Europe*, pp. 114–119.

12. Wiklund and Sundelius, "Nordic Cooperation in the Seventies," p. 112.

Further Readings

In view of the likely audience for this book, I have limited the notes and references almost entirely to publications in English. A substantial and growing body of works in Danish has been very helpful for my understanding of politics and government in Denmark.

Chapter 2

Anderson, Robert T. *Denmark: Success of a Developing Nation*. Cambridge, Mass.: Schenkman, 1975.

Anderson, Robert T., and Barbara Gallatin Anderson. *The Vanishing Village: A Danish Maritime Community*. Seattle: University of Washington Press, 1964.

Bach, H. C., and Jørgen Taagholt. *Greenland and the Arctic Region: Resources and Security Policy*, 2nd ed. Copenhagen: Information and Welfare Service of the Danish Defence, 1982.

Bure, Kristjan, ed. *Greenland*. Ringkjøbing, Denmark: A. Rasmussen, 1961.

Fullerton, Brian. *Scandinavia: An Introductory Geography*. New York: Praeger, 1972.

Gad, Finn. *The History of Greenland*. 3 vols. London: C. Hurst, 1970, and Montreal: McGill-Queen's University Press, 1970, 1973, 1982.

Kandel, Denise B., and Gerald S. Lesser. *Youth in Two Worlds: United States and Denmark*. San Francisco: Jossey-Bass, 1972.

Koch-Nielsen, Inger. *New Family Patterns: Divorces in Denmark*. Copenhagen: Danish National Institute of Social Research, 1987.

Körmendi, Eszter. *Refugees in Denmark*. Copenhagen: Danish National Institute of Social Research, 1987.

MacHaffie, Ingeborg S., and Margaret A. Nielsen. *Of Danish Ways*. Minneapolis: Dillon Press, 1976.

Malaurie, Jean. *The Last Kings of Thule: A Year Among the Polar Eskimos of Greenland*. New York: Thomas Y. Crowell, 1956.

Miller, Kenneth E. *Denmark*. Vol. 83, World Bibliographical Series. Oxford and Santa Barbara: ABC-Clio Press, 1987.

Millward, Roy. *Scandinavian Lands*. London: Macmillan, and New York: St. Martin's, 1965.

Sømme, Axel, ed. *A Geography of Norden: Denmark, Finland, Iceland, Norway.* London: Heinemann, 1968.

West, John F. *Faroe: The Emergence of a Nation.* London: C. Hurst, and New York: Paul S. Eriksson, 1972.

Williamson, Kenneth. *The Atlantic Islands: A Study of the Faeroe Life and Scene.* London: Routledge & Kegan Paul, and New York: Fernhill House, 1970.

Wylie, Jonathan. *The Faroe Islands: Social Change and Cultural Continuity.* Lexington: University Press of Kentucky, 1986.

Chapter 3

Brøndsted, Johannes. *The Vikings.* Baltimore, Md.: Penguin, 1965.

Derry, T. K. *A History of Scandinavia: Norway, Sweden, Denmark, Finland and Iceland.* London: Allen & Unwin, and Minneapolis: University of Minneapolis Press, 1979.

Flender, Harold. *Rescue in Denmark.* New York: Simon and Schuster, 1963.

Foote, Peter G., and David M. Wilson. *The Viking Achievement: A Survey of the Society and Culture of Early Scandinavia.* London: Sidgwick & Jackson, 1980.

Goldberger, Leo, ed. *The Rescue of the Danish Jews: Moral Courage Under Stress.* New York: New York University Press, 1987.

Hæstrup, Jørgen. *Secret Alliance: A Study of the Danish Resistance Movement.* 3 vols. Odense, Denmark: Odense University Press, 1976–1977.

Jones, W. Glyn. *Denmark.* New York: Praeger, 1970.

Kendrick, T. D. *A History of the Vikings.* New York: Barnes & Noble, 1968.

Mentze, Ernst. *5 Years: The Occupation of Denmark in Pictures.* Malmö, Sweden: A-B Allhem, 1946.

Nordstrom, Byron J., ed. *Dictionary of Scandinavian History.* Westport, Conn.: Greenwood, 1986.

Oakley, Stewart. *A Short History of Denmark.* New York: Praeger, 1972.

Outze, Borge, ed. *Denmark During the German Occupation.* Copenhagen: Scandinavian Publishing Company, 1946.

Petrow, Richard. *The Bitter Years: The Invasion and Occupation of Denmark and Norway, April 1940–May 1945.* New York: William Morrow, 1974.

Randsborg, Klaus. *The Viking Age in Denmark: The Formation of a State.* London: Duckworth, and New York: St. Martin's, 1980.

Roesdahl, Else. *Viking Age Denmark.* London: British Museum Publications, 1982.

Toyne, S. M. *The Scandinavians in History.* Port Washington, N.Y.: Kennikat Press, 1970.

Chapter 4

Arter, David. *The Nordic Parliaments: A Comparative Analysis.* New York: St. Martin's, 1984.

––––––. *The Danish Criminal Code.* Copenhagen: G.E.C. Gad, 1958.

Elder, Neil, Alastair H. Thomas, and David Arter. *The Consensual Democracies?: The Government and Politics of the Scandinavian States.* London: Martin Robertson, 1982.

Fitzmaurice, John. *Politics in Denmark*. New York: St. Martin's, 1981.

Ginsburg, Ruth Bader. *A Selective Survey of English Language Studies on Scandinavian Law*. South Hackensack, N.J.: Fred B. Rothman, 1970.

Iuul, Stig, Åke Malmstrom, and Jens Søndergaard. *Scandinavian Legal Bibliography*. Stockholm: Almqvist & Wiksell, 1961.

Miller, Kenneth E. *Government and Politics in Denmark*. Boston: Houghton Mifflin, 1968.

Søndergaard, Jens. *Danish Legal Publications in English, French and German*. Uppsala, Sweden: Almqvist & Wiksell, 1964.

Chapter 5

Berglund, Sten, and Ulf Lindstrom. *The Scandinavian Party Systems*. Lund, Sweden: Studentlitteratur, 1978.

Borre, Ole. "Critical Electoral Change in Scandinavia." In R. J. Dalton, S. C. Flanagan, and P. A. Beck, eds. *Electoral Change in Advanced Industrial Democracies: Realignment or Dealignment?* Princeton, N.J.: Princeton University Press, 1984.

Carstairs, Andrew M. *A Short History of Electoral Systems in Western Europe*. London: George Allen & Unwin, 1980.

Castles, Francis. *The Social Democratic Image of Society: A Study of the Achievements and Origins of Scandinavian Social Democracy in Comparative Perspective*. London: Routledge & Kegan Paul, 1978.

Einhorn, Eric S., and John Logue. "Continuity and Change in the Scandinavian Party Systems." In Steven Wolinetz, ed., *Parties and Party Systems in Liberal Democracies*. London and New York: Routledge & Kegan Paul, 1988.

Esping-Andersen, Gøsta. *Politics Against Markets: The Social Democratic Road to Power*. Princeton, N.J.: Princeton University Press, 1985.

Logue, John. *Socialism and Abundance: Radical Socialism in the Danish Welfare State*. Minneapolis: University of Minnesota Press, 1982.

Miller, Kenneth E. "Danish Socialism and the Kansas Prairie." *Kansas Historical Quarterly*, 38:2 (Summer 1972), pp. 156–168.

Pedersen, Mogens N. "The Danish 'Working Multiparty System': Breakdown or Adaptation." In Hans Daalder, ed. *Party Systems in Denmark, Austria, Switzerland, the Netherlands and Belgium*. New York: St. Martin's, 1987.

Thomas, Alastair H. "Social Democracy in Scandinavia: Can Dominance Be Regained?" In William E. Paterson and Alastair H. Thomas, eds. *The Future of Social Democracy*. Oxford: Clarendon Press, 1986. Pp. 172–222.

Chapter 6

Damgaard, Erik, and Kjell A. Eliassen. "Corporate Pluralism in Danish Law-Making." *Scandinavian Political Studies*, 1:4 (new series, 1978), pp. 285–313.

Laux, William E. "Agricultural Interest Groups in Danish Politics: An Examination of Group Frustration Amidst Political Stability." *Western Political Quarterly*, 21:3 (September 1968), pp. 436–455.

Pedersen, Clemens, ed. *The Danish Cooperative Movement*, 3rd rev. ed. Copenhagen: Det Danske Selskab, 1977.

Raffaele, Joseph A. *Labor Leadership in Italy and Denmark*. Madison: University of Wisconsin Press, 1962.

Skard, Torild, and Elina Haavio-Mannila. "Equality Between the Sexes—Myth or Reality in Norden." *Dædalus*, 113:1 (Winter 1984), pp. 141–167.

Chapter 7

Aaron, Thomas J. *The Control of Police Discretion: The Danish Experience*. Springfield, Ill.: Charles C. Thomas, 1966.

Allardt, Erik, et al., eds. *Nordic Democracy: Ideas, Issues, and Institutions in Politics, Economy, Education, Social and Cultural Affairs of Denmark, Finland, Iceland, Norway, and Sweden*. Copenhagen: Det Danske Selskab, 1981.

Bishop, Norman, ed. *Scandinavian Criminal Policy and Criminology 1980–85*. Copenhagen: Scandinavian Research Council for Criminology, 1985.

Bruun, Kettil, ed. *Controlling Psychotropic Drugs: The Nordic Experience*. London: Croom Helm, and New York: St. Martin's, 1983.

Buksti, Jacob A. "Policy-making and Unemployment in Denmark." In Jeremy Richardson and Roger Henning, eds. *Unemployment: Policy Responses of Western Democracies*. London: Sage, 1984. Pp. 271–273.

Danish Ministry of Labor. *Description of the Danish Unemployment Insurance System*. Copenhagen: Danish Ministry of Labor, 1987.

Danish Ministry of Social Affairs. *Pensioner: What Are Your Possibilities? An Introduction to Danish Old Age Policy*. Copenhagen: Danish Ministry of Social Affairs, n.d.

Einhorn, Eric S., and John Logue. *Modern Welfare States: Politics and Policies in Social Democratic Scandinavia*. New York: Praeger, 1989.

Esping-Andersen, Gøsta, and Walter Korpi. "From Poor Relief to Institutional Welfare States: The Development of Scandinavian Social Policy." In Robert Erikson, Erik Jørgen Hansen, Stein Ringen, and Hannu Uusitalo, eds. *The Scandinavian Model: Welfare States and Welfare Research*. Armonk, N.Y., and London: M. E. Sharpe, 1987. Pp. 39–74.

Heckscher, Gunnar. *The Welfare State and Beyond: Successes and Problems in Scandinavia*. Minneapolis: University of Minnesota Press, 1984.

Johansen, Lars Nørby. *The Danish Welfare State, 1945–1980: Institutional Profile and Basic Tables*. Odense, Denmark: Odense University, Institute for Social Science, 1982.

Lønberg, Arne. *The Penal System of Denmark*. Copenhagen: Danish Ministry of Justice, Department of Prison and Probation, 1975.

Marcussen, Ernst. *Social Welfare in Denmark*, 4th ed. Copenhagen: Det Danske Selskab, 1980.

Svare, Annika, and Ulla Bondeson. "Criminological Research in Scandinavia." In Michael Tonry and Norval Morris, eds. *Crime and Justice: An Annual Review of Research*. Chicago: University of Chicago Press, 1985. Vol. 6, pp. 237–259.

Chapter 8

Buksti, Jacob A. "Bread-and-Butter Agreement and High Politics Disagreement: Some Reflections on the Contextual Impact on Agricultural Interests in EC Policy-Making." *Scandinavian Political Studies*, 6:4 (December 1983), pp. 261–280.

―――. *Conciliation in Industrial Disputes*. Copenhagen: DA, 1988.

Federation of Danish Industries. *Drive for Growth: A Statement on Industrial Policy in the 1980s*. Copenhagen: Industrirådet, 1984.

Flanagan, Robert J., David W. Soskice, Lloyd Ulman. *Unionism, Economic Stabilization, and Incomes Policies: European Experience*. Washington, D.C.: Brookings Institution, 1983.

Gustafsson, Bo, ed. *Post-Industrial Society*. New York: St. Martin's, 1979.

Hasselbalch, Ole. *Worker Participation in Decision-making Processes*. Copenhagen: DA, n.d.

Katzenstein, Peter. *Small States in World Markets: Industrial Policy in Europe*. Ithaca, N.Y.: Cornell University Press, 1985.

Lafferty, William M. *Economic Development and the Response of Labor in Scandinavia*. Oslo: Universitetsforlaget, 1971.

Madsen, Henrik Jess. "Class Power and Participatory Equality: Attitudes Towards Economic Democracy in Denmark and Sweden." *Scandinavian Political Studies*, 3:4 (1980), pp. 277–298.

Mikkelsen, Arne. "Denmark: Economic Tensions and Changing Priorities." In Det Økonomiske Råd. *Economic Growth in a Nordic Perspective*. Copenhagen: Det Økonomiske Råd, 1984. Pp. 73–99.

Ølgaard, Anders. *The Danish Economy*. Brussels and Luxembourg: Commission of the European Communities, 1980.

Sløk, Axel. *Participation and Cooperation on the Danish Labour Market*, 2nd ed. Copenhagen: DA, 1979.

Uhr, C. G. "Economic Development in Denmark, Norway, and Sweden." In Karl H. Cerny, ed. *Scandinavia at the Polls: Recent Political Trends in Denmark, Norway, and Sweden*. Washington, D.C.: American Enterprise Institute, 1977. Pp. 219–248.

Chapter 9

Bamberger, Ib Nathan. *The Viking Jews: A History of the Jews in Denmark*. New York: Shengold, 1983.

Boesen, Gudmund. *Danish Museums*. Copenhagen: Committee for Danish Activities Abroad, 1966.

Bordwell, David. *The Films of Carl-Theodor Dreyer*. Berkeley and Los Angeles: University of California Press, 1981.

Cowie, Peter. "Scandinavian Cinema: Denmark." *Scandinavian Review*, 72:2 (Summer 1984), pp. 76–84.

Harrison, K. C. *Libraries in Scandinavia*, 2nd ed. London: Andre Deutsch, 1969.

Hunter, Leslie Stannard, ed. *Scandinavian Churches: The Development of the Churches of Denmark, Finland, Iceland, Norway, and Sweden*. London: Faber & Faber, and Minneapolis: Augsburg, 1965.

Idorn, John. *Sport in Denmark: The Development of Danish Physical Education and Training.* Copenhagen: Det Danske Selskab, 1978.

Knudsen, Johannes. *A Danish Rebel: A Study of N.F.S. Grundtvig.* Philadelphia: Muhlenberg Press, 1955.

Marker, Frederick J., and Lise-Lone Marker. *The Scandinavian Theatre: A Short History.* Oxford: Basil Blackwell, 1975.

Rørdam, Thomas. *The Danish Folk High Schools,* 2nd ed. Copenhagen: Det Danske Selskab, 1980.

Rossel, Sven H. *A History of Scandinavian Literature (1870–1980).* Minneapolis: University of Minnesota Press, 1982.

Sauerberg, Steen, and Niels Thomsen. "The Political Role of Mass Communication in Denmark." In Karl H. Cerny, ed. *Scandinavia at the Polls: Recent Political Trends in Denmark, Norway, and Sweden.* Washington, D.C.: American Enterprise Institute, 1977. Pp. 181–216.

Secretariat for Nordic Cultural Cooperation. *Adult Education in the Nordic Countries: Denmark.* 1976.

Struwe, Kamma, ed. *Schools and Education in Denmark,* 3rd ed. Copenhagen: Det Danske Selskab, 1981.

Stybe, Svend Erik. *Copenhagen University: 500 Years of Science and Scholarship.* Copenhagen: Bianco Lunos, 1979.

Thodberg, N.F.S., and A. Pontoppidan, eds. *N.F.S. Grundtvig: Tradition and Renewal.* Copenhagen: Det Danske Selskab, 1983.

Von Haven, Mogens. *The Royal Danish Ballet,* 2nd ed. Copenhagen: Gyldendal, 1964.

Chapter 10

Auken, Svend, Jacob Buksti, and Carsten Lehman Sørensen. "Denmark Joins Europe: Patterns of Adaptation in the Danish Political and Administrative Processes as a Result of Membership of the European Communities." *Journal of Common Market Studies,* 14:1 (September 1975), pp. 1–36.

Dreyer, H. Peter. "Scandinavia Faces Europe." In Peter Christian Ludz, H. Peter Dreyer, Charles Pentland, and Lothar Ruhl. *Dilemmas of the Atlantic Alliance: Two Germanys, Scandinavia, Canada, NATO and the EEC.* New York: Praeger, 1975. Pp. 73–149.

Einhorn, Eric S. *National Security and Domestic Politics in Post-War Denmark: Some Principal Issues, 1945–1961.* Odense, Denmark: Odense University Press, 1975.

Espersen, Mogens, et al. *Denmark's Defence.* Copenhagen: Information and Welfare Services of the Danish Defence, 1986.

Flynn, Gregory, ed. *NATO'S Northern Allies: The National Security Policies of Belgium, Denmark, the Netherlands, and Norway.* Totowa, N.J.: Rowman & Allanheld, 1985.

Haagerup, Niels Jørgen. *A Brief Introduction to Danish Foreign Policy and Defense,* 2nd ed. Copenhagen: Information and Welfare Services of the Danish Defence, 1980.

———. "The Nordic Peace Movements." In Walter Laqueur and Robert Hunter, eds. *European Peace Movements and the Future of the Western Alliance*. New Brunswick, N.J., and Oxford: Transaction Books, 1985. Pp. 144–165.

Haskel, Barbara G. *The Scandinavian Option: Opportunities and Opportunity Costs in Postwar Scandinavian Foreign Affairs*. Oslo: Universitetsforlaget, 1976.

Holbraad, Carsten. "Denmark: Half-Hearted Partner." In Nils Ørvik, ed. *Semi-alignment and Western Security*. New York: St. Martin's, 1986. Pp. 15–60.

Miljan, Toivo. *The Reluctant Europeans: The Attitudes of the Nordic Countries Towards European Integration*. London: Hurst, and Montreal: McGill-Queen's University Press, 1977.

Møller, J. Ørstrøm. "Danish EC Decision-Making: An Insider's View." *Journal of Common Market Studies*, 21:3 (March 1983), pp. 245–260.

Petersen, Nikolaj. "The Security Policies of Small NATO Countries: Factors of Change." *Cooperation and Conflict*, 23:3 (1988), pp. 145–162.

Sundelius, Bengt. *Managing Transnationalism in Northern Europe*. Boulder, Colo.: Westview, 1978.

Taylor, William J., Jr., and Paul M. Cole, eds. *Nordic Defense: Comparative Decision Making*. Lexington, Mass.: Lexington Books, 1985.

Wendt, Frantz. *Cooperation in the Nordic Countries: Achievements and Obstacles*. Stockholm: Almqvist & Wiksell, 1981.

Acronyms

AC	Central Organization of Danish Professional Workers (Akademikernes Centralorganisation)
AOF	Workers Educational Association (Arbejdernes Oplysningsforbund)
ATP	Labor Market Supplementary Pension Plan (Arbejdsmarkedets Tillægspension)
CAP	Common Agricultural Policy
CFP	Common Fisheries Policy
DA	Danish Employers' Confederation (Dansk Arbejdsgiverforening)
DJ	Danish Union of Journalists (Dansk Journalist Forbund)
DK	Danish Women's Society (Danske Kvindesamfund)
DKN	National Council of Women in Denmark (Danske Kvinders Nationalråd)
DR	Radio Denmark (Danmarks Radio)
EC	European Community
EEC	European Economic Community
EF	Folkebevægelsen mod EF (People's Movement Against the European Community
EFTA	European Free Trade Association
FTF	Joint Council of Salaried Employees and Civil Servants (Fællesrådet for Tjenestemænd og Funktionærer)
GDP	gross domestic product
GNP	gross national product
HF	Higher Preparatory Examination (*højere forberedelseseksamen*)
LO	Danish Federation of Trade Unions (Landsorganisationen i Danmark)
MCA	Monopoly Control Authority (*monopoltilsynet*)
MF	Member of the Folketing
MRC	Market Relations Committee (*Markedsudvalget*)
NATO	North Atlantic Treaty Organization
OECD	Organization for Economic Cooperation and Development

OOA   Organisation til Oplysning om Atomkraft (Organization for
        Information on Nuclear Power)
OPEC   Organization of Petroleum Exporting Countries
SF   Socialistisk Folkeparti (Socialist Peoples party)
U.N.   United Nations
VAT   value-added tax

About the Book and Author

The Denmark of the 1990s contrasts sharply to that of the immediate postwar years. Once detached politically, if not economically, from Europe and interested primarily in Scandinavian regional cooperation, Denmark has emerged from its neutral status to become a member of both the European Community and NATO. Once a model of a politically stable, advanced welfare state, the nation has become a divided polity. These international and domestic changes have affected the level of consensus in the society, brought divisive issues to the public agenda, complicated decision making, and stimulated the formation of new political parties as well as new interest organizations and popular movements.

Despite the controversies and divisions, Denmark maintains its vibrant democratic society and rich cultural life. The welfare state endures, although with marginal changes and some reductions in government spending. Pioneering efforts have been undertaken in new fields, including consumer protection and the promotion of equal rights for women; and new departures, such as economic democracy, are widely debated. This mixture of social welfare, economic planning, political democracy, and labor-market and industrial-relations policies marks Denmark as a prime example of the "Scandinavian model," as well as a modern industrial society.

In this critical introduction, Professor Kenneth Miller delves into the society, government, and public policies of Denmark, focusing on the changes that have transformed this nation in the last forty years. He presents a story of stability and change, of a welfare state in times of challenge and adversity, and of a small nation—though buffeted by international political and economic storms—striving to maintain its own identity and autonomy.

Kenneth E. Miller is professor of political science at Rutgers University. As a Fulbright senior research scholar, he has been a visiting professor at Copenhagen University. He is the author of *Government and Politics in Denmark* and other books as well as numerous articles on politics, international relations, and government in Nordic countries.

Index

In Danish, the letters æ, ø, and å come at the end of the alphabet, but for convenience, they have been alphabetized in this book as *ae, o,* and *a.*

209